Complex
Humanitarian
Emergencies

Complex Humanitarian Emergencies

Lessons from Practitioners

MARK JANZ AND JOANN SLEAD
Editors

ISBN 1-887983-18-X

Published by World Vision International, 800 W. Chestnut Avenue, Monrovia, California 91016-3198, U.S.A.

Printed in the United States of America. Senior editors: Edna Valdez and Rebecca Russell. Copy editor and typesetter: Joan Weber Laflamme. Cover design: Steven J. Singley. Cover photo: Rod Curtis/World Vision.

Contents

Contributors

Ayotunku Olabanji Abifarin is director of the Food Security Program for Africa for World Vision. "Ayo" has been with World Vision since 1995, holding such positions as agricultural manager in Liberia and acting director of the World Vision Liberia Program. Previous experience included consultancies with government agencies, and positions as a rice breeder with the West Africa Rice Development Association and the International Institute of Tropical Agriculture. Ayo has a doctorate from Purdue University, a master of science degree from the University of Nebraska, and a bachelor of science degree from University College of Ibadan, Nigeria. He is a member of six professional associations and has had over 60 publications.

James Chapman is an agricultural economist with more than 15 years of experience in economic development, research and policy analysis in Asia, Latin America, Africa and the United States. James is currently the team leader, Latin America and the Caribbean, WVUS Program Group, based in Washington, D.C. Prior to this, James served as director for the Southern Africa Transition Programs as well as the El Niño task team leader, based in Johannesburg, South Africa, for World Vision. He was also a regional programmes director, providing direct strategic, management and technical support to World Vision's largest relief/development programmes in Africa, Asia, Latin America and the Caribbean. James holds a doctorate and a master of science degree in agricultural economics, as well as a bachelor of arts degree in mathematics.

Rebecca Dale was a policy department researcher and lobbyist for Oxfam UK in 1994. During 1995-98 she worked in Rwanda in various capacities: she was seconded by Oxfam UK to the Rwandan Ministry of Rehabilitation and Social Integration to assist in setting up government/UN/Co-ordination Systems to prepare for refugee return; she served as information and liaison officer for the international NGO forum; then she was special assistant to the UN Resident/Humanitarian Co-ordinator for Rwanda. She has just received her master's degree from the Fletcher School of Law and Diplomacy, Tufts University, where she specialised in conflict negotiation and organisational learning.

Brigette Delay is currently working as a chief technical advisor for International Rescue Committee's Youth and Children's Program in Rwanda. She has worked for more than 10 years in Africa in both development and relief situations. Her work has primarily focused on assisting children in difficult circumstances, women and other vulnerable groups. She has also managed participatory community development programmes and has extensive training in participatory techniques. She is the author of "Participatory Action and Research for the Rights of the Child: A Grassroots Approach to Promoting the Convention on the Rights of the Child" and has conducted a number of studies on displaced children for the UN, NGOs and other advocacy groups. Brigette has a master's degree from Columbia University in international social work.

John Fawcett has worked for World Vision for 10 years, joining World Vision New Zealand in 1989 as national director for Love Inc. Between 1993 and 1995 he was the human resources manager for World Vision Cambodia, and he joined World Vision's Partnership Office Human Resources team in 1996 as international recruitment co-ordinator. In 1998, John began a three-year project as stress and trauma support services co-ordinator, to assist the organisation in developing sound practices and policies to support adequately all staff as they work with people in need.

M. A. Hamalouta worked as one of the few professional Taureg development workers in the North of Mali before seeking refuge in Mauritania in 1991. As a refugee, he continued his work, initially as an agricultural extension agent, and in 1994 as the project officer responsible for the World Vision support program for refugee women. He actively participated in cross-border work to transfer the Malian Refugee Program and World Visions experience back to the North following the period of repatriation in 1994–95. Following his return to Mali, he continued to contribute to efforts to rehabilitate the North with World Vision.

Wolfgang Jamann assumed the role of head of the relief group within the International Programs Division in World Vision Germany in August 1999. For four years previous to that, he was the senior programme officer for World Vision Sudan. He also has worked for a university, DSE (the German bilateral development agency), and UNDP (United Nations Development Programme). He has work experience in East and Southeast Asia, and Southern and Eastern Africa. Wolfgang earned both a master of arts and the doctorate in development sociology.

Mark Janz was born and raised in the former Republic of Zaire and appreciated from a young age the dynamics and challenges of humanitarian work in difficult, isolated locations. He worked in Zaire for 10 years with the Zaire Council of Churches before obtaining a master of professional studies degree in international agriculture and rural development from Cornell University. Mark has worked for World Vision's Relief Division since 1989, responding to emergencies in all the regions where World Vision is working. His interest and focus are implementation of relief programmes that provide essential developmental foundations and demonstrate high standards and good practice.

Heather MacLeod is a registered nurse from New Zealand. She has worked predominantly in community-based settings with a focus on child, family and community health. She has worked with World Vision for eight years with children in especially difficult circumstances, including the design and management of programmes in Romania, Rwanda/Eastern Zaire/Democratic Republic of Congo. Currently World Vision's advisor on child protection, Heather is leading the work in advocacy for children with an emphasis on child protection, leading the assessment, programme design, implementation and evaluation of World Vision programmes for children. Her work has taken her to countries such as Sierra Leone, Burundi, Somalia, Liberia, Tanzania, Ghana, South Sudan, Albania and Kosovo. She is a member of

World Vision's Staff Stress Management Team, Child Rights Information Group, and represents World Vision on a number of Regional Forums for children in especially difficult circumstances.

Walter Middleton, who joined World Vision 12 years ago, began his food-aid career with CARE in his home nation of India. Now, 30 years down the line and with food-aid experience in 35 countries, he is regional director of WV's food-aid activities based in Johannesburg. Besides providing guidance to national offices around the Partnership as they establish and expand food-aid programmes, he also focuses on capacity building and professionalism of food-aid staff. In the last few years he has been instrumental in starting up World Vision food-aid programmes worth millions of dollars in several countries.

Claude Nankam is programme officer for Latin America and Caribbean with World Vision US, based in Washington, D.C. For four years prior to that, he was director of the agriculture programme with World Vision Angola. Claude's past work includes 10 years as a senior research officer in Cameroon, and three years as a research assistant at the University of Illinois, where he earned his doctorate in plant pathology/breeding. He also holds a master of science degree in plant pathology from Iowa State University and an undergraduate degree in agronomy from the University of Cameroon. Claude has published more than 22 scientific papers, abstracts and technical papers.

Lincoln Kinyanjui Ndogoni has served since July 1997 as leader of the World Vision Rwanda team setting up and delivering psychosocial support services in the post-genocide re-adjustment phase. The programme aim is to facilitate, support and assist victims of the 1994 genocide as they come to terms and process their traumatic experiences and hopefully begin the journey of healing and reconciliation. Before joining World Vision, Lincoln was a lecturer at the University of Nairobi (faculty of social sciences) for six years. In addition, he worked as a part-time counsellor and trainer for a number of NGOs and private institutions in Nairobi. Lincoln holds a bachelor's degree (hons.), a master's degree in development planning, a post-graduate diploma in counselling psychology and an advanced practitioner's certificate in NLP (neuro-linguistic programming).

Solomon Nsabiyera is project co-ordinator, reconciliation and peacebuilding, World Vision Rwanda Programme. He has a bachelor's degree in psychology.

Warren Nyamugasira is a Ugandan economist with 20 years' experience working with NGOs and has written widely on development issues. He has worked in development programmes within adjusting countries and completed service in 1999 as country director, World Vision Rwanda Programme.

Johnson Olufowote serves as associate director of the Food Security Program for Africa for World Vision. He holds a bachelor of science degree in agriculture from the Ahmadu Bello University in Nigeria, a master of science degree in agronomy from the University of the Philippines at Los Banos and a doctor of philosophy degree in plant breeding and international agriculture/ rural development from Cornell University, USA. Johnson joined World Vision in 1995, bringing 26 years' experience working as a rice breeder with the Nigerian government, sub-regional research co-ordinator/rice breeder with the West Africa Rice Development Association and research associate with Cornell University. He has more than 50 scientific publications, of which 13 are peer-reviewed papers in scientific journals and 5 in books.

Charles Rogers is director of corporate security for World Vision. During his previous 18 years with World Vision, he served as executive vice president as well as executive director of Euro Vision, and director of Eastern European Operations. Charles holds a master of divinity degree from Trinity International University. He has written several publications and is a member of the American Society for Industrial Security and the Overseas Security Advisory Council (US State Department).

Joann Slead has 16 years' experience in relief work, and a number in staff development as well. She travelled and worked extensively in complex humanitarian emergencies as a relief associate for World Vision. She has been involved in a number of publication efforts for World Vision. She currently has her own business providing key services to non-profit organisations in the areas of emergency relief and disaster mitigation, staff development, board development, design and facilitation of international events and writing on various topics. She is also writing a handbook for national governing boards, editing a staff development newsletter, and creating multi-media learning materials on food aid. Joann has a master's degree from the University of Southern California in political science, and has completed course work for the Ph.D.

Alan Whaites has worked in relief, development and advocacy for more than 10 years, including time spent living and working in Pakistan, Laos and Thailand. After post-graduate studies in the politics of Africa and Asia at London's School of Oriental and African Studies, he became policy and research manager for World Vision UK before moving to the World Vision Partnership Offices as director for international policy and advocacy. A regular contributor to development journals and conferences, he is based in his home country, the United Kingdom.

Jon White is an agronomist with 25 years of experience in rural development in various countries of Europe, Africa and Latin America. Currently providing leadership in multilateral funding for the National Office in Brazil, Jonathan also served with World Vision in Mozambique as national director for four years and as manager of agricultural recovery and emergency programmes for six years. Work experiences prior to this were in the private sector of agricultural research. His main interest is production and marketing support for smallholder farmers.

Introduction

Changing Parameters

Challenges for Practitioners
and
the Humanitarian Response Community

MARK JANZ

With the passing of the Cold War era, a once rather straightforward bipolar world is today an insecure multi-polar world.[1] As a result, the number of complex humanitarian emergencics[2] is continuing to increase and the humanitarian work environment has become much more dangerous.[3] Neutrality of humanitarian workers is in serious question, to the point that they have actually become targets.[4] Factors that must be taken into consideration when mounting humanitarian operations in such an environment have correspondingly increased in number and complexity. Given all of these changing parameters, NGOs such as World Vision need to be much more thoughtful and analytical regarding humanitarian operations in order to assure we "do no harm" and have a positive rather than negative impact.[5] For appropriate timely interventions, this analytical emphasis must also be balanced with operational know-how. The following chapters demonstrate the more reflective learning style and needed new skills demanded by the challenges of implementing humanitarian assistance in this increasingly hostile and complex world.

SUMMARY OF CHAPTERS

The contexts of emergencies described in these chapters exemplify the complexity and difficulty encountered by practitioners from multiple perspectives—for whom geographic isolation, lack of infrastructure, lack of security and war are only the most striking elements among many that must be considered. The cases demonstrate that NGOs must consider that in future interventions they are likely to confront the following parameters:

- High risk—insecurity—war—civil unrest
- Large scale—high death rates and trauma
- Ethnic and/or religious factors
- Multiple factions—weak or dissolving government structures may require negotiation with numerous factions
- Dissolving or damaged economy, institutions and infrastructures
- Difficult access or denial of access to areas of need
- On-going, long-term crisis or escalating series of crises
- Potential to increase suffering through inappropriate aid assistance
- Increased competition for limited resources

These parameters are very different from those for traditional responses to natural disasters, which generally occur in stable working environments and where project areas often experience a rapid return to normal conditions. The majority of World Vision's humanitarian responses in the past ten years have increasingly incorporated the above parameters. This challenge has necessitated ongoing learning. The case studies in this book—which cover approximately ten years, beginning in 1989—describe the urgency of learning to work within these parameters and the essential combination of an analytical and experiential approach actively linked with appropriate operational know-how to achieve effective humanitarian work.

In responding to the Rwanda genocide described in chapter 1, World Vision came across thousands of unaccompanied children, many suffering from physical injuries and trauma. Because children have been WV's focus for more than 50 years, we engaged in a programme to address the needs of these children and, working alongside other agencies, developed principles to guide this work. These principles informed efforts with local government, institutions, donors and communities to promote community responsibility for these children by tracing families on behalf of lost or unaccompanied children, assisting foster families, and strengthening child-headed households.

Chapter 2 describes the challenges of accessing an isolated, starving population in war-ravaged Mozambique. The chapter covers the airlift of emergency food and supplies, as well as important integration of food programming with nutrition, health care and agricultural recovery programming. Also discussed is the innovation (for that time—1989) of using national staff to conduct therapeutic feeding in this life-saving operation.

Liberia has endured an on-going cycle of violence since the early 1980s, beginning with the Samuel Doe takeover and reaching a crescendo from 1990 to 1996. Insecurity for NGO actors and periodic evacuations of staff have been the norm. In this setting, described in chapter 3, World Vision has struggled and learned in the painful process how to be better prepared for working amid such insecurity. Important lessons learned include setting risk thresholds and taking appropriate monitoring and preparedness precautions for continuing work in insecure locations.

The setting for chapter 4 is Cambodia, the Khmer Rouge genocide, the subsequent resettlement and violent political flare-ups, including the civil unrest around the attempted coup in 1997. Experienced field worker and sociologist John Fawcett describes the struggles and traumatic events experienced by both expatriate and national humanitarian workers. Fawcett investigates two different models for addressing psychosocial trauma—a traditional Western approach, and a community development approach—suggesting innovations for providing appropriate support for national staff in particular.

Agricultural recovery programming, described in chapter 5, has proven a complementary asset to enhance food programming in humanitarian action. Agricultural recovery programming engages a range of participants including agricultural researchers, local

government ministries, communities and institutions in promoting
improved varieties and practices for increased production. This
chapter describes the process in Mozambique, Angola, Congo and
West Africa, where outcomes have included building community
stability, contributing to fundamental development and increasing
local food security for the long term.

Chapter 6 addresses the on-going conflict in South Sudan and
the challenges of implementing humanitarian interventions that—
rather than fuel conflict—build connectors between opposing
groups. The author discusses applying the Local Capacities for
Peace (LCP) analytical framework to planning and implementation in World Vision operations in Yambio County, South Sudan.
Some lessons and challenges while implementing this framework
in operations included implications for organisational policy, opportunities for significant community participation opened by use
of the framework, and practical applications that engaged the community in deciding modes of intervention and selection of staffing.

In the aftermath of the Rwanda genocide, chapter 7 concludes
that most of the population had been affected by aspects of the
traumatic events. To engage in effective reconciliation work, World
Vision had to acknowledge the effects of this trauma on staff out-
looks and work performance. Comparable outlook and performance symptoms were observed among communities and partners. While seeking to find effective ways forward, World Vision
discovered two similar but different approaches to address trauma
and healing for WV operations staff, partner institution staff and
communities, both rooted in the idea that (to quote Ivan Illich)
"if you want to change society, you must tell an alternative story"
and leave behind the old inherited narratives that feed conflict
and violence.

The 1990–96 Tuareg uprising in Mali and the subsequent refugee flow into Mauritania provide the background to the women's
group skills-training project described in chapter 8. Included are
discussions of the repatriation of these women's groups back to
Mali in 1996, preparations for this return, the impact of skills
transfer to women's groups after resettlement, and lessons
learned from this process. The findings provide striking evidence
of the importance of skills transfer, as well as the resilience and

creativity of women as they use these skills through the repatriation process.

Chapter 9 articulates the dilemma non-governmental organisations (NGOs) face when working in countries with repressive regimes or factions. This chapter is especially relevant to the future of humanitarian interventions, as evidence suggests that complex humanitarian emergencies (CHEs) most often occur in countries with repressive governments. It is the responsibility of NGOs to avoid becoming part of those mechanisms of repression. This may well create tension in important relationships with governments or ruling factions. Chapter 9 examines several means by which NGOs may keep from being used as political tools while creating opportunities for community participation and empowerment.

PURPOSE OF THIS BOOK

In developing this book, our goal was to disseminate lessons learned and best practices from the perspective of the practitioner. Thus, each chapter documents varied dimensions of implementing humanitarian work in complex emergencies. We hope this material will contribute to practitioners, academics and policy influencers, and donors who are currently grappling with these same issues and seeking to promote best practices. This book focuses on the "how to" rather than "why" questions. In reviewing existing literature on humanitarian emergencies, we found that much of what is available focuses on broad-brush analysis of issues arising from humanitarian emergencies. Analysis is critical, but we specifically sought to fill a gap in documenting how practitioners actually address these challenges while responding to emergencies. Their experiences and approaches often called for ingenuity and moral acuity in weighing the risk of doing nothing against the risk of learning-on-the-go in order to appropriately tailor humanitarian programmes for effective outcomes. Our motivation for engagement in this on-going learning process is to accrue benefits to populations in crisis through more appropriate, thoughtful and effective humanitarian interventions.

WORLD VISION'S
ACTIVIST MOTIVATION

In responding to today's complex humanitarian environment, World Vision as a Christian organisation is motivated by its regard for the sacredness of human life and by a desire to mitigate the terrible assault humanitarian emergencies wreak on the physical, psychological and spiritual well-being of millions today. Our work is also motivated by our love for a God who commands us to love and serve all people in need, whether they share our religious beliefs or not. World Vision does not allocate humanitarian assistance in a coercive or selective manner. We administer all of our assistance regardless of race or ethnicity, beliefs or religion of the recipients. Aid priorities are calculated on the basis of need alone. We are signatories to and adhere to the *Code of Conduct: Principles of Conduct for the International Red Cross and Red Crescent Movement and NGOs in Disaster Response Programs* in our operations. As a belief-based organisation, World Vision is strongly cognizant of its responsibility for stewardship of resources. This includes transparency with donor publics, both private and government, as well as with the populations served.

Motivational mottoes are not to be trusted unless staff values and beliefs become visibly incarnate in our work. These chapters merely begin to demonstrate the extraordinary motivation, commitment and compassionate love of staff who work in complex emergencies—those willing to bind wounds, to deliver food and to share heartaches in some of the most stressful and difficult work environments in the world. Our continuing challenge on behalf of the brutalised and damaged communities with which we work is to provide hope by meeting immediate physical needs, as well as restoring the foundations on which tomorrow's aspirations may be built.

In the early work of belief-based organisations such as ours, staff motivated by strong moral and ethical humanitarian values mobilised relief efforts based on good intentions. As in any industry which has matured, however, the humanitarian response community has now developed internationally accepted standards to measure the impact of its work and outcomes. World Vision has grown more professional, with many sectoral specialists striving to achieve high standards, as demonstrated in these chapters. What was once a gaggle of well-intentioned people with a mixed group of skills responding to emergencies is today a professional industry requiring specialised skills and standards.

The significant changes in the humanitarian environment of recent years have resulted in expansion into cutting-edge theory and praxis, including peacebuilding, security, psychosocial trauma and staff well-being. Limited humanitarian experience in these *soft* non-traditional humanitarian response arenas has meant that extensive how-to standards and models are not available. Rather, applied research and learning are taking place during programme implementation in the field. Practitioners are learning the path of effective response methodologies as we walk it. This is scary and risky business, but our beliefs engender a humanitarian imperative: We cannot walk away in the face of need; we must respond with what knowledge and expertise we have in the contexts in which we work. This often means linking with outside specialists and institutions to address new programming challenges in operations.

MULTIPLE SKILLS DIMENSIONS

While dimensions documented in the following chapters demonstrate many of the skills required for effective operations, they are not and cannot be exhaustive. Those skills necessary for any given emergency response depend largely on the situation.

All agencies have core competencies, where they focus their operations in emergencies. Transition dynamics flow between relief and development implementation modes in a constantly shifting cycle (see Figure I-1 on page 8). This changing and dynamic cycle between relief and development is important to consider when implementing emergency programmes. Understanding this cycle, its inherent dynamics and precursor indicators of change, may well inform critical programming changes and shifting points between implementing more developmental or more relief-focused programming.

The multi-dimensional skills in Figure I-1 are admittedly daunting. Some experts in the relief and development community be-

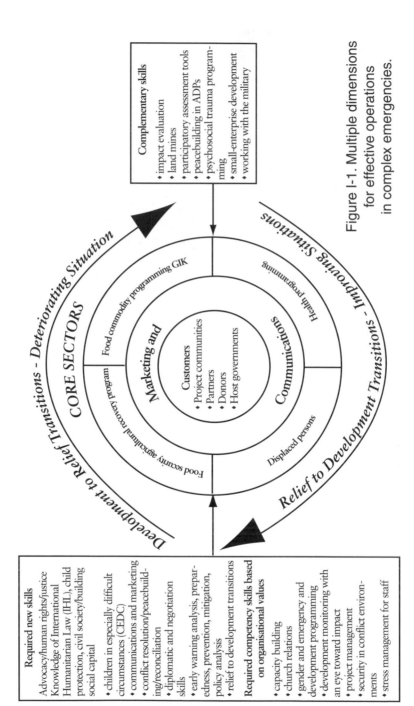

Figure I-1. Multiple dimensions for effective operations in complex emergencies.

lieve that achieving such multiple competencies is unrealistic. Not all these competencies can reside in one programme or agency. Humanitarian workers are not superhuman, able to internalise all needed skills for any given scenario. However, I would like to characterise this lengthy list of competencies as a pantry of required ingredients needed for different contextual recipes. Skilled CHE managers gather those competencies (ingredients) required for appropriate programming to respond effectively to the emergency context. If needed skills do not reside within their own organisations, they will collaborate with outside agencies that can provide the necessary expertise. This underscores the importance of close co-ordination and dialogue among responding agencies to share different competencies for planning and implementing effective interventions.

I have made several observations from the following chapters and my accumulated experience over 20 years of humanitarian work: (1) An increased number of skills are now needed in emergency work, and (2) they require increasingly high degrees of humanitarian practitioner professionalism. (3) In addition, there is a clear need to achieve balance between analytical rigor and operational know-how, which, if combined correctly, allow humanitarian operations to engage effectively on the ground.

OPERATIONAL AND ANALYTICAL BALANCE

Imbalance in the analytical and operational elements of a humanitarian response can result either in inaction, where there is a bias to complete analysis prior to action, or in inappropriate action, where there is an operational bias with little analytical thought.

Recent evidence of *analytical bias* on the international humanitarian front takes for granted the operational skills necessary to implement programmes in difficult environments—the argument being that these operational skills are readily for hire. This, however, has failed to be the case. Building field-based operational know-how requires more than prepackaged skills and a "cookie cutter" or blueprint approach. Complex skills honed by years of experience and adaptation through trial and error are indispensable. For example, mobilizing a cost-effective humanitarian airlift with limited funding in war-ravaged Mozambique or isolated and mountainous Irian Jaya is very different from airlifting goods in a more developed context. Needed skills may be for hire, but only among a limited pool of individuals throughout the world.

On the flip side, an *operational bias* can result in ineffective and even harmful disaster responses. Analytical bias in fact arose partly in response to investigation of past failures of standard operationally biased responses. Some operationally biased responses provided "assistance" that did not meet the real needs of the people in crisis—and in fact made helpful response to the disaster more difficult. For example, airports have become clogged with useless goods, preventing badly need relief goods from getting through; at other times, large amounts of supplies were imported from Western countries when they should have been purchased locally or at least regionally. Some operationally biased responses have exacerbated existing armed conflict. Some have created new problems that could have been prevented if programme designers and implementers had carefully thought things through.

Both analytical rigor and operational know-how are vital. Analytical perspective adds an essential, thoughtful element for effective humanitarian programming. Analytical "knowing what" is, however, of little use without operational "knowing how." In using the "do no harm" LCP framework, World Vision has found that the *kinds* of professionally planned humanitarian interventions are not of *most* importance. While the kind of interventions is indeed key, of even more importance is *how* they are designed and implemented.[6]

In publishing this book, we want to do as much as we can to ensure that NGOs and academic institutions avoid minimizing the importance of operational skills and documenting best practices. The danger with any new trend in development, as with this new analytical bent, is that it may be allowed to overshadow critical lessons that remain from what has gone before. We cannot afford to let operations know-how become the taken-for-granted "poor relation" to analytical thinking and writing. On-the-ground operations, after all, remain critical to ensuring that appropriate life-saving operations take place.

COMMON THREADS

A striking group of common threads recur throughout these chapters, but the patterns reveal different dimensions of implementing humanitarian work. One example is the need to understand the historical, sociopolitical, economic and institutional context in any crisis. This is especially evident in the chapters on Sudan, Rwanda, Mali and the dilemma of NGO responsibility to decide where and how to engage in repressive government settings.

Humanitarian emergency work is not static, with neat, clean prescriptions available directing how to best meet needs within the many dimensions of any given context. The fluidity of a crisis requires on-going analysis in order to tailor programming to respond effectively to new and changing dynamics. It is important to be open to looking for ways forward which differ from those originally planned. The importance of such analysis is even more evident when context requires working under repressive regimes. In any case—whether analysing dimensions for LCP in South Sudan; mobilising an airlift in a complex logistics environment in Mozambique; establishing and monitoring security thresholds in Liberia; responding to the changing agricultural context effected by drought, disease, flood and insecurity in Mozambique and Angola; or understanding the background history of trauma in Rwanda—understanding the social, historical and cultural background is a must for ensuring staff and community (or beneficiaries') well-being when faced with stressful work and living environments.

Emergency crises can be an important impetus for societal change, whether this involves changing roles for women in Mali; changing roles for indigenous organisations, governments or factions in Rwanda and Sudan; or adapting to new crops in Angola and Mozambique.

Genuine co-ordination and co-operation is essential among NGOs, governments, communities, donors and international organisations—whether responding to children's needs and trauma healing needs in Rwanda; the need for cross-border operations resources in the Mali repatriation; engaging the local Sudanese authorities and institutions in LCP training; and government involvement in agricultural programming in Angola and Mozambique. Humanitarian measures taken must be based on what is best for beneficiaries—not necessarily for donor, agency or government agendas.

Participatory processes are needed for effective contextual understanding and effective development and relief programming in all the following phases of emergency responses: pre-emergency (prevention), during emergency, and post-emergency (transitions).

Participatory engagement which enhances humanitarian response is described while promoting LCP in operations in Sudan; identifying the needs of children and healing traumatised staff and individuals in Rwanda; engaging the population in promoting effective agricultural recovery programming in Mozambique and Angola; providing skills development for Malian women for future repatriation; engaging national staff and communities in articulating their world and the stress they face; and also in working under repressive regimes with populations and institutions to find participatory and empowering opportunities. Participatory appraisal tools and skills are as important to good emergency response and transitions programming as they are to development programming.

ON-GOING "BEST PRACTICE" LEARNING

Whether addressing children; building LCPs; or examining how best to approach agricultural recovery, programme security, trauma, roles of women in reintegration programming or gaining access to emergency locations—programming in emergencies requires an ongoing "best practice" learning process that links field knowledge with action.[7] Whether donors, academic institutions and think tanks or humanitarian NGO operations, we all face the multiple challenges to effective work in CHEs. Multiple new skills are needed. New, more intentional partnerships are necessary to identify and document best practices. These partnerships are beginning to emerge, as evident with the Sphere Project standards[8] and the Active Learning Network on Accountability and Performance in Humanitarian Assistance (ALNAP). With best practices thus documented, we must then rise to the occasion together to train a cadre able to implement best practices in increasingly complex emergencies (see Figures I-2 and I-3).

The Changing Humanitarian Response Environment:
new challenges, new skills, new partners

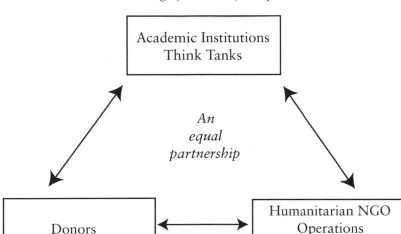

Figure I-2. Moving toward "best practice"
through applied learning.

Standards for many traditional skills such as delivery of commodities, health and sanitation, and water (as documented in the Sphere Project standards) are well established. Many new skills areas, however—such as conflict management, civil society, trauma, care of staff, mitigation and relief-to-development transitions—require further documentation through case studies and applied learning to identify best practice. Subject areas such as peacebuilding are difficult and complicated to test for[9] and quantify; thus there is a lack of significant donor resources or commitment to applied research in such operations.

What is needed is an applied how-to learning and research approach which can be articulated only in the working laboratory of operational realities. Donors, academic institutions, think tanks and humanitarian NGO operations all have a common interest in learning best practice from their own institutional perspectives (see Figure I-3).

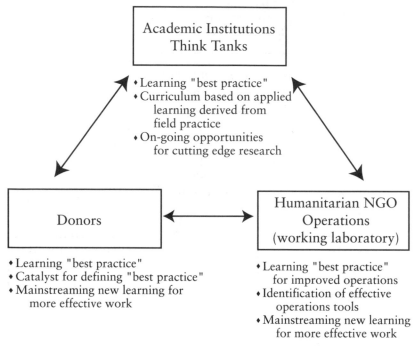

Figure I-3. "Best practice" learning—joint benefits.

Academic institutions and think tanks want to develop effective curricula derived from field practice, as well as cultivate on-going opportunities for cutting-edge research. Donors want to be catalysts for defining best practice to ensure more effective work and mainstreaming of new learning. NGO practitioners, who function in unique operations working laboratories, want to improve operations, identify effective operations tools and frameworks to improve programming, and mainstream new learning for more effective work. This applied learning and research in operations will validate methodologies that have merit and point out weaknesses, successes and failures.[10] What is lacking is equal partnership among these three parties to work effectively on the on-going nature of the learning agenda. Achieving a partnership of equality will entail NGOs, academic organisations, think tanks and donors working closely together. All will need to shoulder a portion of planning agenda costs and seek donor resources to invest in applied learning research in important subject areas.

This is the huge challenge before the humanitarian community. Can we work jointly to identify best practice in the increasingly challenging humanitarian environments where we work? We realise this is a competitive world. Yet in the interest of long-lasting impacts resulting from humanitarian interventions it would seem worthwhile to test theory against reality in field operations, in a co-operative and co-ordinated effort. Mechanisms such as this book may enable more practitioners to contribute to a compendium of best-practice knowledge effectively pointing toward important how-to lessons and next steps.

THE LEARNING EVENT:
BRINGING OPERATIONS AND ANALYSIS TOGETHER

In October 1999, a review process was organised around these chapters. Participants included the authors, editors and a panel of long-experienced consultants and experts with academic, operations and leadership experience. The panel included Mary Anderson, author of *Do No Harm* and director of the Collaborative for Development Action (CDA); Ian Smillie, writer, consultant and former director of several NGOs; Dan Kelly, World Vision Australia Emergency Relief Unit; Dr Milton Amayun, director of International Programs for International Aid; and Larry Minear, director of the War and Humanitarianism Project at the Watson Institute of Brown University. Included was a three-day learning event, rich in dialogue and content, including much consensus and many issues that still require more debate. This exchange of learning provided significant opportunities for operations practitioners to share their wealth of knowledge and experience and test these against the rigors of the academic and professional humanitarian communities.

We would like to express our appreciation to the authors who participated in the learning event, as well as to the review panel members who all exercised candor and brought their strong views, commitment and expertise to contribute toward excellence in life-saving humanitarian endeavours. The learning event proved refreshing as well as challenging as participants sought to find common language in discussing best practice and active ways forward in contexts that may provide few obvious options and only small windows of hope for those affected by emergencies. We hope that this experience and publication will point the way to more active engagement among the humanitarian community and practitioners in documenting best practice in dynamic and changing response environments.

APPRECIATION

I want to express appreciation to my colleagues and friends in World Vision who developed this material, much of it on their own time. Have you ever met humanitarian emergency response workers who actually find extra time to document their experience, lessons learned and best practice? These chapters developed through the "sweat equity" of World Vision practitioners. We are seeking to strengthen organisational commitment to this type of effort and effectively apply lessons to our implementation of humanitarian operations. This project has taken almost three years, having been delayed several times due to emergency interventions including Hurricane Mitch, Kosovo, Sierra Leone, Indonesia, and so on. I deeply appreciate that World Vision has recognised the importance of this work by our field practitioners and allocated the time and resources needed to make this book a reality.

NOTES

[1] Richard Falk, "In Search of a New World Model," *Current History* (April 1993).

[2] We are defining complex humanitarian emergencies as those emergencies that have at least three of following characteristics: (1) presence of pre-famine indicators (such as drought, crop failure and population movements) and starvation; (2) systemic economic collapse (such as mass unemployment, hyperinflation, negative GNP growth, currency collapse); (3) refugee and displaced populations (large size and movement); (4) violence and/or disintegration of government authority (such as civil war or organised resistance movements, ethnic, tribal, or religious violence, human rights abuses and collapse of law and order) (Andrew Natsios, *US Foreign Policy and the Four Horseman of the Apocalypse: Humanitarian Relief in Complex Emergencies*, foreword by George Bush [Westport, Conn.: Praeger, 1997], 7).

[3] Andrew Natsios, "The International Humanitarian Response System," presented at the Humanitarian Support Operations Conference, Honolulu, Hawaii (September 1995).

[4] Hugo Slim, "The Continuing Metamorphosis of the Humanitarian Professional: Some New Colours for an Endangered Chameleon," *Disasters* 19 (Oxford: Blackwell Publishers Ltd., 1995).

[5] Mary Anderson, *Do No Harm: How Aid Can Support Peace—Or War* (Boulder, Colo.: Lynne Rienner Publishers, 1999).

[6] Anderson, *Do No Harm*.

[7] Michael Edwards, "Becoming a Learning Organization, or, the Search for the Holy Grail?" (draft), Save the Children—UK, University of Manchester (May 1996); idem, *Learning from Experience in Africa* (Oxford: Oxfam, 1989).

[8] Sphere Project, *Humanitarian Charter and Minimum Standards in Disaster Response* (Oxford: Oxfam, 2000).

[9] Slim, "The Continuing Metamorphosis of the Humanitarian Professional."

[10] Edwards, *Learning from Experience in Africa* and "Becoming a Learning Organization."

1.

Holistic Care of Children in Complex Humanitarian Emergencies

HEATHER MacLEOD

INTRODUCTION

When people talk about complex humanitarian emergencies, the nation of Rwanda quickly comes to mind. The genocide that swept the country for 100 days beginning in April 1994 stands out as a landmark of evil during the 1990s, perhaps of the twentieth century. According to UN figures, it resulted in the deaths of well over half a million Tutsi and moderate Hutu. More than a million Hutu were forcibly displaced to neighbouring countries, with many dying from the diseases and privations they encountered. In the midst of all this chaos, it is estimated that more than 100,000 children were separated from their families.

Now, imagine this scene in the early stages of the Rwanda emergency. You are recruited to lead a programme and mandated to address the needs of the most vulnerable children. There is a great deal of money available to be spent quickly, due to the high level of attention from the world media. The needs of the children are being particularly highlighted; people expect to see immediate visible results from the generous donations they have made. The magnitude of the crisis is larger than anyone has ever had to face before and seems overwhelming.

As programme manager, you are expected to make assessment visits to various locations and to attend numerous co-ordination and planning meetings. You are collaborating with leaders of the emerging government, with other non-governmental organisations and with United Nations bodies. There are many requests for assistance to children in different parts of Rwanda, and to Rwandan children in neighbouring countries that are inundated with more than two million refugees.

After each assessment or meeting, you return to the office to find lines of people or bundles of letters. Every day you must find time to listen to individual requests and to appeals from groups of people who want help for children. All have heartbreaking stories of suffering endured by the children they represent, and it leaves you, the programme manager, struggling to decide whom to assist, whom to refer elsewhere, and whom to turn away. On top of all this, the situation is changing daily, like a moving target.

In the midst of this crisis management you are aware that what you are doing now affects what happens long term. You want to have development in the forefront of your thinking even as you address the essential needs around you.

Whatever programme you design, you will need staff to implement it. You will have to recruit and orientate new staff in an environment where most records and references have been destroyed. References are not available for you to validate the background of your applicants. It is hard to find staff with the training or experience necessary to help children affected by war.

LEARNING ON THE SPOT

By comparison with this work of targeting the special needs of children, emergency responses to health crises and provision of relief food or household items have a long history. Many people are experienced in these disciplines—but when it comes to specialised assistance for children affected by war, the pool of expertise is extremely small. Most staff are learning on the spot. There is no diploma or degree that prepares people for addressing the holistic needs of children in conflict zones, and this shortage of skilled expertise needs to be considered in planning a response.

In an emergency like Rwanda's post-genocide society, most people would say all children are vulnerable and in need of special attention. Some categories of children are considered more vulnerable however: children with disabilities, children who are separated from their parents or primary caregiver, and children who are in conflict with the law. This is the setting in which World Vision began its work in Rwanda.

There were two immediate challenges. The organisation could choose to focus on one particular type of support for children, such as NGO-managed transit care for children, becoming a specialist in that intervention. Alternatively, it could develop a broad-based programme that included a variety of activities, aiming to be responsive to the changing, unpredictable and prolonged nature of CHEs. World Vision chose the latter course and decided to provide both community-based and institutional support for children in five geographical locations. The decision to opt for a variety of interventions was based on the immediate survival needs of children already gathered in centres and World Vision's commitment to integrated community development. Another factor was the significant media attention on "centres," and the visible needs of large numbers of children gathered in centres demanded a response.

There is a tendency for people to consider Rwanda as an extreme, an anomaly, but it would be unfortunate not to learn the lessons offered by this valuable experience. Some of the things we learned from 1994 were put to good use to improve our work in the repatriation of 1996, and then in other conflict zones such as Burundi, northern Uganda, Sierra Leone and Kosovo. While it is true that each country or CHE has its own peculiarities, there are good practices that can be very helpful for those planning and implementing programmes in other war zones.

INITIAL RESPONSE OF CHILD-FOCUSED NGOS

In Rwanda, in 1994, one of the most vulnerable groups of children identified by the government, communities, UN and NGOs was "unaccompanied children,"[1] which is to say "children separated from both parents and [who] are not being cared for by an adult who by law or custom, is responsible to do so."[2]

Why was there a focus on unaccompanied children? Because many were already grouped together in large numbers. In July 1994, for example, there were well over 1,000 children gathered in the town of Nyamata, in Kigali Rurale Prefecture, and they were in obvious need of food, water, sanitation and shelter. Their trauma needs were also obvious; even though they were in a large group, they were virtually silent. As Phyllis Kilbourn states:

> Central to the children's losses in war is the loss of family and home. Especially for young children, home, together with the family, is the centre of their world. At home children find love, security, trust, belonging, acceptance and care. So when the child has lost home, parents and siblings the loss is immense. . . . Separation from or loss of family members, especially parents, is the worst possible outcome of war for children. Children will tell you that they fear this more than something happening to themselves.[3]

A minority of the estimated 300,000 unaccompanied children in Rwanda ended up in centres. Some children had been taken in and cared for by families they did not know and effectively found themselves being fostered. There were two main groups of unaccompanied children—those in "unaccompanied children centres" (UCCs) and others in "spontaneous foster families."

Initially, the greatest efforts were made for children in centres, with little attention paid to children in foster families—an approach that had clear shortcomings. There was little urgency when it came to tracing families for the fostered children. Reunification was therefore delayed, and their general situations were not assessed. When assistance could be directed to foster families, many people caring for extended family members started to call themselves foster families in an attempt to get more help, a phenomenon that confused the process.

Urgent attention was devoted to children in centres, because they were often living together in large numbers with minimal care and substandard facilities. After huge amounts of food, agricultural tools and seeds were given to communities in 1994, everyone believed that children in foster families would have their essential needs met because foster families had been included in the distributions.

WORLD VISION'S RESPONSE

Avoiding institutions

World Vision's involvement with children in other countries, especially Romania, had demonstrated clearly the harm that could be

inflicted on children by leaving them in institutions, and child welfare experts agree that institutions should only be used as the last
resort. Therefore, from the beginning, our project had no intention
of providing long-term institutional care for children. Rather, the
project set out to provide transit care for children who had no-
where to live while waiting for efforts to trace their families to bear
fruit; for those who were not traced, the project aimed to outline
appropriate community-based alternatives.

Promoting communities

World Vision could have limited its efforts to helping the children
in centres, but from the start managers committed themselves to
look for solutions that would continue to work in the long term.
Keeping children in institutions was not an acceptable option; instead, the local community was adopted as the preferred focus for
sustainable development. An unaccompanied children's programme
was designed that would promote families and communities as the
main agents to provide care for children. The organisation's community workers became familiar in the towns and villages through
their intensive efforts to trace families for the children in centres,
and the many reunifications they were able to organise and follow
up. Health promotion activities, measures to provide food security,
and material and psychosocial support reinforced these contacts
and the commitment to the community.

Follow-up

Support workers quickly found their commitment did not end when
children were reunited with families. Reunified children and their
families often had significant unmet basic needs and faced new
challenges, and the risk of a return to institutional care was high
for the children. Discussions with the community revealed that the
population had developed a dependency on humanitarian organisations for a range of requirements. Absorbing the international
community's constant emphasis on the needs of children in centres, communities had developed a tendency to believe their children were better off in the centres, and they had started to believe
the children were no longer their responsibility. Many poor families

encouraged their children to present themselves to the centres to benefit from better nutrition and health care and education opportunities. Over time, this voluntary separation reinforces a child's alienation from his or her own community. Community workers began to increase their support for children perceived to be at risk of abandonment, and began to develop techniques to challenge and encourage communities to take responsibility and support their vulnerable children.

A common approach

Other key players also recognised the need for a broad approach that emphasised the community. The Organisation for African Unity (OAU) and the 1990 *UN Convention on the Rights of the Child* support such methodologies. In the Continental Conference on Children in Situations of Armed Conflict, held by African Network for the Prevention of Child Abuse and Neglect (ANPCAN) in collaboration with the OAU in Ethiopia from 24–26 July 1997, OAU recommendation 25 was accepted:

> Humanitarian agencies intervening in the interests of unaccompanied children should in principle adopt community-based rehabilitation approaches, so as to take due account of the cultural values and practices of the community. Interim group care arrangements, with adult support, should also be considered as an alternative to institutionalisation of unaccompanied children. Child participation in the making of such arrangements should always be sought. The nature of separation of those children from their families should form the basis for establishing appropriate programmes for them, including tracing activities with a view to family reunification as one of the most important aspects of assisting separated children.

OAU recommendation 23 stated:

> In the delivery of essential services to people affected by armed conflict, relief agencies should involve the participation by local authorities and local community as a way to ensure the sustainability of such interventions.

An inclusive approach

World Vision, in common with many other agencies, chose not to limit its interventions to unaccompanied children. Other vulnerable groups of children identified and helped were:

- those in communities who were showing signs of trauma.
- those at risk of abandonment or separation.
- those living alone or in child-headed households.
- those with disabilities, particularly if they were in centres or with more vulnerable families.
- later on, those who were placed in formally arranged foster families.

WORLD VISION'S PRINCIPLES

Underlying principles on which World Vision designed its broad-based approach emerged over time. At the beginning of the programme, these principles had not been developed specifically in this way. However, in hindsight they summarise the essence of the project design.

The programme was designed according to eight principles:

1. holistic perspective;
2. community perspective;
3. collaborative perspective;
4. integrated perspective.;
5. people perspective;
6. participative principle;
7. peacebuilding perspective; and, to summarize,
8. broad and long-term perspective.

Principle one: A holistic perspective

To promote the healthy development of a child it is necessary to consider the child as a whole. The World Health Organisation in 1948 defined health as "not being merely the absence of disease but also the physical, psychological, intellectual, spiritual and social well-being of a person."

In an emergency, aid workers dealing with children commonly consider as essential interventions those that deal with physical security, adequate nutrition, safe water, shelter, sanitation and health care. It certainly is important that these needs are recognised and that adequate care and attention is paid to them, but to focus exclusively on physical requirements minimises equally important needs in other, less tangible areas.

For example, in refugee camps in Goma in 1994 and during the repatriation of refugees to Rwanda in 1996, there were instances where humanitarian workers made urgent efforts to save the lives of sick mothers. They would whisk the sick mother away to receive health care, without fully considering that they were separating children from their mothers. Some of these children were so small that they could not identify themselves, and to this day they do not know who they are and to whom they properly belong. If aid workers had quickly identified which small children were attached to the woman with whom they were working, and ensured that there was someone who knew their identity to care for the children, there would be more children today who know their real name. Better yet, those aid workers could have allowed these small children to be taken to the health-care posts along with their mother.

Keeping body and soul together

Many argue that saving lives is the priority and that psychological issues are secondary. World Vision's experience is that in many cases both can be addressed simultaneously, with a little extra effort. One example of this is related to the way children were cared for in transit centres as they awaited the outcome of family-tracing operations. Children need good nutrition, but there are some children who, under extreme stress, do not eat. These—and all children—need to have an adult figure who will listen to them, care for them and encourage them. Having enough staff of the right quality to provide care in a transit centre is key to promoting the physical, emotional and psychological health of a child.

An example of what happens when psychological considerations are ignored was illustrated during an assessment by World Vision staff of a centre crowded with more than a thousand children, all

with blank faces, all silent. The staff running the centre said that
local authorities had allocated more space in which the children
could be housed, and that this was desperately needed to provide a
more hygienic environment. When the visitors reached this new
accommodation, however, they found children washing blood from
the floor of a room they were going to sleep in. This was a genocide
site, a place in which people had been murdered. It seemed tragic
that these children were once again so vividly reminded of the terrible violence that had devastated their lives.

Children in war have had their lives turned upside down. Providing an environment with a healthy routine makes a positive difference. If, as a consequence of war, they have been deprived of
social activity, they need to return quickly to familiar events and
routines that will support their psychosocial recovery.

Likewise, support for children's intellectual development through
re-establishment of education was addressed as a priority from the
emergency phase. As effects of the crisis subsequently decreased,
valuable support was given directly to children in the form of uni-
forms and school supplies, and to schools as desks, latrines, supplies and textbooks.

Other elements of programme design that were included to promote the holistic development of children included ensuring that:

- the number of staff in the centres was carefully planned in relation to the number and needs of the children. For example, a
  one-to-five ratio with the under-five children. In two cases of
  children with special needs (physical and mental), there needed
  to be one caregiver specifically assigned to that child.
- basic training in trauma mitigation, health and hygiene was
  given to community leaders and teachers.
- children were placed where possible in a centre close to their
  place of origin.
- children in centres could attend the place of worship with which
  they were familiar before the war.
- there were good programmes that prevented separation of children from their parents during the 1996 repatriation.
- fostering of children was facilitated where no relative could be
  found.
- a strong emphasis was retained on reunification of children
  with their families.

Lessons learned
- ♦ People working in a CHE do not always understand the need for the holistic care of children.
- ♦ The quality of care in transit centres is important. In 1994, World Vision concluded that the training of staff in centres had a lower priority than tracing and reunification, because it was assumed the centres would close quickly. An over-emphasis on training could be seen as implying a need for long-term residential care, and this was not the aim of the UN or most NGOs. In hindsight, however, the children stayed in care considerably longer than was first planned. If staff had been trained in child development and given an appreciation of the need for quality communication with children, they could have better supported the development of the children in their care. That would have helped with the reintegration of the children into the community and would have increased the morale of the staff in the centres by showing they were valued. The OAU conference also supported this conclusion, stating that "priority should be given to the non-material needs of children, including education, training and special programmes for those particularly traumatised by armed conflict and violence." The *UN Convention on the Rights of the Child* also supports this focus.
- ♦ Transit centres should create an environment as close as possible to that of a family.

Principle two: A community perspective

In order to grow and develop normally, children need to belong to a family and community and to interact with adults. Children's programmes should have a community perspective. An agency working with children should know the community well, develop positive relationships within it, and work alongside it to help its members understand the crucial role they play in the development of children. The children of Rwanda are the responsibility of their parents and Rwandan society, not of the NGOs.

As in virtually any culture, the norms of Rwandan culture affirm that children are valued by society, and this gave community workers a solid foundation from which to educate the community on the needs of children. Development writer Chris Roche from

Oxfam confirms the need for capacity building, community focus and advocacy early in CHEs:

> Capacity Building can and should be as much a need in the face of severe crisis as in a more settled situation. Similarly the strengthening of local coping mechanisms and political protection and lobbying are needed just as much by communities dealing with long-term trends as those dealing with crisis.[4]

Understanding the community is key to determining the real needs of children. In Rwanda, it was assumed those children in spontaneous foster families or children living alone would be cared for by the community around them, and would receive the same food ration and support as others during distributions. Indeed, a child head of household reported in 1996 that the household did receive tools and seeds in a distribution; the problem was that no one taught them how to grow the crops properly. The "food for work" programme down the road was more attractive to them than gardening, and consequently their own harvest was poor. Had the community been more involved, and the various specialists working together more closely, these interventions would have been better focused on the real needs of the vulnerable groups they were targeting.

In 1997, when focus group discussions were held in Kanazi with households whose oldest member was a child or a youth, the children said the assumption that neighbours, extended family and community would provide support was not the case in many situations.[5] These children reported that, while neighbours and others would observe them, they would not actively listen and help them on a regular basis. The measure of support offered might include adults employing the children to do casual work for them—at a considerably lower wage than adults.

In one project area, a "prevention of abandonment" programme was implemented which provided food, household items, agricultural implements and seed to spontaneous foster families, and later this was extended to other needy families. After this it was possible to encourage vulnerable families in groups to form community-based co-operative associations that could take advantage of agricultural and micro-enterprise business opportunities.

As outlined earlier, the follow-up of children who had been re-unified with their families became a high priority. Many of these families were extremely poor, and there was risk of the children facing more suffering or even abandonment and forced return to the transit centres.

In countries like Uganda and Sierra Leone, where demobilisation of child soldiers and their subsequent reintegration into society are extremely difficult, our experience in Rwanda has been put to good use. An NGO staff member's understanding of community dynamics and of techniques that can be employed to focus everyone's mind on the needs of their children is often the key to a successful reintegration.

Keeping flexibility

World Vision's provision of essential material items for children and their families was problematic as we introduced the concepts of community development into the programme.

It is important to identify clearly the people you are going to assist, of course; grouping beneficiaries into categories is the only option in the early stages. At the same time, it must be recognised that being overly dogmatic about categories can reduce flexibility when dealing with individual cases, and does not always produce a wide enough safety net to catch some of the most vulnerable children. For example, a two-parent family with three children may have more need for assistance than a family caring for a disabled child.

In addition, when aid organisations categorise children, it becomes more likely that the community will do the same, labelling and stigmatising them and causing long-term harm. There is no easy solution to this. Communities often have to be helped to understand their children, to see their own importance as adults in supporting the healthy development of the next generation. In the rehabilitation phase of a programme, the community can be helped to consider what factors influence whether a child becomes a healthy adult, and that in turn can bring to light the things that make a child vulnerable. Usually, this seems to include education, family income, access to clean water, and the desire of the children to be part of a family with an adult caregiver who can support their emotional needs.

Most NGOs in Rwanda felt strongly that children should be taken out of residential care and put back in family-based care as soon as possible. Transit care centres provided residential care while tracing efforts went on, and other options such as fostering were explored. Centres for children are themselves part of a community, and the connection between the institution and the society around it needed to be acknowledged and developed.

World Vision sought to provide essential care and protection for children who were placed in the four transit care centres it managed through provision of

- good nutrition;
- adequate shelter;
- essential health care;
- opportunity for play;
- psychosocial support through caring, listening and specific activities;
- education at local schools;
- staff training on health, hygiene practices, grief and trauma;
- an environment where love and attention for children was encouraged;
- means to cater to individual needs of children as much as possible; and
- grief and trauma support for the children.

World Vision undertook to pay sufficient salaries in the centres it managed, to ensure the ratios of staff to children would make it more likely that children were given suitable care by an adult. The work of tracing families for the children and of providing reunification support was a high priority. Initially, tracing and reunification was a task solely undertaken by the International Committee of the Red Cross and Save the Children Fund UK, but it was quickly recognised that other NGOs could accelerate their tracing and reunification efforts, and World Vision became involved.

Some transit centres were managed by indigenous organisations, and here the intention was to provide emergency support for the children in care, while building relationships to such a point that the centre and staff would support tracing and reunification. In many cases, this was a major problem because staff resisted reunification efforts. Explanations for their reluctance ranged from their own fears of unemployment or financial loss should the centres close, to more genuine concern that the children would not receive good care in the families in which they were being placed.

As has been noted, to some extent this concern was justifiable. When families are struggling and the centres are providing better food, clothes and health care than the community, the abandonment of children back into centres is common. Interestingly, in 1995, when there were forced repatriations to Rwanda from the Mugunga Camp in Goma (then in Zaire, now the Democratic Republic of Congo), many families came to collect their children from the unaccompanied-children centres. These were children for whom family tracing efforts had from 1994 been unsuccessful, yet their families in the camps had known for a long time that their children were safe in the centres.

Lessons learned

* Helping the community to understand children's needs must have a high priority, with a focus on defining what is a healthy child in the particular community, and then working out what it takes to enable a child to become a healthy adult who will make a positive contribution to society. This may seem obvious, but it is too easy to think about the material needs of children and much more difficult to consider the holistic development of a child.
* Participatory planning methodology could be useful to involve the community in planning for its own future as early as possible.
* NGOs should not make a care centre an attractive alternative to the community around it and should screen children who are to enter it carefully.
* Developing in advance regional teams who have skills in prevention of separation, documentation, tracing, reunification, fostering and appropriate short-term transit care would enhance rapid response to the needs of children in a CHE and reduce the numbers and effects of separation of children.
* The *UN Convention on the Rights of the Child,* which has been signed by every state in Africa except Somalia, is a useful tool for child advocacy with the government and local authorities.

Principle three: A collaborative perspective

In an emerging field of expertise such as children's programmes, the sharing of information and inter-agency planning and learning are essential. When there is so much work to do, it is essential that meetings between agencies are effective. Long meetings without clear objectives can be counter-productive and certainly result in poor attendance and co-ordination.

It should be a priority to include governing authorities in networks and communication, as they have overall responsibility for the population.

In many cases, co-ordination meetings are well attended by the international NGOs and not so well by national NGOs. Reasons for this vary. Many indigenous NGOs are based in rural areas and require transport to attend meetings; in addition, they have few staff, and representatives cannot easily leave their work. Sometimes they do not understand why meetings are important, and they may not feel they are encouraged by international NGOs to attend meetings. There can indeed be a tendency for international staff to dominate discussions.

Networking with other agencies is often done in a social setting or with people who speak a common language well. This is one way relief staff deal with the stress of their jobs. National staff also have day-to-day family commitments, something international staff rarely have in CHEs. So the general tendency is for national staff to talk together in one informal group and for international staff to form other groups according to the common language they speak. While there are obvious problems with this natural division, sharing information among agencies and mutual understanding of each organisation's work accrue many benefits. The collaboration that occurred between child-focused agencies during the repatriation to Rwanda in 1996 was a testimony to the strength of the network that existed and the planning that had been carried out up to then. Those working on the ground had met regularly, both formally and informally, and a close network had developed over two years. Staff were familiar with the mandates for each other's agencies, recognised their strengths and challenges, and planned accordingly. Repatriation came quicker than expected, but each group had a clearly defined role to play; when stresses mounted, there was enough respect to solve problems in a constructive way and to extend forgiveness when necessary. In this case, the best interests of the children remained paramount for everyone, which made co-operation easier.

Communication under stress

It is hard to over-estimate how grief, loss and stress can damage communication among adults, and between adults and children. Adults—including staff—are affected by the war, and in the immediate post-war situation are in distress from their own grief and loss. Their ability to work and to communicate effectively is compromised. This can be compounded when expatriate and local staff are working together for the first time. An understanding of cultural barriers will ease communication.

Training in stress management for NGO staff and their community partners needs to consider how trauma affects communication. This provides an opportunity for individuals to explore cultural differences in a positive environment and helps them identify factors that increase stress. While it is not practical to have this training in the first few weeks of an emergency, it should receive higher priority than it does now. Where possible, it should be included in training for all development workers, because positive relationships are the key to effective work. (See chapters 4 and 7 for a more in-depth examination of stress and trauma management.)

Lessons learned

- Regular meetings among agencies, with clear agendas, objectives and plans of action, are vital for effective work. Whoever facilitates meetings should be trained and experienced in this role. People attending meetings should identify those among themselves who have good facilitation skills and use them.
- Deliberate effort should be made to include national NGOs and relevant government decision-makers in co-ordination meetings. Their voices must be heard so that all the groups involved with children can reach a common understanding and all participants can learn from one another.
- Staff of children's programmes who have no experience in co-ordinating meetings should be encouraged to learn how to participate and facilitate effectively. This is a vital skill often

ignored in training, where more technical skills are given priority.

- Agencies should keep the need for networking in mind when they appoint staff. Not all types of personalities respond well to the pressures of inter-agency co-ordination on children's issues; it takes a commitment to learn, respect for others, a willingness to understand other agencies' mandates and pressures— and, of course, commitment to the well-being of children.
- Differences of language and culture mean verbal messages can often be unclear. Agreements between international NGOs and their local partners should always be written to ensure that expectations and agreed-upon actions by both parties are clear. Ambiguity in an agreement leads to confusion about roles and responsibility for a project. Ensuring clear written agreements are made with the government for particular projects as soon as possible in the process is also recommended, for the same reasons.
- Decentralising co-ordination efforts to the districts in a country is more inclusive, effective and enhances stronger working relationships on the ground. This does not exclude the need for effective central co-ordination but allows for that co-ordination to base its strategies on district realities.

Principle four: An integrated perspective

NGO interventions in emergencies tend to adopt sectoral approaches. One agency may be known as the expert in food distribution, another in water and sanitation, a different one in emergency health, and yet another in psychosocial interventions. This sectoral specialism has strengths and weaknesses.

Looking holistically at the healthy development of a child, all these areas have an effect; unless there is a co-ordinated response, there may not be a sufficiently comprehensive safety net. An integrated approach to addressing the needs of children, weaving together the various disciplines of humanitarian intervention, appears most effective. Ideally, then, specialists in health, agriculture and commodities work together with the children's programme staff in the design and implementation of interventions.

In reality, this is difficult. The increasingly specialised technical focus in emergencies and the desire for efficiency are increasing the tendency toward single-interest programme design. Generalists are harder to find in CHEs these days. Those especially concerned for children need the support of other sectors more than ever.

Donor participation

The dynamics of project funding are a significant encouragement toward sectoral programme design, and donors need to be re-educated to ensure the problem does not persist. While some donors appear to show increasing interest in innovative ideas, this is not always the case.

Competition for government funding is strong, and those who write project proposals often hesitate to include in the budget anything that might seem to be out of the ordinary. This is particularly true in addressing social ("soft") components, as opposed to purely technical interventions. In the emergency phase, it is true that there is often money for specific children's work such as family tracing, support for reunification and managing transit centres. But in the later transitional phases, when some stability has come to a country but life is still fragile, finding financial support for broad programmes that support children becomes harder. Yet this is when the value of community-based programmes is greatest, to provide a safety net for the most vulnerable children.

Demonstrations of how the integration of sectors can provide better care for children came in more than one war zone in Africa in 1997. In each case, it was assumed that children who had been separated from their families would be integrated into the community, as had normally been the case in the past. It was found, however, that some separated children were not treated equally with others and that families were giving greater priority to feeding their own children. This led NGOs to attach a community worker to nutritional feeding centres, working with the centre and the community to follow up children who were not putting on weight at the expected rate. This is not a procedure that was considered in health proposals as a matter of course; instead, it was often left to the agencies that focus on social issues to write a separate proposal for funding. That often comes too late and is not as cost effective as integration of community workers at the start of the health project.

Organisations specialising in food distribution are generally very responsive to requests from orphanages, but if they do not consider the wider implications, this can have a detrimental effect in the long term. If an orphanage receives more regular or better food than families in the community, then those orphanages will become attractive for families who are struggling—and the risk of children being abandoned into residential care increases.

Preventive care

A CHE can cause serious harm to the development of many children. Special attention should be paid to regions which show signs of deteriorating toward instability and crisis; prevention work could be done to mitigate the effects of any increase in conflict. A glance at the extent to which the crisis in the African Great Lakes has affected the entire region suggests that, even in countries which appear to have more political stability, humanitarian agencies could benefit from training staff on the special needs of children in CHEs.

This training should incorporate local organisations working in the community and should be adapted to the country in question. That would establish a range of local organisations that would understand key issues and expectations and the need for accountability.

During the Rwanda crisis, many organisations were new to the country. Regularly updated country profiles, written before an emergency, could indicate the capacity of local organisations and identify those which may have some basic ability to cope with a CHE. In a new political climate, of course, there may be suspicions about established organisations and their bias toward the previous regime, and this needs to be taken into account when selecting partners. But in hindsight, the strongest local associations in Rwanda tended to be those that were present before the war or had local leadership with experience in the international community.

Lessons learned

- An understanding of the factors that influence healthy development of children should not be limited to the child specialists and related programme staff.
- Encouraging creativity in project design includes addressing the developmental needs of vulnerable children and starting the process of addressing funding challenges with donors.

◆ Staff need to be attentive to and track the history of individual children. Simple but effective record keeping of the children's on-going status helps staff learn more about the most effective ways to track the development of children in and after emergencies. This is part of good program design but on the ground in an emergency is not so easy for staff to put into practice. It also requires funding.

◆ Training about the needs of children in CHEs should be extended to staff in countries not considered to be relief situations, as well as those that are so designated.

Principle five: A people perspective

In conflict and post-conflict zones, the first call on the time and energy of senior staff should be investing in people, not structures. A lot of money was offered by a number of private donors and some government donors for building orphanages in Rwanda. These donors were not interested when alternative uses for the money—such as measures to prevent abandonment of children or support for community initiatives—were suggested.

Children need shelter. Providing it is rightly a priority. But when the roof is up, the quality of transit care for children in CHEs will depend on the skills and understanding of the adults involved, not the structures in which children are housed. In war and post-war situations, more trained staff are always needed than are available, and NGOs must train staff as an early priority. Yet capacity building is often last on the list of priorities in a CHE.

Often this is the time when there are many visitors to the programme, and many of these visitors have technical expertise in programme design or evaluation. It is easy to forget to use them to provide a short, informal training experience for staff. If it is argued that everyone is too busy, the counter-proposal is that staff will be more effective if they have more knowledge, and this will save time in the long run. In July 1994, an expert in psychosocial issues for children affected by war was advising UNICEF in Rwanda. During his visit, NGOs were invited to attend a half-day training session in practical issues, and those who were not psychologists gained some basic skills in caring for traumatised children. The investment of time proved its worth, even in the emergency phase, and subsequent programme design was enhanced.

Many managers will be tempted to postpone capacity building for staff until things quiet down, but this traditional relief mindset can remain for years. Quality of staff training will directly affect the care and development of children during the CHE and thereafter.

Several agencies are now making a positive effort to address this training gap, but it will still require a commitment by project managers to support staff and encourage their attendance at training sessions.

Lessons learned

- Invite child development experts who visit projects to run short training sessions for field staff. Look into regional staff exchange programmes.
- Identify areas in which training is needed as soon as possible, and make it a priority to address these needs. Consider key community leaders such as teachers, religious leaders and local authorities as resources and potential trainers in this identification process.
- Joint training with other NGOs, especially indigenous partners, and with government officials makes good use of limited resources even though it requires more time and energy to organise. Such training provides opportunities for people to share practical experiences and to see other models for working with children, and prevents organisations from becoming isolated and narrow in their perspective.
- Tools for stress management should be included as part of staff capacity building.

Principle six: A participative principle

Working with children in Rwanda, the UN *Convention on the Rights of the Child* was the key source for statements on good practice. However, some aspects of the convention were given a lower priority, probably because staff had less understanding, skills and experience. Specifically, articles 12 and 13 of the convention refer to the right of children to participate in decisions which affect them and their freedom of expression. How did World Vision promote an environment where children had freedom of expression, and to what degree did the children participate in the decisions made for them?

In the assessment and planning stage in 1994, staff held informal discussions and asked children (as they did adults) what was happening to them, what concerns they had, and what they wanted for the future. In later planning, staff kept this feedback in mind. As community workers visited families, they were encouraged to include children in discussions. When questioned about child participation in relation to tracing and reunification activities, community workers' common response was that children who had been separated had to consent to reunification. Children were informed of their options when it came to placement with extended family when their parents were not found and were asked what they wanted.

But is this true participation? What more could have been done?

Children in unaccompanied-children centres often participated in public gatherings on key issues. At times, it appeared the children were being used to promote a cause through dramatic performances with little notion of what the cause was really about. This is what Roger Hart, in his Ladder of Participation,[6] refers to as "decoration," really a degree of non-participation.

Two other simple examples indicate that the levels of participation could have made for a better programme.

One case related to a centre where children went on "strike" to complain about the food. They were not eating well because they were tired of the same food, and some children had bad stomach pains as a result of the way food was prepared. They first informally expressed their unhappiness at the diet but were not listened to. Some of the more vocal children then suggested they go on strike, and the others agreed. The children themselves recommended solutions to the problem, which were incorporated in changes that were eventually made.

While it could be argued that the food strike taught some children skills in assertiveness, it would have been better if the children learned negotiation skills that do not require the level of conflict that leads to a strike. If children had been an integral part of planning and implementation of the centre, they would have felt acknowledged and could have been listened to earlier and the conflict avoided.

The second example relates to the 1997 Child-Headed Households Qualitative Needs Assessment. This provided a forum where a specific group of children were intentionally listened to. We had assumed prior to this that by helping the community, these children would automatically benefit, but this was shown not to be the case in many situations. As adults, we also assumed that we knew the problems of children and therefore knew what their priorities should be. We assumed that the children felt supported if neighbours were providing material support, but we found this was not the case. As one girl said, "What we need most is someone to understand what is in our hearts. We need to be guided, loved and supported to cultivate our land."[7] The material support was important, but there was much more. This girl knew what she needed. Adults should listen to what children say as they ask for support. Many children affected by war have developed incredible survival skills and abilities which we need to acknowledge and build on in a positive way.

Discussions on child participation continue today and relate to how we view child development and the democratic process. If we are to be child focused, we need to go far deeper than the tokenism that often takes the place of participation. Roger Hart's Ladder of Participation is a useful tool to help an agency assess how seriously it is committed to participation.

Lessons learned

- Programmes that affect children need to include children in the design, implementation and evaluation process.
- Staff need early training in participatory processes to avoid waste of resources; this training needs to focus on methodologies to ensure effective participation by children.
- We must not assume that children's problems need to be solved by adults. We need to acknowledge the skills that children in conflict zones have developed and build on these in a positive way.
- Children in the wider community should be involved in the participatory assessment process—not just those children in particularly vulnerable situations.
- In many cultures, children are expected to be seen and not heard. Community education on the right to participation by children needs to be incorporated in capacity building initiatives.

Principle seven: A peacebuilding perspective

This is probably the biggest challenge for any programme planner. From a field perspective, there appears to be minimal understanding and commitment by NGOs to supporting peacebuilding skills with children. This is not to say nothing is being done. In Rwanda, UNICEF developed the Peace Education Programme for schools, but this naturally took time to develop, taking into account the local context, and was limited to schools. Developing community-based peacebuilding programmes through churches and other groups would seem to be possible with very sensitive planning and good timing.

This need for NGOs to consider peacebuilding was brought home during a number of instances from 1994 to 1997.

Late in 1994, some children were asked to draw pictures of what they wanted to do in their future. Most pictures had a military theme, guns featured prominently, and the children's heroes were generally soldiers. The children appeared to view soldiers as the people who rescued them and protected them from more danger. This reaction is understandable in light of the events of that year.

In 1995, separated children who came from the IDP (internally displaced persons) camps were to be brought to a transit centre. Residents of that centre refused to admit any of the children over 12 years, in case they had taken part in the genocide. This certainly challenged us to think about issues related to protection and healthy development of children from both sides of the conflict.

In 1996, some children were performing for government visitors. A child confidently read a poem he had written. Translation of one line in particular highlighted the challenge ahead: "We are brave and we are strong and we will fight the enemies at the borders." Once again, children appeared to be concerned about being safe and needing to fight to stay safe.

What can an NGO do to help children develop good conflict resolution skills and promote peaceful community life? Debates surrounding justice and peace issues which relate to peacebuilding with children are too complex to discuss in this chapter. But these complexities should not prevent the issues being explored in more depth. Thus the recommendation for research on such programmes.

One wonders whether the types of programmes described in chapters 4 and 7 could be adapted for children. As with the UNICEF programme, a focus on building self-esteem seems to be an appropriate starting point. The rationale is that children (and adults) need to love and care for themselves before they can truly care for others.

To some extent, the type of care and attention given to children who have experienced war will determine whether these children will become healthy adults who make a positive contribution to a civil society or will perpetuate the hatred they have witnessed and experienced in their childhood.

Lessons learned
- More research needs to focus on understanding how to better support children who have experienced war. The aim could be to help children reach the point when they have the breadth of skills to choose less violent methods of resolving conflict.
- Conflict-prone areas should be targeted for peace education projects as a mitigation response.
- Programmes working with marginalised children and encouraging their social reintegration—such as separated children and demobilised child soldier programmes—should have a peace-building component deliberately written into them.
- Education and vocational-training opportunities should be an integral part of supporting peace efforts.

Principle eight: A broad and long-term perspective

A commitment to children affected by war, as illustrated by the seven previous principles, cannot be taken lightly. To be child sensitive, to address the needs of the most vulnerable children, requires that an organisation design a broad-based programme and make a long-term commitment. Skilled and knowledgeable staff are needed to embrace the holistic needs of children, to integrate the wider society in relevant activities, and to generate a proper degree of collaboration with community leaders and other organisations.

Just as experts design food security and health programmes, programmes for children in CHEs must also to be designed by experts in the field. Specialists must collaborate with those who have knowledge of the local culture, while listening to the children and learning the lessons of the past.

The healing process for children affected by war does not proceed quickly. If we are serious in our concern for the future of a country and region, programmes addressing children need to take the widest possible view of their needs and be planned with the end result in mind—growing adults who will contribute positively to their world.

NOTES

[1] Other terms used to describe this group of children include *unaccompanied minors* (UAMs) and *separated children*. The term *separated children* is more commonly used now.

[2] UNHCR, *Working with Unaccompanied Children: A Community-Based Approach,* rev. ed., Community Services Guidelines (Geneva: UNHCR, 1996).

[3] Phyllis Kilbourn, ed., *Healing the Children of War* (Monrovia, Calif.: MARC, 1995).

[4] Chris Roche, *Development in Practice* 4/3 (1994).

[5] World Vision Rwanda, draft report on child-headed households in Kanazi (Kigali, December 1997).

[6] Roger Hart, *Children's Participation: The Theory and Practice of Involving Young Citizens in Community Development and Environmental Care* (London: Earthscan/UNICEF, 1997).

[7] 1999 World Vision Child-Headed Household Baseline Survey in Kanazi Subprefecture.

2.

The Gile Airlift

Integrated Humanitarian Programming

WALTER MIDDLETON

Is 50 percent enough? The first crop harvested after the beginning of the Gile airlift produced only 50 percent of its possible yield.[1] It may not sound like much, but in the context of nothing, it is quite a lot. The people of Gile were literally starving to death. They had only a few bags of food to feed 36,000 people. Through the airlift, provision of food aid, health care and agricultural inputs (which

---

This chapter is based on World Vision program reports. The health and nutrition section was contributed by Dr Hector Jalipa, who is currently World Vision's Africa Regional Health Advisor based in Nairobi, Kenya. He has acted as advisor for health and nutrition projects in at least twenty countries (ranging from East Timor to Zambia). Prior to that he worked in countries such as Mozambique, Ethiopia and Thailand. In addition to his health work for World Vision, Hector has consulted for UNICEF and was part of a USAID assessment team for Angola. Hector has an MD from the University of Santo Tomas in Manila, and a master of public health degree from Harvard University. The section on agricultural inputs was contributed by Jonathan White, an agronomist with 25 years of experience in rural development in various countries of Europe, Africa and Latin America. Jon also served with World Vision in Mozambique as National Director for four years and as Manager of Agricultural Recovery and Emergency Programs for six years. The author and contributors were the major designers and implementers of the airlift program. We are aware of nothing else that has been published on this particular topic.

produced this first crop, as well as others of much higher yield later) became steps toward self-reliance for the people of Gile. In fact, they recovered so well after the airlift that they became producers of surplus food.

What made such a transformation possible? A resilient people, surely. Also an eight-month airlift of food, medical supplies, seeds and tools. In short, an integrated relief programme.

This chapter presents a case study of World Vision's airlift to Gile, which had been cut off from all relief assistance by road due to military activity and land mines. Landlocked, and with no rail line, airlift was the only option to save tens of thousands of lives. This chapter offers practical advice and guiding principles for conducting successful airlifts and also highlights issues to consider when designing and implementing integrated emergency response.

In an emergency situation, especially when conducting an airlift operation, an integrated approach is not always easy. Careful planning and co-ordination are essential to ensure that people are not only given food and clothing, but also seeds, tools, technical assistance and health care, so that they are enabled to progress from relief to development, thus enabling them to attain food security and self-sufficiency.

BACKGROUND

Mozambique, a large country of 15 million perched at the southeastern corner of Africa, gained its independence from Portugal in 1975 after nearly 400 years of colonialism. Opportunities for advancement among black Mozambicans during those years were so limited that even taxi drivers, postal clerks and plumbers were Portuguese. Samora Machel, who became the first president of Mozambique in 1975, had earlier reached the highest professional position he might have aspired to, that of hospital nurse. In those early days of newfound independence, people with little education or experience tried to make the country run.

One of the most difficult obstacles the country faced was a country-wide civil war in which RENAMO (also known as the MNR—Mozambique National Resistance Movement) forces were pitted against the government. RENAMO publicly enunciated only a vague political intent other than to overthrow the Marxist government.

Some political pundits believed RENAMO's chief purpose was to destabilise the country's economy. Externally backed RENAMO forces targeted attacks on schools, health centres, relief convoys, economic installations, rural villages and towns, as well as private commercial establishments. Hundreds of thousands of Mozambican peasants were killed in rural massacres and assaults. Because of rural terrorism, 1.6 million Mozambicans were displaced within their own country, and another 1 million fled to neighbouring countries. Peasant food production and commerce were greatly reduced due to these war conditions, forcing an additional 2.5 million Mozambicans to depend on food aid. The emergency in Mozambique was further deepened by repeated drought.

The economy of Mozambique was finally so shattered that for some time it was impossible to buy basic necessities such as soap, candles and matches anywhere in the country—even in the capital of Maputo—even if you had hard currency. A five-star hotel at one time had a menu that consisted of only three items for breakfast: coffee, butter and bread. And the hotel often had only two of those items to serve on any given day.

The bottom line: Mozambique was a complex emergency. Its long-term nature, the constantly changing location of the most affected population, the inadequate infrastructure due to the colonial legacy, and destruction by RENAMO forces made re-building the economic and social life of the 5.1 million rural Mozambicans affected by the emergency very difficult. Mozambican families fleeing RENAMO-controlled areas had few resources. Often they would walk for days or weeks to safety and arrive in secure areas severely malnourished and weak. Food aid was the first line of action to save their lives.

Gile, a district in the province of Zambezia in northern Mozambique, was one of the districts under RENAMO control for about two years before the government regained control in June 1988. Even after the government regained control, Gile continued to be extremely isolated due to the security situation. Roads to Gile had been destroyed and mined, making it accessible only by air. Gile was situated 175 kilometres from the provincial capital of Quelimane.

Although there were some supplies of food by air, these were not nearly enough to meet the needs of the estimated 36,000 people, many of them displaced, who had gathered in Gile. Between the months of January and March 1989, 28 metric tons of food was delivered to Gile. This food was enough to feed the people there for two days only.

In early February 1989, reports of widespread malnutrition and starvation-related deaths in Gile began to trickle into Quelimane. At that time, government officials approached food-aid donors for emergency relief to Gile, as the government had neither the resources nor the means to airlift food to the area.

World Vision was the first NGO to send an assessment team to Gile on 17–18 March 1989. The scene was haunting. In the last moments of their lives, people dying from starvation were holding their equally emaciated loved ones in an effort to comfort and be comforted. In the government warehouse, the team found just four bags of wheat and two bags of yellow corn, sufficient to feed only 857 people for one day. Severe malnutrition was rampant, with 15 to 20 persons dying daily.

WORLD VISION'S RESPONSE

World Vision immediately began operations. A team of specialists in health, food aid and agriculture travelled to Gile to assess and quantify needs so that adequate supplies could be arranged and ordered. The people lacked even basic amenities of food, water and sanitation. Disease was rampant, mostly measles, diarrhoea, anaemia and malaria. The assessment team recommended immediate intervention of food aid and medical assistance. This was to include therapeutic feeding and sanitation. This set the stage for one of the most successful life-saving operations in World Vision's history.

The primary objective of the airlift was to control and end the severe malnutrition and high mortality rates in the district of Gile through delivery and distribution of approximately 225 metric tons of food every month to the people concentrated in the town of Gile, over a period of six months. This was not the ideal ration for the malnourished population, but this quantity was derived after taking into consideration resourcing and logistical constraints. In an emergency such as this, the tendency is to set ration scales based on available food stocks and logistical constraints rather than nutritional requirements and other considerations.

In addition, it was decided to carry out a nutritional survey to identify the "at risk" suffering from third- and fourth-degree malnutrition in need of therapeutic feeding, and to establish baseline data for a child-survival project.

The first and foremost task was to put together a proposal to seek funding for the airlift operations. A budget for US$1,259,300 was prepared and submitted to United States Agency for Development (USAID), World Vision's biggest donor in Mozambique, which expressed an interest in funding the airlift operation. The question could be asked, Why not repair the road leading to Gile rather than airlift food at an exorbitant cost? The answer: Security was a critical constraint; the roads were mined. Further, people were dying. Airlift was the only option. To get the operation up and running, World Vision committed US$500,000 of its private monies.

The first priority was to charter a plane and hire an airlift co-ordinator. Protocols were established for co-ordination with the relief arm of the government, the Department for Prevention and Combat of Natural Calamities (DPCCN). An airlift co-ordinator with significant experience in logistics was immediately hired and based in Quelimane to co-ordinate and implement the airlift operation.

AIRSERV, an NGO involved in providing air transport in Mozambique, mostly to organizations involved in relief work, was contracted to do the airlift. AIRSERV had just one small cargo plane, a Caravan Cessna with a carrying capacity of 1.3 metric tons. It turned out to be a mistake to undertake the airlift operation with only one plane, as several problems were encountered as soon as the airlift got under way. On the third day of operation, the plane hit a land mine when it landed in Gile and had to be grounded for several days. Other problems included engine problems, regular maintenance trips to Maputo (which took four hours plus time to work on the aircraft), rain, erratic supply of fuel, and the crush of requests to fly visitors (high-profile donors, technical and marketing personnel) to Gile.

In the first month of operation, because of the above problems, against the target of 225 metric tons, only 92 metric tons of food were airlifted. World Vision was compelled to look for additional planes to meet the monthly food-delivery target that lives were depending on. Getting cargo planes suitable for landing on the small airstrip in Gile was not easy. In August 1989, World Vision hired a second aircraft, a CASA, from the Mozambican airline company, Linhas Areas de Mocambique (LAM), with a carrying capacity of 2.5 metric tons. With the second plane, World Vision was able to average 10 to 15 metric tons per day, depending on the weather, location of commodities and plane down time.

Two food-aid monitors were based in Gile to oversee and co-ordinate operations on the ground. Along with them were two nurses to do the therapeutic feeding. At the therapeutic feeding centre, wet feeding provided four feedings per day for the severely malnourished. The centre was run only by day; patients were not allowed to remain in the hospital by night because they would have been vulnerable to attacks by bandits.

Bandit activity, even in those pathetic conditions, was still a re-ality and often resulted in the cutting off of people's ears, noses and lips. Women were abducted and raped. Huts were burned. Staff slept fully dressed, ready to run and hide in the bush should an attack occur at night.

In addition to providing therapeutic feeding, health agents treated complications of severe malnutrition. Before long, people's health started to improve. In a September 1989 report, staff noted that at the onset of the programme, an incessant crying could be heard, but after the first couple of months of feeding, sounds heard were happy ones and a difference could be seen in the faces of the benefi-ciaries. The dramatic difference in those children who had been fed for four months was visible assurance that other children would recover also—and this lent hope to the whole scene. If World Vi-sion had not started the therapeutic feeding programme, a segment of the population could not have benefited from the regular emer-gency food donated (maize, beans and vegetable oil).

Clinical records indicated that after food, medicines and soap arrived in April, a steady decrease in death rates from diarrhoea, anaemia and malnutrition occurred. Deaths from diarrhoea were down from 152 in March to 28 in July. Deaths from malnutrition were down from 119 in April to 18 in July. There was still a need to lower death rates further, however.

The airlift had been in progress for six months when, in early November, a mentally ill local man was killed when he walked into the spinning propeller of the LAM CASA at Gile. An inquiry into the incident revealed that security was lax and that at the time no one was actually controlling the crowd. There was no fencing around the airstrip. After this incident, security personnel were put on duty during off-loading of the aircraft and a fence was constructed where the discharge of cargo took place.

PROBLEMS ENCOUNTERED

An airlift operation during an emergency is difficult, especially when facilities are limited, officials are corrupt, food is scarce, manpower is limited, and there is no certainty of continuous funding. During the eight months of the airlift operation, we experienced innumerable problems. Some could have been avoided or minimised had we not been working in emergency mode. Very often we did not put into practice the "P5" formula we preached: Proper Planning Prevents Poor Performance. The following are some of the problems we encountered.

Erratic fuel supply

We could start work in the morning with the understanding that there was ample supply and by evening be told there was none and no more would be available for days. We managed to mitigate this by creating our own emergency reserve of fuel in 55–gallon drums. However, from time to time, fuel depot officials refused to pump fuel into the drums. At one point we restructured our programme to bring the fuel into Gile from Nampula, another province approximately 350 kilometres from Gile. This was only about 60 percent as productive as flying fuel from Quelimane, but at least we kept the planes flying when fuel was unavailable in Quelimane.

Then there were days when there was no diesel for the truck carrying the fuel from the depot to the airport. At times the fuel pump would break down. And at times there would be no electricity at the depot, and it would take hours to fill up the truck manually.

Thefts

When the airlift first started in Gile, soldiers assigned to protect and guard the commodities were often found opening sacks of grain and stealing the contents or running away with containers of vegetable oil. On one occasion, when food monitors intervened, the guard was taken to police, interrogated and intimidated for six hours, then put into prison accused of being a member of the secret police. Thefts by the soldiers could be attributed in part to the fact that they received their supplies directly from the government, and very often their supplies were delayed two to three weeks. Hence they were tempted to steal. They were also very poorly paid and often didn't receive salaries for months.

Lack of commodities

In several instances, no commodities were available in the warehouses. At times, there would be cereals, but no pulses[2] or oil. There were occasions when DPCCN would take days to ship food up from Maputo to Quelimane.

We started exploring ways and means to overcome the lack of commodities. Through contacts we learned that Alto Molocue, a district 60 miles from Gile, had a surplus of maize, beans and rice from local production, and that this surplus was going to waste because of the inability to ship it out due to security problems. We were able to swap the commodities in Alto Molocue with our own commodities in Quelimane on a kilogram for kilogram basis. However, there was still a problem. There was no fuel in Alto Molocue. This problem was overcome when a ground support area was set up in Alto Molocue. The Caravan would fly to Gile in the morning from Quelimane loaded with drums of fuel and make seven flights a day between Alto Molocue and Gile. The four flights from Quelimane carried 1,250 kilograms each, for a daily total of 5 metric tons. Because of the lighter fuel load, the flight from Alto Molocue carried 1,450 kilograms, so the daily lift was over 10 metric tons, with a corresponding reduction in cost. As the days got longer, we were able to increase to eight flights, so the day capacity went up to 11.5 metric tons. Not only was there a reduction in cost, but the tonnage of food delivered into Gile significantly increased. Agricom, the Mozambican government-owned company from which the commodities were taken in Alto Molocue, was extremely happy to receive commodities in Quelimane. Had the swap not taken place, their commodities would have rotted.

Land mines

The airlift had barely started when the AIRSERV Caravan hit a land mine in the Gile airstrip, damaging the plane's port undercarriage. This put us out of operation for three weeks. When the town of Gile had been liberated, a mine sweep removed 61 land mines from the airstrip alone. Unfortunately one was missed—the one that damaged the AIRSERV plane. A thorough mine sweep was carried out again by the army, and this time they found just one additional land mine. Once the airstrip was cleared, the operation resumed.

Labourers

When the airlift first started, it was very difficult to find labourers with enough strength to unload the bags and containers of oil from the aircraft. In Quelimane, the labourers were very demanding. In a few instances, there were not enough labourers to load the aircraft on schedule in the morning. This happened most often when the DPCCN took our trained labourers for other activities. We eventually began loading the aircraft the previous evening, after it had made the final trip for the day.

Arrangements were also made to store two 20-foot containers at the airport, which always had a stock of food commodities. In case food trucks did not arrive on time from the warehouse, food could quickly be taken from the containers. This helped ensure a quick turn-around time for the planes. Within a month after commencement of the airlift operation, staff in Quelimane had trained a group of labourers to load the AIRSERV Caravan in less than four minutes. Off-loading in Gile took approximately three minutes. Once, a pilot jokingly stated that he did not get enough time on the ground to visit the restroom.

On a few occasions labourers at the Quelimane warehouse shut the warehouse down at 5 P.M., refusing to work extra hours unless they were paid a significant amount for overtime.

Proper use of the aircraft

When the airlift began a number of passengers—mostly government officials—took rides to and from Gile on the AIRSERV plane.

It did not take us long to ban passengers from the cargo planes. There were a few medical evacuations, along with flying our airlift monitors in and out. There were also a few occasions on which we flew senior officials, but these were rare and occurred only when we judged it expedient. This policy of "no passengers" helped us maintain control of aircraft payloads but did not please government officials in Gile and Quelimane, who frequently asked for lifts.

MOVING PEOPLE FROM DEPENDENCY
TO SELF-SUFFICIENCY

From the outset of the airlift operation, World Vision provided people with seeds and tools in order to move them from dependency on food imported at high cost toward food self-sufficiency. Initially, the majority of the displaced families were too weak and traumatised to engage in agricultural activities. However, after several months of food aid, the population was able to take up land preparation following the distribution of basic hand tools. This ability of farmers to return to a more normal life helped to restore their hope in the future and to heal some of the trauma of war. This was also a crucial factor in improving security and minimizing the public health risk for a crowded population living under conditions of precarious sanitation. As the population slowly moved out to bring land under cultivation, the security radius improved and daytime military patrols extended their range of protection. This wider population presence provided early warning of rebel incursion. When we first distributed hand tools, farmers' fields less than 1 kilometre from Gile town could be visited only with a heavily armed military escort. The spreading out of the population was quite dramatic.

It is of obvious importance to ensure the appropriate combining and sequencing of interventions in the target areas. For example, hungry farmers will eat seeds rather than plant them, unless they receive a prior food distribution and the seeds are distributed to coincide with the onset of the rains. Adequate food distributions should always precede seed distributions and continue in order to protect the seed until it is in the ground. To minimise seed eating, seeds were coated with a dye and a low-toxicity seed dressing with an unpleasant odour. In harmony with the cool, dry agricultural season—and in recognition of the initial high risk of seed eating, the limited airlift capability and the need for a qualitative supplement to the staple distribution of maize, beans and oil—the first seed distribution was of vegetable seeds for planting in the water-retentive river margins. Small packs of vegetable seeds, called Horti-Paks, consisted of leaf cabbage, chinese cabbage, squash, carrots, tomatoes, onions and green beans, with a total weight of 150 grams. Vegetables and legumes provide an important qualitative supplement to diet in terms of vitamins and minerals and complement both food aid and agriculture production. A total of 2,800 Horti-Paks were delivered, and this encouraged the people, who were eager to grow their own food.

Farming represented their whole identity—historically and emotionally. Being involved in their fields was a way of restoring their sense of identity and self-worth. Their lives centred around the land, the seasons, and their crops. Agricultural intervention, even in deteriorating security, allows social reintegration after the trauma of war displacement. Technicians provided technical support and also encouraged multiplication of small stocks of cassava and sweet potato available in the area.

Later, at the start of the rainy season, an additional distribution of hand tools was made to ensure that each family had at least two hoes. Seeds of the major staple crops were distributed in Ag-Paks consisting of maize, sorghum, cowpeas, sugar beans, groundnuts, pigeon peas, squash and okra. Each Ag-Pak contained approximately 14 kilograms of seed, enough to plant 0.75 hectare. A total of 8,000 Ag-Paks were delivered to women considered to be heads of household. The Ag-Paks provided many months of food security, drastically reducing the need for free food distribution, reducing costs, and allowing us to respond to newly arrived displaced persons who as yet had no access to locally produced food. The cost benefit of the seeds intervention is clear when considering that every metric ton of seed provided (airlifted at a cost of about US$800) could result in approximately 50 metric tons of staple food production (transport valued at US$40,000). To ensure that the quantities of seed and the crop varieties chosen were appropriate, participatory evaluation with farmers and key informants such as the district Department of Agriculture were conducted. The goals were to increase understanding of traditional farming systems and how these might be modified for the emergency situation, for example, short-season maize to alleviate hunger. Nutritional value of crops in relation to the priority dietary requirements of malnourished children and adults was also considered.

During emergencies, it is difficult to balance the need for sound methodology (representative sampling, reliable survey instruments) with the need for timely information and intervention. Given the critical situation of the people, it was a foregone conclusion that every family in Gile would benefit from distribution of seeds and tools.

HEALTH AND NUTRITION

Surveys indicated that more than 30 percent of the population in Gile had global acute malnutrition,[3] and about 3 percent had severe acute malnutrition.[4] This was far above the rate at which general food distributions are started. World Vision staff carried out surveys among the displaced population in secure areas in and around Gile. Populations outside this secure zone could not be included. Children under five were used as the baseline for estimating the entire population's malnutrition level. The system of using the body mass index as an indicator for adult malnutrition was not as systematically used then as it is now. Severely malnourished children requiring intensive (wet)[5] feeding initially numbered more than 100.

Co-ordination with other NGOs was an important feature of the Gile programme. To avoid duplication of efforts, agreement was reached among the NGOs operating in the area, whereby responsibility for water and sanitation was carried out by Oxfam, health training and education by Save the Children Fund, medical care by Medecins Sans Frontieres (MSF), nutrition and food distribution by World Vision. In most cases, the NGOs made their own arrangements to bring in their supplies.

The feeding protocol for severely malnourished children consisting of milk, sugar and oil was first developed and tested in the 1984 Ethiopian famine. The famine in Mozambique became the testing ground to check the protocol's applicability and repeatability in other contexts. There were many changes and adaptations to the protocol as the Mozambique programme progressed, among them inclusion of micronutrients, distribution of antihelmenthics,[6] and blanket antibiotic treatment against infections.

Gile was one of World Vision's pioneering large-scale therapeutic feeding programmes, validating the importance of incorporating micronutrients in the food. Positive results included reduction in respiratory tract infections and restoration of atonic intestines.[7] Controlled studies in South African hospitals later confirmed the importance of vitamin A in increasing survival rates of patients with measles and diarrhoea.

High Energy Mixture (milk, sugar and oil) was the main food given to newly admitted patients (days 1–3) and fortified porridge (maize meal, beans, oil and sugar) was started on day 4 to substitute the mid-day dose of milk. Quantity of distributed food was determined by demand. Only in subsequent programmes was food quantity calculated based on body weight and caloric requirement. Only day feeding was allowed in the Gile centre because of insecurity.

To consolidate the system in Gile, staff opted to include supplementary feeding in the therapeutic feeding programme. In hindsight, it would have been better to separate them as we now normally do. Separate systems for therapeutic and supplementary feeding programmes better define beneficiary groups and lead to better administration of resources at lower overall programme cost. Supplementary feeding could easily be administered in homes, thereby limiting the number of children coming to a centralised location. In addition to lowering cost, limiting the number of children at a central site reduces the public health hazard. Fewer people gathered at a central site results in a lower possibility of spreading disease.

In previous programmes, accompanying persons (an adult accompanying two or three children) were not included in food calculation and were not given their own rations. As a result, pilferage was very high and food given to admitted patients was often shared with relatives. The adverse effect was a prolonged stay in the feeding programme for those who were severely malnourished. These observations led to development of an adjunct feeding protocol for accompanying persons, consisting of maize, beans and oil, with dried fish added for variety three times a week.

The feeding of the one patient plus accompanying persons led to greater compliance and shorter stays in the programme. While it seems that more food was being consumed, use of high-value food like milk and sugar was drastically decreased.

It was calculated through clinic records that the average length of stay in the feeding programme was 21 days. Reduction in the mortality rate was one of the most dramatic observable changes in the programme. Patients who were on the verge of death seemingly sprang back to life overnight simply because they received food. Clinic records showed mortality rates going down from 20 to 2–3 a week within two weeks of operation, eventually going down to 1–2 a month until the programme was closed down six months later.

One shortcoming was the lack of an exit survey to document accurately the impact of our nutritional intervention. We relied on clinic records in making the decision to close down the feeding programme, which occurred when the number of children needing therapeutic feeding went below 20. Thereafter some support was given to the district hospital in the form of milk, sugar and oil. Clinic records provide adequate criteria for making programming decisions but do not constitute an adequate measure of public health.

Many feeding programmes relied on expatriate staff, as it was believed that therapeutic feeding was a specialised field requiring highly trained and experienced health personnel. The Gile programme opted to use national staff who had basic nursing training and to give them intensive hands-on training. Subsequent follow-up and monitoring of staff was carried out once every five to seven days. This had dramatic impact on local capacity building and savings in overhead and administrative costs. These staff members eventually became the backbone of future interventions in Mozambique. As the programme moved toward rehabilitation, more and more responsibilities were handed over to district health authorities.

Malnourished children are very vulnerable. Mortality rates rise quickly if simple infections like diarrhoea, malaria and respiratory infections are not managed early. Public health interventions like provision of water and latrines are essential to overall recovery. Distributing bars of soap and requiring patients to bathe before attending clinics controlled the spread of eye and skin infections.

Additionally, the role of a health logistics person cannot be overemphasised. It is critical that a support base be established for smooth operations in the field, leaving technical staff free to concentrate on clinic work. It can become very frustrating for people working in the field when supplies are not delivered on time. It is already very stressful to work in this environment, and if staff needs are not provided on time, burnout results.

NEED FOR CONSTANT MONITORING

From the very first day, we had monitors in Gile on the ground. The monitors' role was to assist DPCCN staff to take delivery of food at the airstrip, to ensure its safe transport to the warehouse and proper storage, to assist in preparation of the distribution plan, and to monitor distribution and verify that this was in fact taking place according to the plan. The monitors also had the responsibility every morning of sending by radio a weather and security report to Quelimane, the location from which planes were flying into Gile. Security was especially fluid, and we needed to ensure planes were not flying into an attack.

From our on-site monitoring, as well as periodic visits of World Vision staff and an audit, we believe that to a very large degree all of the food airlifted into Gile did in fact reach the population. Two or three situations required the attention of the local administration, but by and large we received no long-term complaints from the population. When the health programme got under way, health personnel were assigned to Gile, and an agriculture extensionist was added when the agricultural seeds and tools were airlifted in. So we had several sets of eyes at all times on the situation, as well as periodic visits from World Vision Mozambique's management team. Teamwork and team support characterised the programme. Each sector supported the other when need arose. Food monitors assisted the health staff with logistics needs. Likewise, the health staff time assisted the commodities staff in monitoring. The commodities and agricultural staff worked side-by-side during distribution of seeds and tools.

IMPACT OF THE AIRLIFT OPERATION

This airlift operation was one of the longest in the history of World Vision, lasting from 20 April 1989 to 21 December 1989. During these eight months we airlifted into Gile a total of 1,667 metric tons of food and some medicines and clothing for the 36,000 people there. By the end of December 1989, the situation in Gile had experienced a marked transformation.

The obvious impact of the operation was the saving of lives. The number of deaths was significantly reduced by December. Infant malnutrition was down to 10 percent. People who were walking skeletons when the airlift began were now healthy and strong and even smiling. Three months into the operation, a small market sprang up, and the local community even opened a disco where young folk would flock by night to dance. Children were bubbling with energy, a sharp contrast to the early days. People were aggressively tilling their soil, building houses and repairing bridges and roads. Two water wells were recovered and equipped with manual pumps. The airstrip was levelled, and the approach cleared back an additional 100 metres. A hospital kitchen was built, and a new roof was put on the maternity clinic.

Impressions

Administrator of Gile: "In July 1988, the people had gone for two years without medical attention and food. They began to come in bringing the sick. I felt ashamed because the people had to live like this. In December 1988, Medecins San Frontieres brought in nurses along with some medicines. The airlift of food began in April 1989, and when the planes came and kept coming, we knew then that the world had not forgotten us. Now Gile is 5 or 10 times better than in August of 1988. Now there is music and dancing at night in Gile."

Barlinda Alberto Danas, Secretary of DPCCN: "In August of 1988 they brought us here because it had been liberated, but there was little food. Everything is better now. We have food, clothes and medicines."

Leonardo Eduardo, primary school teacher: "When I came here the children in the class were all skinny and sick. It was difficult to teach. It took a long time for them to understand—they were slow because of hunger. Now the children are receiving a high-protein milk mixture once every other day (there is enough milk mixture for feeding every day, but we lack cooking pots and cups). We are noticing that their motivation to learn has returned. Their bodies are strong, and they grasp ideas more rapidly. Now what we need is physical education equipment to help them with their physical development—we don't even have one ball."

Jonathan White, World Vision agricultural manager in Zambezia: "Twenty-eight thousand Horti-Paks were distributed in Gile and have produced an estimated 50 percent of crop yield. They were given in response to an emergency need, and therefore there was not enough technical support available. . . . The provincial Department of Agriculture was not able to offer any technical help either. Two other factors which lowered the yield were low water availability, and green fly attacks."

Tanya Brenneman, part-time reporter for World Vision who made occasional trips to Gile: "Every person I asked gave me the same ration per month per person that they were receiving: 5–6 kilos of maize, to 1 kilo of beans, and, if it came in, 0.5 kilo of oil. They indicated that it was enough. They also said that the delivery had been regular. I was very impressed with the efficiency of the pilots and the loading and unloading of the planes. They were very serious about their jobs and were highly professional."

Author: On 24 April 1989, when I went into Gile, four days after commencement of the airlift operation, it was like a ghost town. The only noise one could hear was the arrival and departure of the AIRSERV plane. What surprised me most was that there was absolutely no emotion in the faces of the little children, not even on seeing the plane come in. I tried to talk to them, smile at them, shake their hands, but all I got in return were blank stares. Almost all of them, as well as the men and women, were skin and bones. When I went to the warehouse, I saw a man lying at the side where there was a little shade. He must have been in his mid-40s but looked old and haggard. I went over to speak with him. He kept staring at me. I repeated my questions, and in a very feeble voice he responded in Portuguese, "Quero morrer [I want to die]." I learned that he had been through immense suffering and torture and had lost all of his family—three had died due to starvation and two at the hands of RENAMO. He said life was not worth living. I informed him about the arrival of food in the town and asked one of the staff to take him to the therapeutic feeding centre. His name was Mario.

Four months later, on my third visit to Gile, I was walking through the small market area when someone from behind came and put his arms on my shoulder and greeted me. He politely said, "I am Mario. Do you remember me?" There was no way I would have recognised him. He had put on weight and now held my hand and led me to his little shop where he was selling dried fish. He was proud of it and wanted to present me a handful of fish. He was so thankful that World Vision had saved his life: "I have just got married again and I want to enjoy life."

When I landed that morning at the airstrip, several dozen children were cheering and clapping on seeing the plane landing. This transformation of Gile is something I will never forget. The district is now producing enough food to feed not only itself, but also to feed nearby districts. Surplus maize is being exported.

The airlift operation came to a close 21 December 1989, when the road to Gile finally had been repaired and opened up. Trucks began to ply the route between Nampula and Gile. A round-trip took two days. The DPCCN assumed responsibility for food shipments into the area, as it had developed capacity to handle the operation. Gile was back on its feet. In the morning you could hear the sounds of corn being ground, and the singing of children in the school. Both were new sounds—sounds of life.

The district agricultural department reported that due to the assistance provided by World Vision, 12,000 hectares of land had come under cultivation and the people had a good harvest to look forward to.

LESSONS LEARNED

Lessons learned from this operation were applied to other airlift operations we undertook in other districts/provinces. Let us look at some of these:

Airlifts

+ To maximise productivity and minimise lost flying days, it is essential to develop and control the fuelling process and have an ample supply of fuel reserve at all times. When this was done, we were able to fuel and load the Caravan in about four minutes.

- If possible, hire your own ground crew. In the beginning we used labourers from the DPCCN pool at Quelimane airport. They were good, but when DPCCN fell months behind in paying them, they would come to us for help. We had the same trouble early on in Alto Molocue, until we went ahead and paid our own crew.
- Select an appropriate aircraft. The ability of the Caravan to fly out in the morning with a day's fuel supply makes it an excellent aircraft for airlifts that include swaps between districts or picking up loads from distant locations. Its fuelling and loading are simple enough so that it is feasible to train and manage crews in remote areas.
- Security arrangements on the airstrip *must* be put in place before actual flying begins.
- To limit hassle, delay and lost productivity, establish a vigorous "no passenger" policy right from the beginning. This gave us some tension with local officials, but in the long run it paid off.
- Plan realistically. An aggressively managed airlift means that, over the life of the airlift, you should only plan on actually transporting goods that will fill 80 percent of the theoretical capacity of the aircraft. Days and flights will be lost due to bad weather, lack of fuel, mechanical and labour problems. We were able to reach the 80 percent level often enough to believe this is a realistic target when planning future airlifts of similar length and nature.
- To remain productive, an experienced and competent airlift coordinator or manager is vital from the very beginning. Technically, an airlift is relatively simple; it might appear that it can run with just technical staff. In practice, in an environment such as Mozambique, the number and frequency of problems that arise to threaten to ground the plane demand constant attention and intervention.
- To help assure rapid turn-around during daylight hours, always plan complex loads for the first flight of the day. That way, the aircraft can be loaded the night before and not slow down productivity.
- Mix loads of high-bulk items with heavy items to maintain maximum utilization (e.g., only 800 kilos of blankets fit into

the Caravan; by mixing 650 kilos of beans with 600 kilos of blankets the full lift and cubic capacity of the aircraft was used.)

* In any swap or other situation involving 90-kilo bags, always plan to re-bag into 50-kilo bags. Ninety-kilo bags take 50 percent longer to load than 50-kilo bags. The cost of re-bagging is less than the cost of the additional block time of loading. From time to time, the lost minutes on each flight will add up to one lost flight for the day. In addition, the large bag makes for less loading flexibility. (The flight from Alto Molocue carried 16 bags of 90 kilos, for a total of 1,440 kilos. It was also loaded with 29 bags of 50 kilos, for a total of 1,450 kilos. The 10-kilo difference in 242 flights comes to more than four tons.) Further, it is easier for a beneficiary to carry a 50-kilo bag from the distribution site than a 90-kilo bag.

* Maintain a two- to three-day reserve of storage space at the airport. Without this, there will be times when cargo will not be at the airport when the plane arrives. Also, this allows flexibility for change of plans and for shelter from rain.

* Have a monitor on the ground at the receiving district to verify that food and non-food items are being distributed according to an equitable plan. Also, it is desirable to have the monitor have control of a radio to call in early security and weather reports. Depending on government officials for this is not always timely and reliable.

Integrated food/agricultural/health programming

* The integration of emergency food, agricultural inputs, and health intervention combined with wet feeding create a remarkably positive synergy. If we had not been delivering food and health interventions for months, beneficiaries would never have been physically able to cultivate their fields. Neither would they have believed our promise that seeds would be delivered. Consequently, preparation of the soil would have waited for the arrival of the seeds, and planting might have been delayed past the optimum time, thereby reducing yield.[8] As it was, when we promised that seed would arrive in two months, beneficiaries believed us and began to prepare extensive amounts of land that were ready for planting when the seeds arrived. If the seeds

and tools had *not* been taken into Gile, the situation would have reverted, once the airlifted ended, to what it had been before our intervention.

♦ Adequate distribution of food should always precede seed distributions. Also, in certain situations distribution of hand tools should precede seed distributions to allow for ground preparation.

♦ Beneficiaries should be encouraged to save their own seed to supplement seeds provided from Ag-Paks during a second year of recuperation.

♦ In addition to the quantitative impact of agricultural production, certain crops—particularly vegetables—can provide a valuable nutritional supplement to food aid. Vegetable production also helps farmers generate some cash income.

♦ The value of adding micronutrients, including those in vegetables, to the food cannot be over-emphasised. Micronutrients decrease mortality and morbidity rates.

♦ When starting a health programme, a logistician should be assigned to the health team so technical staff are free to concentrate on clinic work.

♦ Develop the capacity of local health staff and use them to staff feeding programmes rather than relying on expatriate personnel. This will help build the skills of local individuals, better equip the community to do future feeding programmes if necessary, and cut staffing costs.

♦ It is extremely important to co-ordinate with all NGOs working on the ground. There is also a clear need to integrate food aid, infrastructure, water, health and nutrition activities with the provision of basic agricultural inputs in order to maximise complementarity and rapidly restore food security.

♦ This multi-sectoral approach with programmes working closely together can ensure that the complete needs of affected populations are addressed.

CONCLUSION

Our integrated response provided self-reinforcing complementarity among the three sectors (food aid, agriculture and health), resulting in rapid restoration of food security and allowing for a gradual and planned phasing-out of food aid and emergency feeding centres for malnourished children.

Lessons learned in the Gile airlift operation are widely applicable to other situations in which an airlift is required. Airlifts are not the first choice in food relief/emergency programmes. They are very costly. It would be more costly, however, to lose the lives that can be saved in those instances where airlifts truly are the only means to reach people in need. In Gile, the airlift made the difference between life and death for 36,000 people. These are people who have names and faces, who are loved, who are continuing to live and raise their families in what was once war-ravaged Mozambique. These are people who now live in peace. People who would have died without the airlift.

NOTES

[1] There were a number of reasons for this initially low yield, including green fly attacks, lack of water and the urgent intervention without follow-up technical assistance that would normally accompany agricultural inputs caused by the emergency.

[2] *Pulses* are the edible seeds of peas, beans, lentils or any other plants having pods.

[3] *Global acute malnutrition* is defined as less than 80 percent weight for height. In lay terms, this may be considered *moderate* malnutrition.

[4] *Severe acute malnutrition* is defined as less than 70 percent weight for height. In lay terms, this may be considered *severe* malnutrition.

[5] *Wet feeding* means prepared food served from a centralized kitchen.

[6] Antihelmenthics combat intestinal parasites.

[7] An atonic intestine does not properly contract to move food through it.

[8] The reader might remember that yields of this first crop were substantially reduced by green fly attack, lack of water and the fact that, due to the extremely urgent nature of providing agricultural inputs, agricultural follow-up assistance was not possible. Delayed planting could well have reduced yield even further.

3.

Risk and Security Essentials
for Humanitarian Operations

Liberia

MARK JANZ, CHARLES ROGERS, JOANN SLEAD
AND AYO ABIFARIN

INTRODUCTION

6 April 1996. Monrovia, Liberia. Chaos seemed to reign. Smoke
from burning buildings hung in the air. Bodies lay in the streets
during a bloody 42-day killing spree. When it was over, an estimated 5,000 people had been killed. Staff and families hid for days
wherever they could—under tables, in garages, behind toilets. The
endless discharge of weapons told them it was not safe to venture
outside. They were trapped.

After several days of harrowing experiences, they were finally
evacuated from Monrovia. They were now safe but were traumatised and had lost most of their personal property. In addition,
most NGOs had lost vehicles, electric generators, communications
equipment, computers, printers and photocopiers. In effect, they
had at least temporarily lost their ability to work in Liberia.

The story of the Liberian civil war encapsulates nearly all of the
adverse elements and complexities that characterise the post–Cold
War CHE. In the absence of any external restraints, local warlords
engaged in a bloody power struggle that, in addition to producing
large numbers of refugees and internally displaced persons, involved

the sinister targeting of innocent civilians and the treatment of the local population as instruments of war.

In the midst of this chaos and violence, NGOs gamely attempted to respond to the needs of the victims of the conflict. In doing so, however, they placed their staff, both national and expatriate, at considerable risk.

The essential question before all the agencies involved in this context, and those in similar conflict zones, is this: How much risk is too much?

This chapter presents a case study of World Vision's experience in Liberia and the lessons we have learned from it and similar experiences.

The Liberia case was indicative of security risks WV faced in a number of other countries. Together they brought to light the changing world of humanitarian operations and our lack of preparedness to protect our people and our assets. From these experiences we began to take security issues more seriously. We redefined them as our moral and ethical imperative. As a result, WV created an office to monitor security risks and develop protocols which would help ensure staff and asset protection, as well as set and review risk thresholds to help guide our operations in deteriorating situations. A security manual was created and distributed to all appropriate staff. Training courses were developed and implemented which simulate the dangers of working in CHE environments and help trainees learn the best means of dealing with them. The following list of topics included in these materials and courses forms a safety net which enhances our ability to protect our staff and operations:

- country risk ratings
- standard security plans
- safety guidelines
    - -when travelling in vehicles (in convoys, at checkpoints, etc.)
    - -when walking
    - -when using public transportation
    - -for women
    - -in the home
- situational awareness
- surviving attacks, clashes and abductions
- conducting security assessments

- implementing standard security procedures (including communications)
- responding to emergencies (evacuations, hostage negotiations,
  medical crises)
- working effectively with the media
- managing stress and maintaining mental health

EMERGENCE OF SECURITY AS AN ISSUE FOR NGOS

In the last decade, security has become a major issue for NGOs
working in a large number of countries. Although it was not readily
apparent at the time, international humanitarian-aid work changed
dramatically after the end of the Cold War in the late 1980s. A
number of factors may have been involved in this, including

- The end of the Cold War itself. The new geopolitical order, or
  perhaps disorder, that resulted from the cessation of fifty years
  of superpower rivalry brought an abrupt end to the "rules"
  that had defined humanitarian-aid operations for the second
  half of the twentieth century. Gone forever were the artificial
  lines of demarcation that had characterised the post-war world,
  that had separated spheres of influence between East and West.
  Gone, too, were the client states in the developing world that
  had dutifully lined up beside their superpower benefactors in
  the global jockeying for power.
- Increased media coverage of CHEs. This was especially problematic when warlords received large amounts of press coverage, as they did in Somalia, possibly adding to the warlords'
  sense of personal power, the legitimacy of their positions and
  their attitudes of impunity.
- Lack of NGO solidarity when humanitarian conventions were
  violated.

With previous constraints removed, warlords and regional
powerbrokers unleashed a flurry of conflicts that defied all attempts
at diplomatic or military resolution. Tactics employed by belligerents
came to include targeting civilians, and by association, those who
come to their aid. Humanitarian-aid workers accustomed to responding to the needs of victims of natural disasters now found

themselves caught in the crossfire in their efforts to help innocent victims of conflict. Viewed by combatants as just another faction in the fighting, NGOs have largely lost their long-cherished status as neutral deliverers of humanitarian assistance. In some cases, as in Somalia, host governments have expressed resentment at what they view as NGO encroachment on their national sovereignty.

This scenario poses a difficult and dangerous challenge to NGOs that respond to the needs of civilian victims of conflict. Humanitarian-aid workers are exposed and vulnerable to danger as never before, raising serious questions among NGOs about staff safety, psychological well-being and operational security. As John Fawcett writes in chapter 4:

> In a report dated 15 August 1997 the UNHCR (United Nations High Commissioner for Refugees) noted that fully two-thirds of all staff, international and local, now work in security risk areas with one-third serving in particularly hazardous duty stations. Further, the report claims that "humanitarian workers are more and more often deliberately targeted." *The Los Angeles Times* noted that "it is more dangerous to be a U.N. humanitarian worker handing out food than to be a soldier on peacekeeping duty in a war zone." During 1998 alone 17 civilian aid workers of the UNHCR had died in separate incidents during the course of their duties compared with only eight military peacekeepers.

The story for NGOs, while not well documented, is not much different from that of the UNHCR. There is an abundance of anecdotal evidence clearly indicating that all aid workers are increasingly the victims of violence.

LIBERIA: THE CASE STUDY

Liberia's natural environment

Liberia enjoys one of the highest annual rainfall amounts in the subregion. With a landscape that is almost perpetually a lush green, Liberia seldom suffers from the droughts that plague its neighbours, especially during the planting season. An abundance of rice, the nation's food staple, and low-cost American food aid more than meet any occasional shortfalls. Liberia's natural resources include large amounts of iron and some gold, diamonds and timber. Once home to one of the largest virgin rain forests in West Africa, Liberia also claimed the world's largest rubber plantation.

Liberia before its civil war

Established by approximately 5,000 freed slaves from the United States during the mid-1800s, Liberia was the first republic in Africa. These settlers were identified as America-Liberians. They brought with them a southern US culture, much of which was confined to the coastal areas that they settled. They felt a distinct superiority over African Liberians and engaged in a "civilising" mission that resulted in justifying the development of an elite with exclusive control of political, economic and social functions similar to colonial administrations.[1] This elitist system discriminated against African Liberians, breeding resentment and anger. For indigenous groups, the system limited social services, such as education, and participation in government. It was not until the mid-1970s that a few "safe" outsiders (African Liberians) were allowed to enter the governing clique.[2]

Liberia's neighbours had somewhat recently gone through the politically charged process of decolonisation. Their newfound independence left Liberia in a volatile vacuum. Once a bit of participation through education and President Tolbert's development policies was opened up in the mid-1970s, past inequality and discrimination led to an intensive scramble to engage politically by unions and working class influences.[3]

By 1980, many America-Liberians were considered to be middle income, their prosperity fuelled by Liberia's maritime and rubber interests. The huge economic disparity between America-Liberians and African Liberians blinded the former to grievances that were building. In reality, Liberia was a nation with a dangerous history of inequality, repression, skewed wealth distribution, corruption and a newfound voice calling for the end of Americo exploitation. Samuel Doe violently took power in April 1980, not long after serious populist food riots in 1979 caused widespread damage.[4]

At the time he took power, Doe was a junior officer with an eighth-grade education. Doe, a member of the Krahn tribe, perpetuated the culture of fostering inequities by placing his fellow clansmen in government positions.[5] The Doe takeover aimed in a violent and corrupt manner to address Liberia's troubled history and was itself the seed bed for many more years of struggle. Scores were being settled between African Liberians and Americo-Liberians, as well as between vying tribes who were targeted and oppressed before 1980 and in the years after the Doe takeover. The 1980s were characterised by corruption and an economic downturn. With the assistance of Medecins Sans Frontieres (MSF), Africa Watch documented a number of serious human rights violations beginning in 1983. Victims of abuse were military and civilian alike and were found mostly along ethnic lines. Doe's years in power were characterised by extra-judicial executions of civilians and soldiers, torture, arbitrary arrests, detentions without trial, convictions on false charges, suppression of a free press, looting and burning of civilian homes by soldiers and constraints on freedom of association.

This set the stage for a messy stew of multiple factions, some with foreign influence, and began the waves of vying for control and violence which characterised the 1980s. This was the volatile and complex environment into which humanitarian NGOs entered during the 1990s.

The civil war

Nimba County, December 1989. Civil war began and spread within six months to encompass the entire country. The goal of the war, led by Charles Taylor, was simply to depose Doe. Taylor's forces made good progress initially, despite confronting the better trained and armed (though poorly motivated and disciplined) Doe army. Taylor was able to cut off the main road to up-country areas and extend his control down to the outlying areas of Monrovia. It was there that he bogged down, and two other factions within his forces were formed. ECOMOG (monitoring group set up by the 16-nation Economic Community of West African States—ECOWAS) became involved at this point, creating a buffer and potential mediating mechanism. Most of the killing, especially of civilians, occurred in the interfactional fighting that then arose. The first factions split again, so eventually there were seven or eight main groups. These were loosely organised along ethnic lines.

Huge migrations of people during the war resulted in roughly half the country's population residing in the capital of Monrovia. Unemployment there was as high as 50 percent. Throughout the country, public facilities and infrastructure were destroyed and the vast majority of civil servants had abandoned their posts within six months after the beginning of the war. Manufacturing, formal service and agricultural sectors were essentially non-functional. Access to the interior of the country was especially difficult due to destruction of roads, numerous military checkpoints and clashes between the armed forces of rival factions. Liberia's economy and its physical infrastructure were shattered.

By the end of the war in July 1996, an estimated 200,000 people had been killed and more than two-thirds of the country's approximately two million people had been displaced from their homes.

Various transitional governments, with multiple agendas and alliances, lacked the ability to govern, and there was no infrastructure able to deliver relief and rehabilitation assistance to the people, who were in dire need.

Vulnerabilities resulting from early choices

WV funded relief assistance and work in Liberian orphanages through other agencies in the 1980s. In 1995, WV became operational in the country, implementing humanitarian relief and recovery programmes.

WV made choices early in its operational work that made it exceptionally vulnerable to the violence of the civil war. *These were choices neither naively nor easily made.* We realised this work was risky. In retrospect, however, security plans were inadequate.

Work in areas of military action

WV has a commitment to meet the needs of those who most desperately need assistance. Thus, in 1995, WV began work in the southeastern part of the country, where no international NGO had worked since the beginning of the civil war. In the initial phase of the work, the primary focus was on nutritional rehabilitation through therapeutic feeding, targeted food distribution and agricultural recovery assistance in the counties of South Nimba, Grand Gedeh and Bong. South Nimba and Grand Gedeh counties were exceptionally insecure.

Part of WV's strategy was to access Grand Gedeh County through its work in southeast Nimba County. After six years of war, roads were non-existent. The first team that went to Zwedru in Grand Gedeh County had to clear its way through the bush and the first medical doctor had to be dropped by helicopter. Supplies also had to be sent by air. Once the road was cleared sufficiently to allow for vehicle passage, the journey to Zwedru from Monrovia took about two days. Armed teenagers and even children, who were frequently on drugs, manned checkpoints on the road. They were far from their commanding officers in the towns and villages and could do essentially what they pleased. They were warlords. The tall grass and trees in the area provided perfect cover for factional military activity, making vehicles travelling on the road vulnerable to attack.

Relationship with factions on the ground
The NGOs, with assistance from ECOMOG and the UN, did their best to maintain neutrality and independence in their work. However, much of that neutrality had to be negotiated through relationships with different factional commanders on the ground rather than with what civil government existed. Military commanders were the people in power. Civilian authority was non-existent or controlled by military commanders.

Crossing factional lines
Transporting resources across factional lines was an especially harrowing experience. Staff would cross two to three of these factions where we worked.

Stockpiling relief supplies
Stockpiling relief supplies and equipment is a necessary element for the effectiveness of relief operations. It can make NGOs a target of theft or robbery, however. Further, equipment and vehicles needed to mount emergency operations also became targets.

Distress and loss: The costs of neutrality

Staff worked under official agreements with the various parties to the fighting in Liberia. They carried official documents identifying them as NGO workers. With these papers, staff ideally should not have had problems. But the word *ideal* and the term *complex humanitarian emergency* can hardly be said to have anything in common. With the total breakdown of law and order and non-existent military command structure, such documents meant nothing to local thugs acting as the military.

Local military commanders made it difficult to maintain neutrality, often insisting on a share of the relief assistance meant for targeted beneficiaries.[6] Refusal often resulted in theft of relief supplies and further insecurity for staff. Free movement for NGO staff was also often prohibited, with commanders citing "orders from above."

At checkpoints

Warring factions at checkpoints often stole relief goods being transported.[7] Combatants at checkpoints also claimed that relief workers were supporting the other faction and often delayed convoys for hours or days. In some cases combatants would check every container or bag to satisfy themselves that arms were not being transported. It did little good to mark vehicles NO ARMS ON BOARD. One incident included detaining a convoy of international staff. They were taken to a village where they were kept until the next day. Checkpoints were also prime locations for staff to be robbed of their personal possessions, such as watches, rings, gold chains and cash. Such experiences did not help ease tensions in an already hostile environment.

The threat to stockpiled relief supplies

Circumstances resulted in stockpiling large amounts of supplies such as food, seeds or farm tools in warehouses, sometimes even in tents. Bad weather, poor road conditions and delays in project and donor approval all contributed to this problem. When supplies were stockpiled in large amounts, hungry combatants and civilians on more than one occasion succumbed to the temptation to steal the food or tools.[8]

In addition to such events, it sometimes appeared as though warring factions would purposely give aid agencies enough time to obtain relief supplies and equipment before triggering a crisis during which they looted NGO facilities. This occurred in the past as related anecdotally by other NGOs, as well as when WV was working on site in April 1996 and yet again in September 1998, when there was evacuation of NGO staff and looting. The warring factions seemed to create instability so they could "harvest" relief supplies and equipment during the civil crises they created.

Loss of communications

Tappita was a key base for World Vision Liberia in the southeastern part of Nimba County. High-frequency radios (including base and mobile units) linked staff to the Monrovia office and Zwedru in Grand Gedeh County. These were necessary to maintain staff security and effective operations. In March 1996, an NPFL (National Patriotic Front for Liberia) general accompanied by a large number of other soldiers came to the World Vision Tappita post and forcibly removed the base radio and two mobile units from our vehicles. He claimed he was obeying a directive from above. The soldiers accused WV of using the radios to communicate with another warring faction, the LPC (Liberia Peace Council). In spite of our formal protests, the radios were never returned. Lack of this key equipment further increased staff vulnerability to attack. In such situations, it is understandable that staff begin to fear for their lives.[9]

Disappearance of staff

Issues discussed above are trivial when compared to the loss of a person's life. Staff from some NGOs disappeared or were killed during implementation of emergency responses in Liberia. Not long before the battle that required the evacuation of WV staff from Monrovia in April 1996, two WV staff were lost between checkpoints. They had to cross from one warring faction into another and never reached their destination. These staff are still officially missing today and believed to be dead. In these cases, joint protests were lodged, and the UN Department of Humanitarian Affairs took up the problem with the government. No satisfactory resolutions were reached.

Loss of staff who are permanently declared missing or killed in the line of duty is not new to operations in CHEs. However, this incident made it clear that more precautions were required to protect NGO staff.

It is common in such settings for families to sue the NGO in question for large sums of money. It is also common for NGOs to settle out of court for smaller sums.

Intensive fighting and evacuation

In early April 1996, there was an extensive resurgence of hostility in and around Monrovia, the capital city of Liberia, where two warring factions were pitted against two others. NPFL and ULIMO-K (United Liberation Movement for Liberia—Kroma faction) united to arrest Roosevelt Johnson, leader of ULIMO-J (Johnson faction). The LPC joined ULIMO-J to resist the arrest. The result was many days of widespread killing, looting and burning. Warring factions seemed not to care whom they killed, military or civilian. Like the staff for all the other NGOs with offices in Monrovia, WV staff members were caught in this mayhem. Those who were in the interior could not return to Monrovia, and no one could leave the city. It did not help WV staff morale to know that their director was in the interior investigating disappearance of staff.[10] For five days WV staff were trapped in Monrovia, with danger lurking behind every shadow. Staff were spread across the entire city and unable to reach each other. They hid wherever they could, in offices trying to guard assets and protect themselves, in homes where they were located, hoping to find ways of reaching safe locations.

We were unable to arrange evacuation of staff for five days because of the heavy fighting among warring factions. Finally, evacuation was arranged through the US Embassy.

Staff were extremely grateful to escape with their life. Many nationals did not. Given that, it sounds trivial that staff lost most of their possessions. Possessions can be replaced. But their loss often has a distinct psychological effect on people. We are all tied to our possessions. They express who we are. They represent safety. Without them, we feel invaded. For these staff, it was but one more piece of evidence of how vulnerable, how close to death, they had been.[11]

Staff were traumatised and terrorised, and thus NGOs lost much of their ability to meet the devastating human need in the country. Humanitarian assistance to those in need was virtually impossible due to the fighting within the city from 6 April to 17 May 1996. Many of the lives that the NGOs had originally hoped to save through emergency services, including food aid and medical care, were lost.

In response to the above events, WV lodged protests with factional leaders. However, none of the warring factions investigated any of the events, nor were any of the culprits arrested and punished. In most cases the vehicles and stolen goods were neither recovered nor returned. Interventions by UN groups on our behalf did not lead to satisfactory responses from factional leaders.

Loss of equipment put at risk our ability to begin operations again. Going to private and public sector donors to replace what has been looted is difficult to justify. This underscored our lack of preparedness in protecting our assets.

This is obviously an extreme example of aid workers in an insecure environment. It is not as unique as we would like to think, however, and is representative of other events (for example, Cambodia in July 1997). Hugo Slim said that working in such environments has led to professional frustration, personal insecurity and adverse effects on the emotional health of staff working in such conditions.[12] Risks to NGOs' staff are enormous. Staff are often unable to work due to war or civil strife. They are prime targets for robbery. Some are even killed. The effects on the work they hope to do are just as deadly. If the means to provide assistance are stolen, if staff are forced to restrict their movements due to threats, if their lives are taken, how then can NGOs fulfil their mandate to meet the physical, emotional and spiritual needs of people who have been devastated by war?

Co-ordination among NGOs

In all complex humanitarian settings, co-ordination of NGO efforts is vital along a number of important dimensions, including security. In especially volatile settings, such as Liberia, an on-going challenge before the humanitarian community is the need to create mechanisms that reinforce NGO co-ordination with *realistic* measures.

While it may not seem reasonable after such a dreadful description of difficult security issues, an ethical framework is absolutely essential to decision-making in these types of environments. Ethical frameworks and principles can help guide and inspire decisions that preserve the humanitarian ideal and help minimise the possibility of being manipulated by warring factions.[13] Maintaining an ethical approach is a challenge in an insecure and fluid environment when staff are trying to get a job done, often under the pressures of harassment and threat. It is very clear, however, that inappropriate ethical actions by NGOs can have a great impact, causing difficulties for other agencies' work and safety.

As early as 1995 the UN and NGOs in Liberia developed the *Principles and Protocols of Humanitarian Operation* (PPHO) to reinforce agency unity and to address continual problems of security and harassment and concerns regarding fuelling the war.[14] Soon after, in April 1996, the crisis and mass NGO evacuation from Liberia resulted in a US$20 million loss in humanitarian assets.[15] Due to this crisis and a history of factional manipulation of NGOs, twelve NGOs, including World Vision, took the unprecedented step of restricting their work to life-saving operations only. This approach included restricting capital and input investments and carefully targeting interventions. The resulting *Joint Policy on Operations* (JPO) was designed to demonstrate to manipulative faction leaders that NGOs were serious about their commitment

- not to fuel the war;
- not to allow the misappropriation of humanitarian supplies and equipment; and
- to reinforce respect for humanitarian principles.[16]

It is important to note that the PPHO and the JPO were established as the result of a crisis. The Liberia case study describes a chaotic, insecure environment in which NGO staff were abused while crossing factional lines and humanitarian supplies were looted from warehouses and convoys. This context required development of measures such as the PPHO and JPO to demonstrate the unwillingness of NGOs to work in such an abusive context where there was no respect for humanitarian principles.

The PPHO/JPO protocols sought to achieve better co-ordination for all operational NGOs through two mechanisms:

- sharing information on factional tactics; and
- establishing the rationale for provision of only minimal inputs.[17]

For these principles to be effective, they needed to be translated into codes of practice or protocols for the specific operational conditions in Liberia. Setting the security criteria under which we could engage in and continue humanitarian work was important. Some of the PPHO/JPO principles which applied most directly to security dimensions of humanitarian work in Liberia include the following:

1. "Our work should have independent access—i.e., it should be neutral in respect to political and military concerns."

Respect for this principle by warring factions would have greatly facilitated our free movement across factional lines and our communications with our different operational sites. It would have literally saved the lives of humanitarian workers moving between work locations and greatly reduced staff stress levels.

2. "Armed escorts should be minimised. Armed personnel should not be carried in or on humanitarian vehicles."

Armed escorts can give the perception that the humanitarian agency is allied to a warring faction, thus making the agency a target for attack. One purpose of this measure was to reduce the risk of civilians and humanitarian workers being caught in a crossfire. Another purpose was to retain the neutrality of humanitarian workers.

3. "There should be no payment for access to any area."

This was often a demand placed upon agencies. Giving in to this practice, even under threat at road blocks, fuelled an environment that encouraged these demands and endangered staff.

4. "The safety of staff and property should be ensured."

We realise there will always be risk to staff working in CHEs. However, a reasonable level of staff safety is a pre-requisite. How do agencies determine what constitutes a "reasonable" level? The material presented in the "Lessons Learned" section below, numbers 3 and 4, should prove helpful. Agencies also need to be thoughtful and aware whether the current form of assistance is fuelling the fighting and thus making the agency a target.

5. "Taking unilateral action which violates agreed humanitarian principles or protocols for operations can jeopardise another agency's work or safety."

One area of solidarity which the PPHO/JPO addresses continues to be problematic—the competition among agencies for donor resources when jockeying for access to new locations, sometimes in areas of higher risk. NGOs can be tempted to take unacceptable risk just to get into the action and obtain donor funds.

6. There should be "maintenance of a 'minimum input' policy and maintaining a high degree of co-ordination and sharing of (capital) assets between agencies."

This refers to keeping NGO inputs, especially capital ones, to a minimum, thus preventing a large build-up of material which factions would find tempting targets for looting. It also refers to sharing vehicles, generators, and other equipment among NGOs. In Liberia this created tensions among agencies regarding what should be included as a minimum asset and who should decide what would be considered a minimum asset. Tensions were also experienced regarding the actual sharing of assets. Scheduling use of vehicles by various NGOs became quite complicated, for instance. Some agencies experienced difficulty in obtaining transport for relief supplies. WV had to rent vehicles from transporters who charged high rates for their vehicles.

Some sharing of assets has been done in difficult locations, such as Somalia and Liberia; however, this is not the norm. Resolving types of issues that emerged in this context in Liberia is a great challenge among NGOs, who have great pride in their independence.

The PPHO/JPO mechanisms frequently were used to defend agency space rather than to promote a principled approach to defend humanitarian space in general. Agencies respected the mechanism in a variable manner, often seeming to abide by the mechanism when it was in their respective interest to do so. The JPO co-operative agreement and approach which resulted directly from the 1996 crisis dissipated over time with the reassertion of respective agency interests.[18] It is normal human behaviour to band together in times of calamity and then see co-operation dissipate as things normalise.

Problems with the PPHO and JPO aside, agencies need to work co-operatively in areas of conflict to ensure that security issues are properly known and addressed.

LESSONS LEARNED

There are many lessons we can learn from the Liberia experience and other similar experiences. Many of them can be stated along the lines of what *should* have been done. Many ameliorative steps have already been taken since our problems in Liberia. They are meant to ensure thoughtful and effective WV relief operations in a world of increasing insecurity. There are even more that can and should be taken, however.

1. Recognising the problem

NGOs first need to realise we can and need to take preventive measures that will minimise risk and loss of life. Valuing people is one of WV's core values. We value our beneficiaries, our donors and our staff. After instances like those in Liberia, we realised we have a moral obligation to them all to ensure we take no foolish risks with their lives, their money or the assistance we provide. Our new recognition that we are morally and ethically obligated to provide adequate security for our staff and projects was based upon our commitment to these groups.

Typical NGO commitment to saving lives is very similar to WV's, and we believe all NGOs share the same moral obligation to provide sufficient security to ensure the safety of beneficiaries, staff and operations.

There will always be times when lives are at risk. Work in CHEs is dangerous. Yet we need to ensure that the risks we take are well reasoned and well informed. Otherwise we would indeed be foolish.

Certainly such a recognition in the Liberia case would have changed our approach.

2. Preventive measures

As with anything else, recognising a problem by itself is inadequate. We need to identify and implement appropriate preventive measures. An organisation assigning staff to areas of conflict and violence can tangibly express its concern for the safety of its workers in many ways. One of the most important is to ensure that basic security procedures are encoded and strictly adhered to at all times.

The security requirements of humanitarian-aid organisations vary greatly from those of transnational corporations and the military. For transnational corporations, security is usually a matter of cost. If commercial opportunities exist in areas of conflict and violence, international business firms will calculate the cost of providing the necessary security for their employees and factor it into the overall cost of doing business. In extreme cases, this can even involve hiring private armies. The military, on the other hand, uses a deterrence model for security, ensuring the safety of its troops and the success of its mission by mobilising sufficient forces and weapons to deter any threat.

The humanitarian-aid community, by virtue of its mission and mandate, must employ security strategies that are uniquely suited to its needs and realities. While agencies have struggled to find the best strategies—some have even hired private protection—the preferred model is gaining the acceptance of the local population, including the factions and combatants involved in the conflict. Failing to achieve that, NGOs will either operate under the protection of international security forces, such as the UN, or they may opt not to intervene in the humanitarian crisis. The choices become few and difficult.

Generally speaking, international humanitarian-aid agencies have been slow to integrate professional security management practices and procedures into their staff training and professional development programmes, while continuing to hold line management responsible for staff safety and operational security. This is beginning to change. Increasingly, the issue of security is finding its way onto the agendas of major international aid conferences and consultations. Security training programmes are being offered by a growing number of aid agencies to help field staff acquire the skills necessary to manage security in a more effective and professional manner.

The curriculum developed by World Vision subsequent to our security problems in Liberia and elsewhere, and now used in our security training programme, places the emphasis on prevention rather than protection. Skill sets include risk assessment, stress management, contingency and evacuation planning, personal security awareness, communications networking, land mine awareness and vehicle safety.

Security training will have little effect, however, in CHEs if it does not translate into a systematic approach to security management where it is needed most—on the ground, in the field, in areas of conflict and high risk. As a matter of organisational policy, NGOs should require all aid programmes operating in areas of moderate to high risk to have in place standard security operating plans that incorporate generally accepted standards and best practices in critical areas of security management.

With regard to the Liberia case study, if we had put a security operating plan in place, we would have been better prepared. Some people believed that there were signs the security situation was beginning to disintegrate prior to April 1996, when the Liberia crisis exploded again, yet no preparedness steps were taken.

Several recent programmes (such as Kosovo) have hired experienced, full-time security officers to develop, maintain and implement security plans. Security officers also monitor and appropriately respond to signs that security is deteriorating.

Donors must realise additional resources will be required to provide additional staff and take appropriate security precautions.

Mandatory components of a security operating plan include:

- threat assessment procedures
- incident reporting protocols
- communications standards
- security briefings
- site selection and physical-plant security
- cash management and transfers
- vehicle and convoy safety procedures
- visitor security
- contingency and evacuation planning
- hostage taking/kidnapping policies and procedures

3. Risk assessment: Key to effective security management

The foundation that supports all good security planning and management is the ability correctly to assess risk. Without properly identifying potential risks to staff and operations, all of the plans and procedures that follow will miss the mark and likely fail in a crisis. The tendency of most NGOs in the past has been to invest minimal effort in assessing risks and spend almost all our energy on designing and mobilising operations. This was true in the Liberia case. NGOs often pride themselves in being able to work under extremely difficult circumstances, circumstances which demonstrate the "can do" spirit in meeting urgent needs. NGOs tend to do this to "win their stripes" with other NGOs, donors and the media. WV has been forced by events to step back from that position.

Humanitarian-aid organisations must get this right from the very beginning, which means integrating security assessments into over-all operational assessments before the programme is launched. Aid agencies must determine not only if they have the capability to carry out a prospective programme, but also whether it is safe to do so.

Historically, CHE programme managers have utilised informal methods of risk assessment, depending mostly on local sources of information and making judgments based on intuition and subjective analysis. The preferred method involves the use of tools that help objectify the process by quantifying risks and threats, such as the one below.

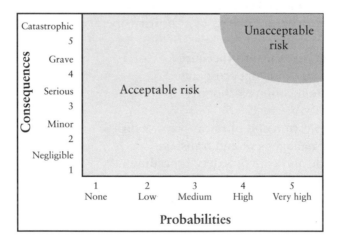

Figure 3-1. Risk assessment.

The process begins with exhaustive inquiry concerning local threats from a variety of reliable information sources. These range from foreign embassy personnel to village tribal elders. Once specific threats have been identified, each is assigned a rating based on probability and consequences. The categories listed on the left axis must be defined by each individual locale (what is catastrophic for one programme may not be for another). Once the threats have been plotted, the responsible programme manager will determine where the programme's risk threshold lies. Only then can meaningful and effective security plans and procedures be developed and implemented. Because of the dynamic nature of conflict situations, the need to assess risk and to change security plans and procedures accordingly is on-going.

This analysis, if applied to the Liberia case, may have helped us better plan, implement, and perhaps even halt programming. WV has been known to pull back from operations because of insecurity and then re-engage after the situation improves. We have done this many times in South Sudan. This is costly but decreases risk. Inter-NGO monitoring and exchange of information on risks at regular intervals could have provided an early warning so we could make the decisions necessary.

4. Analyzing risk tolerance: Counting the human cost

It is safe to assume that as long as CHEs persist as by-products of regional conflicts, NGOs will continue to respond to the needs of the victims of those conflicts. Consequently, aid workers will continue to find themselves in harm's way while delivering aid to the affected population, as they did in Liberia. Because NGOs cannot provide absolute protection to their workers, it can be argued that agencies operating in conflict zones have a moral responsibility to determine their tolerance for risk by establishing an organisational threshold for staff safety and security. An assessment of risk tolerance was not in place in the Liberia case study, leaving staff to "fly by the seat of their pants." Hardly the best means of making decisions.

Once an appropriate risk assessment has been done, an analysis of risk tolerance can be accomplished by defining in general terms a clear line of demarcation between acceptable and unacceptable risk. Such a determination is best made at the highest levels of organisational management and decision-making rather than leaving the decision for line management to make in a high-pressure, situational context. Expressed in the form of broad guidelines, organisational security policies effectively relieve field management of at least some of the heavy burden of responsibility for making life-and-death decisions in a crisis situation and provide for the consistent practice of staff-safety management based on objective organisational guidelines.

One difficulty regarding application of such guidelines is staff resistance. Staff are committed to projects and in a sense "own" them. When they are too committed and too close to a programme, they may need outside advice to distance them from the situation. Outside parties should advise programme managers with respect to especially dangerous situations. A decision-making process in which the programme manager is only one party, though the one whose vote carries the most weight, may prove useful.

5. Corporate liability: Security as a bottom-line issue

In Liberia, the disappearance of two WV national staff while in transit through disputed territory led to legal action by the families seeking compensation for the loss of their loved ones. Though the lawsuits were resolved in terms very favourable to WV, the experience serves as a poignant example of an organisation's exposure to liability arising from issues of staff safety.

In most organisations, programme managers and country directors have primary responsible for staff safety and operational security. But all NGO staff choose their jobs, and do so with the knowledge that their work entails a certain amount of risk. Still, NGOs are responsible to ensure that no foolish risks are taken with the lives of their staff. In some circumstances, the consequences of security-related decisions can reverberate to the highest levels of the organisation's executive leadership. The higher the profile of security incidents in the field, the greater the potential for adverse impact on the agency as a whole. It is incumbent upon all NGOs working in insecure areas, therefore, to demonstrate that security is taken seriously and that due diligence is exercised in making decisions affecting the safety of programme staff. The inability of an agency to demonstrate in a court of law that prudent and reasonable security measures were taken in a high-risk environment potentially exposes that agency to serious liability. The cost to the agency could be enormous, as could the public-relations damage.

In addition to the relevant moral arguments, it can be argued that NGOs cannot afford *not* to take security seriously.

Historically, NGOs such as WV have been known to take risks to meet humanitarian needs under the banner of our protective blanket of neutrality. In the past this was always justified with minimal risk to agencies. It is clear, however, that this laissez faire humanitarian environment has changed and neutrality can no longer be our protection.

6. Inter-NGO co-operation

Joint protocols between NGOs, while they have their limitations, can be helpful in maintaining humanitarian operations in extremely hostile, multi-factional environments. Such protocols can help reinforce to warring factions the principles of humanitarian assistance and reduce the likelihood of NGOs being attacked or manipulated into situations where they can be looted.

To prevent as many difficulties as possible in the implementation of these protocols:

- All key terms should be clearly defined in the protocol. The Liberia JPO did not clarify well enough what was considered to be "minimal input," resulting in disagreements among agencies.
- Protocols should clearly designate where decision-making power resides regarding implementing terms of the protocol. An inter-agency body which was active in Liberia helped keep tensions at a minimum. However, more clarity was needed regarding who determined what was "minimal input" and who allocated use of shared resources.
- Use of shared capital resources may not be the most appropriate solution to some problems. If designers of a given protocol decide to include it, they need to ensure that the resources available are adequate to meet the minimum needs of all signatories to the protocol. Beyond that, they need to ensure that all signatories are aware of the issues they will likely face in sharing capital assets, such as delays in transporting relief goods, the need to rent trucks at very high prices, and so on. Finally, the signatories to the protocol need to ensure a fair and impartial allocation of the use of shared assets.

There will no doubt always be difficulties in implementing such protocols. The most challenging issue, due to the competitive nature of obtaining operational territory and donor funds, will probably be "variable" adherence to the protocol by agencies, depending on agency self-interests.

It should also be noted that protocols are most useful when a crisis exists. When the situation starts to normalise, the impetus for NGOs to abide by the protocol diminishes considerably and quickly.

Inter-agency agreement at head-office levels regarding standards for operation in CHEs may be helpful *before* new CHEs and operations in response to them begin. This could minimise confusion and speed co-ordinated action when new crises occur that threaten operations.

7. Lobbying for international political action

We need to lobby decision-makers in governments and the international arena to create a secure environment for NGO operations. NGOs are often put on the front lines in CHEs as a substitute for major national or foreign policy action. While NGOs can do much more to protect themselves and set clearer guidelines for the conditions under which they will work, these are but a "Band-Aid" compared to the larger dynamics affecting security. National governments and international bodies like the UN should be taking the lead in these situations. Clarification of NGO security needs is key to enabling the UN and various governments to take appropriate action.

8. Inclusive security: Casting a wider net of safety

One possibility which *may* (or may not) have been helpful in Liberia involves advocacy for beneficiaries.

In situations of violence and conflict, organisational security policy and strategies may encompass not only agency staff but the beneficiaries of aid programmes as well. NGOs lack the mandate and the means to physically protect the civilian population that receives their aid. However, they have the capacity to advocate vigorously in the political arena within the international community on behalf of the rights of the victims of war, including their right to safety and security, by appealing to the Geneva Conventions and to

International Humanitarian Law. As a matter of principle, such a fundamental commitment to the rights of aid recipients should be integral to the mission of any agency that operates in war zones and areas of violence. Moreover, it is in the agency's own self-interest to adopt such a mandate, for in those instances when advocacy on behalf of refugee and civilian rights proves effective, it provides another mantle of protection for NGO staff serving in insecure environments. Local Capacities for Peace initiatives can provide a similar layer of safety. Whether such a strategy would have worked in Liberia remains an open question, but the issue could have significant impact on the ability of NGOs to work in such environments in the future.

9. Required for improved security: Management initiative and support

Initiatives aimed at enhancing staff safety and operational security are effective only when executive leadership champions the cause in all dimensions, including availability of financial resources. In many organisations, this requires nothing less than a change in culture.

CONCLUSION: SECURITY AND THE TWENTY-FIRST CENTURY

Incidences of conflicts that give rise to CHEs such as that in Liberia are expected not only to continue in the twenty-first century but possibly increase. While Africa is likely to retain a disproportionate share of future CHEs, it is expected that other regions of the world, particularly Asia, may experience an increase in humanitarian disasters resulting from conflict and violence. Given this scenario, we need to learn from our experiences in Liberia and elsewhere. NGOs most likely to succeed and remain viable in the twenty-first century will be those that employ innovative and effective security strategies to cope with the mounting threats to staff safety and operational security. In other words, security issues will fundamentally alter the way NGOs do business in the years ahead. Those organisations that fail adequately to address and manage risks to their staff in future CHE contexts will likely not survive.

NOTES

[1] Philippa Atkinson, "NGOs and Peace Building in Complex Political Emergencies: A Case Study of Liberia," Institute for Development Policy and Management, working paper no. 5, The University of Manchester (October 1998), 13.

[2] Charles H. Cutter, "The Republic of Liberia," *Africa 1998*, 33d ed. (Harpers Ferry, W.V.: Stryker Post Publications, 1998), 54.

[3] Atkinson, "NGOs and Peace Building in Complex Political Emergencies," 14.

[4] Cutter, "The Republic of Liberia," 54.

[5] Ibid., 55.

[6] This is a phenomenon common to work in many relief settings. For an example with regard to work in Afghanistan, see J. Goodhand and P. Chamberlain, "'Dancing with the Prince': NGOs' Survival Strategies in the Afghan Conflict," *Development in Practice* 6/3 (1996), 39–50.

[7] It would be easy to point a finger at these soldiers and correctly assert they had no right to these relief goods. In their actions, however, they were no different from many civilians. In the desperate struggle for survival, both civilians and combatants yielded to the temptation to steal, threaten, harass and make demands that increased insecurity for NGO staff. Both civilians and combatants were extremely poor; no one was receiving salaries. These people looked to NGOs to meet their needs. When NGOs did not meet their expectations, people resorted to such behaviour. In turn, their behaviour resulted in restricted NGO staff movement and relief response.

It can be noted that confiscation of relief resources at check points is a good example of the transfer of resources in conflict zones which results in unintentionally supporting war efforts, as well as increasing the vulnerability of aid workers (see Mary Anderson, *Do No Harm—Supporting Local Capacities for Peace Through Aid*, research report [Cambridge, Mass.: Collaborative for Development Action, 1996]).

[8] This is a good demonstration of what Chris Roche has called the "butterfly" effect ("Operationality in Turbulence: The Need for Change," *Development in Practice* 4/3 [1994]). Small changes or events can trigger much larger events. For want of a tire, the convoy couldn't move on time. Because the convoy couldn't move on time, it encountered a long delay due to sudden rains making the roads impassable. Because of the delay, the food had to be stored under makeshift situations in a village that had not been targeted for distribution. Because people were hungry in that village, they took the food. The lack of the tire did not *cause* the theft of

the food by hungry villagers; it simply set the stage whereby the theft could occur.

[9] Communications equipment used by NGOs often creates tension in situations where poorly equipped, power-seeking factions exist. Factions become suspicious as to what is being communicated, and they fear other factions or the government are benefiting. As a result of such a situation, in South Sudan the SRRA, the relief wing of one of the power-seeking factions, controls NGO communications equipment there. This created a dilemma for NGOs seeking to ensure staff security. Without being able to control radio confidentiality, monitoring and reporting deterioration of security may be sensitive.

[10] The director was forced to leave the country by road without any of his travelling documents and, like many of the rest of WV staff, lost all his properties in Monrovia.

[11] Looting was extensive. It was reported that combatants took first choice when they went through an area. Whatever they left behind, civilian looters took. In many cases goods were not only removed, but also the roofs, floor tiles, toilets, electrical fixtures, doors and windows. In some cases, even the walls were demolished.

[12] Hugo Slim, "The Continuing Metamorphosis of the Humanitarian Professional: Some New Colors for an Endangered Chameleon," paper presented at the 1994 Development Studies Association Conference (Challenging the Orthodoxies), Lancaster, UK (9 September 1994).

[13] Nicholas Leader, "Humanitarian Principles in Practice: A Critical Review," Humanitarian Policy Group, Overseas Development Institute (ODI), Relief and Rehabilitation discussion paper (December 1999), 4–5; this paper is available at www.odihpn.org.uk/discussion/principles.

[14] Ibid., 2.

[15] Philippa Atkinson, "Do No Harm or Do Some Good? NGO Coordination in Liberia," Relief and Rehabilitation Network 6 (November 1996), 13.

[16] Ibid.

[17] Ibid., 14.

[18] Leader, "Humanitarian Principles in Practice," 4.

4.

Managing Staff Stress and Trauma

JOHN FAWCETT

On Saturday, 5 July 1997, civil war broke out in Cambodia. After two days of fighting in and around Phnom Penh, the airport was re-opened and people began to flee the country. Thousands of expatriate families from the business and NGO communities crowded onto aircraft and headed for the safety of Bangkok, Singapore or Kuala Lumpur. In the weeks that followed, an uneasy calm settled over the city while sporadic fighting continued in the rural and provincial areas. Assassinations of key members of the losing side continued for months, while the international donor community suspended political and social investment in the country.

Such precipitous events are altogether too commonplace in CHEs. NGOs now regularly send staff to work in these situations, and it is imperative that they equip their staff to do more than survive. They need to flourish, grow and mature in these scenarios, as well as do their work. Toward that end, adequate field support needs to be given to both international and local staff to help them develop the skills and coping mechanisms that will enable them to withstand the continual assault of violence on their senses. Field support needs to encompass specific portions of field infrastructure, such as evacuation plans, provision of adequate materials, transportation, communication and information, and psychosocial means of processing all that staff see, hear and feel. If adequate field support is not provided in the project infrastructure from the beginning, programmes will fail and lives could be lost.

Why would an NGO wish to commit scarce funds to this type of enterprise? The financial answer is unequivocal. Preventing traumatic injury is far cheaper than treating the impact of trauma— cheaper in terms of individual health care, and cheaper in ensuring that programme objectives are attained. For instance, a person suffering post-traumatic stress disorder may require up to 24 months intensive trauma therapy, with all the consequent costs. A staff stress and trauma management programme would cost only a small percentage of treatment costs. Professional field staff are an increasingly scarce commodity, and no NGO can afford to lose essential staff through preventable causes. Programme viability is essential for the communities being served, donors providing the funding, and credibility of the NGO providing the service. We all wish to reduce the risk of losing key staff. Finally, and maybe most essential, NGOs will wish to provide comprehensive staff support programmes because this "service of care" is directly linked to the values that drive the whole organisation. Any NGO that presents itself as an entity valuing people will wish to demonstrate that same quality inside as well as outside. Staff working for a humanitarian agency that demonstrates sound support and care practices will carry that value through to the day-to-day work they perform in the field. Consistency and transparency are everything in humanitarian work. Staff care proves we are who we say we are.

This case study will examine the psychosocial support that needs to be provided to staff working in CHEs if they are to cope adequately with the crises they face. Noting that most programmes and, regrettably, most of the published literature have focused on expatriate staff, this discussion will encompass both expatriate and local staff. Local events have as much impact on local staff as on expatriates, if not more, and we need to be consistent in acting on the moral imperative to care for those in need.

Whatever the final shape of the service, we are convinced that humanitarian-aid and relief organisations need to plan and act deliberately to provide the resources and capacity to assist staff who have chosen to live and work in the most dangerous, challenging and ultimately rewarding environments on earth.

The assumption in the past has been that expatriate and local staff have similar psychological needs after living through the same crisis, and that perhaps local staff will suffer even more psychological trauma, since they seldom have a safe place to which to evacuate. A like assumption has been made that "talk" therapy is the best means of meeting the psychological needs of local staff. In fact, our case study shows this may not be true, due to differing sociocultural perceptions, beliefs and the way in which war itself is experienced.

THE CONTEXT
OF INTERNATIONAL RELIEF OPERATIONS

The dramatic social and cultural shifts of the last two decades of the twentieth century caused workers in international relief and aid to examine closely many aspects of the objectives and the process of "doing the right thing."[1] Assumptions that provided firm foundations for programme development in the 1970s are proving shaky in the light of post–Cold War restructuring and the collapse of regional economies. Even the shape of conflict has changed with the old "rules of engagement being usurped by an increasing prevalence of factional fighting, intra-social conflicts and religious campaigns. It is no longer clear who the enemy is or where the next conflict will break out.

As the shape of international relationships has changed dramatically, the role of international relief and aid organisations has had to change as well. This has proved problematic for many first-world agencies as activities previously perceived as neutral become viewed by aid recipients as being supportive of one group over another, whether for political, economic or religious reasons. A common discussion in international relief work at present is the loss of neutrality and subsequent targeting of international relief and aid organisations by armed groups of various kinds. In a report dated 15 August 1997, the UNHCR (United Nations High Commissioner for Refugees) noted that fully two-thirds of all staff, international and local, now work in security risk areas, with one-third serving in particularly hazardous duty stations.[2] Further, the report claims that "humanitarian workers are more and more often deliberately targeted." *The Los Angeles Times*[3] noted that "it is more dangerous to be a UN humanitarian worker handing out food than to be a soldier on peacekeeping duty in a war zone." During 1998 alone, 17 civilian aid workers of the UNHCR had died in separate incidents during the course of their duties, compared with only eight military peacekeepers.

At the same time, international spending on relief programmes has increased dramatically.[4] NGOs, the UN and other humanitarian organisations are being given an increasingly prominent role in both the distribution and implementation of aid programmes, especially governmental funds. As international political and economic influences become apparently more linked to the provision of relief and aid resources, it becomes increasingly difficult for recipients to distinguish between the political and practical donors. This becomes even more difficult in the most dangerous of relief environments (such as Somalia in 1997) where relief resources are guarded by heavily armed soldiers of a foreign nation.

International relief organisations have adopted a variety of different strategies in order to continue operations in the new world environment. Operationally they have become much more security conscious. Organisations have developed recruiting and orientation procedures to guide staff appropriately (for example, the International Red Cross[5]). In terms of providing staff with support service, many organisations are either hiring specialist psychological services or developing such resources for staff in conjunction with other health programmes.

To a large extent, however, the focus of these initiatives has been international expatriate staff. Relief organisations do, of course, care for the well-being of local staff as well, but the reality is that the employment of international staff is characteristically different from the conditions under which local staff are hired. For a whole variety of reasons, some good and some not so sound, international staff often have enhanced security provisions, including evacuation procedures, full health and insurance coverage, plus higher salaries which increase options in times of insecurity.

Humanitarian organisations, both religious and secular, have become increasingly aware of the costs to both staff and families working in these environments. The rapid growth of the international relief profession has meant that many workers have had wide exposure to intense and difficult situations. While many people continue to thrive, organisations are noticing a steady increase in those exhibiting symptoms directly associated with traumatic stress reactions. Resilience literature is beginning to hint that prolonged continuous exposure to multiple, significantly traumatic events may not increase general resilience, as was previously thought, but rather lead to people becoming more vulnerable to the development of intransigent trauma symptoms.[6] Somewhat disturbingly, however, these same people may also become more adept at hiding their symptoms from colleagues and friends.

Christian relief and aid workers, along with all those with strong spiritual beliefs, may be significantly affected by exposure to such events. Rigidly held belief structures may not hold up under exposure to complexity and ambiguity. The "ambiguity factor" appears to be critical here. The more black and white the belief structure held, the more strain it is under in contact with new and unusual conditions. However, even those who have developed more flexible and ambiguous spiritual world views have found extreme environments a real challenge. Many experience the crisis as the destruction of a world view, a tearing out of their "hearts." A person's world view is the foundation for crafting a life and mission. In situations of complexity and violence, especially indiscriminate killing of innocents, questions of meaning inevitably arise. For those who have a predominantly positive world view—for instance, that God is a God of love and healing—the evidence of their own eyes can create internal conflicts of a profoundly traumatic nature. The need to resolve these apparent contradictions and the amount of psychological and spiritual energy required to manage the confusion can lead to some workers needing to leave the field. For a few, the choice has been suicide.

Gina O'Connell Higgins argues that resilience is not achieved so much by belief but by "faith," an analysis that holds promise and requires more consideration in future studies.[7] In summary, Higgins's research indicates that a person's strength of faith (in self, in the goodness of people, in the goodness of God, in the future, in a sustaining religion, and more) is more an indicator of "overcoming" past trauma than adherence to a particular religious code or structure. Faith, she argues, should be separated from religiosity when considering resilience and the potential for psychological damage as a result of trauma. Religious humanitarian organisations may wish to consider how staff are selected and evaluated when it comes to recruiting for complex and difficult working locations. The ability to speak knowledgeably about religious prescriptions may not be as sound an indicator of inherent resilience as some leaders may wish.

In recent years, responses from relief organisations themselves to the phenomenon of trauma and stress have generally been quite positive. Drawing largely from the psychological professions, relief organisations have found ways to assist staff to care for themselves and to increase resilience and stress-management capacity. Western models of individualised health care have proved most effective in providing a foundation for the delivery of staff support for international relief staff and families. Organisations have begun to incorporate strategies in four main areas in order to cope with the changing relief environment.

- Staff preparation: selection, recruitment, organisational orientation, pre-field briefing, in-service support.
- Security: personal and corporate security plans and guidelines.
- Evacuation procedures: ensuring staff are able to leave a crisis environment safely and promptly.
- Mental health services: provision of counselling, debriefing, defusing and on-going psychological services. Some Christian NGOs include provision for spiritual counselling as well.

There is increasing, although largely anecdotal, evidence that such provisions are directly responsible for reducing the potential for violence directed at workers and for supporting workers during and following difficult field assignments. The UNHCR, for example, has decided to reinforce its Medical and Staff Welfare Unit by employing professional welfare and counselling officers in high-risk areas.[8] Other organisations, such as the International Committee of the Red Cross and WV, are developing internal resources for necessary staff care and support.

Most of what has been written in the field of humanitarian trauma and stress has focused on people recruited from one (generally first-world) country and assigned to another (generally third-world). What has been written for local staff who have lived and worked within the country where services are being performed has been largely anecdotal or added to programmes designed for expatriates. We believe this approach has tended to marginalise local staff, moving them to the periphery of the population of concern, or even

out of sight completely. A disturbing tendency is to reduce humanitarian disasters to an examination of two groups: the local affected
population and the international humanitarian workers who have
come to assist. However, for many international NGOs, the bulk
of staff are in fact locally hired, in many cases for the long term.
WV, for example, has approximately 10,000 locally hired staff compared with approximately 300 international staff. Yet, for many
years, staff care and support services for local staff have been mar-
ginal, to say the least.

For these reasons, this chapter will address the issue of caring
for and supporting local staff first. An examination of WV's developing programme to assist international staff occurs later in the
chapter, but it will be observed that the two programmes address
two markedly different groups, with different needs and requirements.

PROGRAMME 1:
A DEVELOPMENTAL APPROACH
TO LOCAL STAFF SUPPORT

In order to develop appropriate trauma interventions, we need to
be clear as to the nature of the trauma experience for the victims.
Cultures may not experience trauma in the same way, and some
cultures may experience trauma as a group phenomenon rather
than an individual one. It is necessary to examine the nature of war
and civil conflict, and discuss how communities and individuals
respond to such events.

War as a psychosocial phenomenon

Organisational responses to crises, whether civil strife or war, will
be determined by assumptions as to both cause and effect. War is a
social event experienced by communities.[9] Yet the modern NGO
response has been to measure effect in terms of impact on the *individual*. In fact, the extent of studies on the impact of war on civilians other than as individuals is somewhat limited.[10] Raymond B.
Flannery notes that for individuals, the social context may be as
important as internal psychological strengths in determining responses to trauma,[11] but a review of the literature reveals very few

studies of the relationship between social support and impacts of trauma. There can be little doubt that war, or an event that approximates war, has dramatic impacts on individuals within a given community or society. What remains unclear, however, is whether individuals experience such events as private or public. For instance, people will regard a physical assault as either an offence against their own person or as an offence against their community or group. Offenses against a group will be experienced largely as public trauma where a clearly identified group has been wronged or damaged. The response to that wrong is often seen in the form of a community action, like the creation of freedom fighters or the development of specific interest organisations. An individual who is assaulted has little recourse to a public expression of trauma and may find it necessary to utilise private means of trauma mitigation or stress reduction. Derek Summerfield asks whether war is a community event largely experienced in public as a community phenomenon. In a wide-ranging analysis, Summerfield argues that to use individual psychosocial models in order to respond to the community event of war is to make a leap that logic and study do not support. He further suggests that a more accurate paradigm to operate from is found within a sociological rather than psychosocial framework.[12]

To appreciate fully this difference in approach, we need to examine in some detail the history of psychological trauma investigation and how influential the psychological definitions have been in affecting trauma-recovery programmes in recent years.

Psychological literature abounds with research findings, discussions and proposals relating to the complex area of individual psychological reactions and responses to traumatic events. Within the last 20 years, the investigation of stress and trauma has become well established in both the academic and operational areas of human care. Literature on stress in both the professional and the popular press is extensive. General understanding of traumatic stress has also been widely covered for some years and is generally accepted by most people as a recognisable condition. Indeed the official psychological organ of definition for psychological conditions, the DSM-IV, includes post-traumatic stress disorder as a recognisable and treatable condition.

To arrive at a diagnosis of post-traumatic stress, a series of criteria must be satisfied. First, there has to be an identifiable traumatic event. This event must occur in the "real world" and not be imagined or psychological. Second, there has to be a readily identifiable group (or individual) who has experienced this event. Third, treatment of post-traumatic stress will always include some kind of public telling of the event from the individual's experience. Fourth, treatment of post-traumatic stress will focus on the "normalisation" of the individual's symptoms or reactions. Treatment is largely an education process to help individuals understand that their personal reactions to the event are normal—it is the event that is abnormal.

Traumatic stress is, by definition, the result of exposure to an event that is so catastrophic that the individual's normal psychological coping capacity is overwhelmed and the individual is no longer able to function effectively. A number of physiological and emotional indicators can signal traumatic stress in an individual, but these on their own are insufficient to render a diagnosis of post-traumatic stress disorder or even the lesser stress reactions that occur from time to time. The key to an adequate diagnosis of this condition is the ability to identify the event that triggered the symptoms. A professional diagnosis will always include an analysis of the actual precipitating event.

A key component of the treatment method is the individual's ability to describe the traumatic event from beginning to end and to achieve an understanding that any emotional and psychological reactions being experienced are normal responses to an abnormal situation. The professional (Western) psychological community generally regards this kind of talk therapy as effective when applied immediately after a traumatic event. Studies indicate a reduction in post-trauma disorders when such procedures are used.

If we believe this to be true for individual events of major impact then, on the surface, it appears logical to apply the same reasoning to CHEs. It is only a question of magnitude. It stands to reason that in a greater and more widespread event, such as a war or civil violence, the psychological trauma will be both more widespread (more people will be affected) and the reactions more extreme (deeper and more serious post-traumatic stress). It seems reasonable to assume that an event such as a military coup, a civil war, or a genocide will give rise to large numbers of individual cases of traumatic stress among the populations experiencing those events. Indeed, this logic has led to demonstrable conclusions. For instance, it has been reported that up to 700,000 people in Bosnia-Herzegovina and Croatia were suffering from severe psychic trauma and in need of urgent attention.[13] Given the relative lack of psychological services in that area, it then became incumbent on the international community to provide resources to meet the needs of this "traumatised" population. The UNHCR in particular has promoted numerous psychosocial projects in Bosnia and Croatia in response to this kind of assessment. Many other NGOs responded likewise.

It would appear to be almost universally accepted that war and similar experiences result in very high numbers of psychologically traumatised individuals, all requiring intensive psychological interventions. The situation requires a more in-depth analysis. The literature on psychosocial interventions within environments of war and violence is limited. However, we have a valuable resource in the experiences from South Africa during the apartheid years. Gillian Straker and her colleagues at the University of the Witwatersrand in Johannesburg have written extensively on the theme of doing therapy while under oppression. In a brief report Straker notes that most psychological interventions rely on two presuppositions: that the environment a person lives in is post-traumatic, and that there exists a relatively peaceful world.[14] However, these presuppositions do not apply in the context of current civil conflict and political oppression. Straker also notes that therapists who live and work within the same environment of oppression and violence suffer the same effects as others in the community, and that self-care, as well as client-care, could effectively include interventions of a political or social nature.[15] Political and social activities are not generally prescribed psychological interventions in Western environments, nor do first-world therapists and clients generally act together either socially or politically in attempting to resolve psychological conditions. Quite correctly, however, Straker and her colleagues refused to adopt a narrow therapeutic approach, recognising the ultimate futility of such a path.

Mental health professionals, as a group, are not experienced in either the assessment of or interventions with large populations. By training, most Western psychologists view the individual as the primary point of both assessment and intervention. Even group therapies have a central focus on the individual within the group. In the few instances where the group is considered ahead of the individual, assessment and interventions tend towards the "mind" rather than the "social" or "physical." The powerful combination in Western culture of the centrality of the individual and the role of the psyche (mind) almost inevitably leads mental health professionals to develop paradigms of intervention founded on *individual* and *mental* health principles. It is critically important to note that other professionals, such as sociologists, anthropologists, economists and historians, examine societal-wide events such as civil conflict from the perspective of the community rather than the individual. War and its offspring—genocide and ethnic cleansing—are considered in these frameworks as social phenomena rather than psychological ones. War is born and borne in the context of a society, a culture, a race, a politic or an economy, not as an individual private affair but as a very public and community dynamic.

Another way to appreciate this is to consider past historical responses to war. While it would be irresponsible to suggest that the events of 1935–45 did not significantly traumatise individual Jews, the overwhelming evidence is that Jewish survivors and descendants see the Nazi genocide in social, religious and justice terms. Furthermore, the subsequent actions of the Jewish people and the state of Israel have been societal, political, cultural and religious. The Jewish people-group has viewed the Nazi annihilation attempts as one more, albeit extreme, manifestation of thousands of years of persecution based solely on race. Single, group and community events are contextualised and managed by reference to history, society and Scripture rather than by individual psychotherapy. Jeffrey Jay states that "in the midst of a recent psychological renaissance of interest in trauma, psychotherapy has been silent on the moral, political and spiritual grappling of the community. In that silence we might turn to traditional communities that have lived with a variety of tragedies and disasters throughout the ages." Jay goes on to suggest that "psychotherapy responds to the seeming meaninglessness of trauma by exploring the individual's personal psychology while Judaism ties the knowledge of trauma to a history and communal purpose, giving it a meaning that stretches back in history as well as forward with precepts for ethical behavior."[16] Judaism has developed community ways of drawing the trauma out of individuals and making it become a part of the core of the culture, its religious and communal workings. Trauma becomes part of the corporate memory, the story of existence, and is structured into both ritual and celebration. Memory—not forgetting—becomes the path towards the future. And placement of the memory and the story within the context of the community gives both the individual and the community power over the effects of the event, in essence normalising community experience.

The contrast between this framework and the paradigms developed by psychotherapists is extreme. In a well-developed paper, Summerfield asserts that modern psychological trauma work is based on a number of assumptions, mostly untested and unsupported:

1. Experiences of war and atrocity are so extreme that they do not just cause suffering on a large scale, they also cause trauma.
2. There is a universal human response to highly stressful events.
3. Large numbers of victims traumatised by war need professional help.
4. Western psychological approaches are relevant to violent conflict worldwide. Victims do better if they emotionally ventilate and talk through their experiences.
5. There are vulnerable groups and individuals who need to be specifically targeted for psychological help.
6. Wars represent a mental health emergency; rapid intervention can prevent the development of serious mental health problems, as well as subsequent violence and wars.
7. Local workers are overwhelmed and may themselves be traumatised.[17]

By challenging these assumptions, Summerfield encourages us to take a broader view of complex humanitarian emergencies and to question the assumptions underlying any interventions organisations may undertake on behalf of their staff and local populations. Summerfield concludes that civil conflict is not a private, individual event treatable in psychological terms, but a public, community experience. If Summerfield is correct, then we can postulate that local staff of international relief and aid organisations are more likely to experience CHEs as members of a community than as traumatised individuals. Local staff are, after all, primarily members of the wider community affected by the critical event, whereas international staff are generally not.

One international NGO which has made significant progress in addressing such complexities in practice is the Transcultural Psychosocial Organisation (TPO). The TPO is a World Health Organisation (WHO) collaborating centre supported by the government of the Netherlands and associated with the Free University of Amsterdam. In addition to its work in Cambodia, TPO has on-going programmes in nine centres around the world. The TPO programme in Cambodia commenced in 1995 with the intention of training local community workers in mental health. However, two years of experience led TPO to the conclusion that many parts of the original training programme were inappropriate for the local culture and situation. Therefore,

> we [TPO] have been trying to find out how trauma affects not only the individual but also the family and the community. Given the massive trauma, it seems more appropriate to look at collective trauma and how the community has responded, coped with trauma as a whole, and survived. We have attempted to identify whole families and communities, in addition to individuals, at risk of developing problems. *A community-based approach that encourages rebuilding family and village structures, networks and processes is emphasized.*[18]

Case study: Cambodia—A community-development framework

In July 1997, following a psychological debriefing in Thailand of evacuated WV expatriate staff and their families from Cambodia, the author went into the country for three weeks of individual debriefing and trauma counselling for local staff and family members. In this period we also conducted an in-depth survey of staff needs, both physical and psychological, and made immediate financial recompense for staff who had suffered material loss. There was general agreement that trauma recovery services should be provided for the local staff who had remained in the country. The World Vision International Partnership raised a significant amount of money to fund a planned and well-designed trauma programme for local staff. In taking such action, it is absolutely essential to avoid the mistake in thinking that the *speed* of the response is more important than the *nature* of the response. By intention, this programme was to be directed by the local staff themselves and, in order to ensure that it was done right, we knew it would take time to develop.

It was determined that as soon as the situation in Cambodia had stabilised, a team of mental health professionals should return to the country to provide appropriate psychological support and treatment. The team assumed that the events of 5–6 July had been traumatic and stressful for the WV staff as well as the Cambodian people. It was theorised that a percentage of the staff would be suffering the effects of post-traumatic stress and that some of the staff would have been affected sufficiently to require significant psychological interventions. The history of the country and 20 years of conflict would have echoes in the present, and the events of July 1997 were linked closely to the period of genocidal rule under the dictator Pol Pot. Our initial plan was to provide a kind of debriefing environment for local staff with the addition of local specialist psychological resources available for longer-term interventions and therapy.

The team[19] originally planned to follow established clinical trauma guidelines in designing a programme. First the event would be defined, then the surviving population identified, and finally an intervention plan designed.

The first challenge came with the identification of the key event, the critical occurrence that defined the impetus for the conclusion that traumatic stress could exist. Although Saturday, 5 July 1997, appeared to be the commencement of the traumatic event, it was not very clear when, if ever, the event had really ended. Certainly the brutal street violence in the capital, Phnom Penh, had ceased, but there was still fighting in the countryside and, more ominously, reports of regular assassinations of people associated with the losing sides in the conflict. As such associations were quite common (almost half of those in the voting population in 1993 were associated with Khmer Rouge–affiliated political parties), the potential for violence being visited on staff and families remained very high.

There are even difficulties with determining the specific time the event commenced. Certainly the first explosions in the capital are noted in time and place. But the build-up to the violence had been going on not only for months but for years. In fact, apart from the brief period when the UN peacekeeping forces ran the country, political violence had been occurring throughout the country for decades. In 1996, for instance, there was a mini-coup, and street violence was quite common from 1993 to 1997.

Without a clear start and with no end in sight, it became harder to label what had happened as a critical event according to the definition of the trauma professions.

Critical incident debriefing models of care generally follow the Mitchell and Bray prescription that, as far as possible, all the people who experienced the critical event should go through a debriefing together.[20] This allows the group context to validate others' experiences, and facilitators can begin the educative process of normalisation. This process helps participants understand that their physiological and psychological responses to the event are normal, while the event is abnormal. But this model fails early on in the context of country-wide civil war. Obviously the whole population of the country is affected by this war. Certainly all the inhabitants of Phnom Penh were touched. The local staff of one NGO were no different from other staffs in the city. Furthermore, most of the actual experiences did not occur in the context of the work environment but in the home. The fighting broke out on a Saturday, when most staff were with their friends and families. Because WV's objective was to assist its own local staff, the population for any intervention was defined by employment status, not by exposure to any specific event. It could be presumed that individual staff experienced different events with different groups of people over the weekend. This alone weakens the utility of a clinical debriefing approach.

The situation becomes more complex because within the staff group there will be different political alliances. By association at least, some of the staff might be perpetrators of the events, others directly targeted victims, and still others neutral, if there can be any such thing in a civil war.

Psychological debriefing of an event of critical nature not only relies on the relative uniformity of the group (all experiencing the same event as neutral participants), but also on the ability to proclaim such an event as abnormal and the individual psychological response as normal. Understanding this will significantly reduce psychological and emotional stress for individuals, and they will then return to a stable state sooner rather than later. Unfortunately, violence in Cambodia is quite normal; it is not unusual. For the vast majority of the population, civil war—or variations of military conflict—has been the norm for nearly 40 years. In some contexts, such as Oklahoma City, a bomb blast can be described as abnormal, but in a country where bomb blasts, gun shots, grenade attacks, armed robbery and even factional fighting between groups of police are everyday occurrences, it is difficult to describe an increase in fighting as abnormal. Indeed a historical review shows that for much of the twentieth century, Cambodia had been at war.

To expatriates who had never seen tanks in the streets or felt the thud of rockets falling, the events of July 1997 were abnormal. But could we make the same assumption for Cambodians?

With our increasing inability to identify either a discrete population or a specific traumatising event, design of an appropriate intervention or treatment plan became problematical. It became more and more difficult to frame staff-support actions purely within the context of individual mental health care. A new approach was clearly required.

We found ourselves asking very basic questions. For instance, What is stress in Cambodia? What is trauma? In a country where nearly two million people were systematically murdered by their co-citizens, what does trauma entail? A translator brought this to our attention in the simplest of ways by inquiring about the word *stress*. The English word *stress* does not translate well into Khmer (the language of Cambodia). This led us to ask whether stress as a condition was easily identifiable within the Cambodian context. Physiological responses may be normative across human beings, and changes in internal bodily functions may be measurable in all people. But we already know that different people respond to the same stimuli in different physiological ways. What causes pain in one person may cause joy in another. What increases blood pressure in one may reduce it in another.[21] Can we assume that a single identifiable event will result in the same response, or a response of the same magnitude, across human beings? It would seem not.

On this basis, it is difficult to say with confidence that the condition known as stress in the West exists in Cambodia. Further, while application of recognised psychological trauma and stress instruments certainly resulted in "scores," it is not immediately clear what the instruments are really measuring. (It is rather like trying to measure the temperature of a bath full of water with a bare hand. It is possible to say that the water is either hot or cold, but the precise temperature is unknown. It is also possible to "fool" the body's assessment of temperature by either cooling or heating the hand before immersing it in the water. All we can really say about this process is that something was measured; it was not possible to determine exactly what.)

Because of the uncertainty surrounding both classification and therefore an appropriate intervention, it became preferable for the team to conduct an assessment of the nature and extent of trauma rather than deliver an intervention. Adopting this approach opened the door to explore other disciplines in order to create the most effective staff-support strategy.

Sometimes it is difficult to see the forest for the trees. The close-up focus of the professional obscures the wider view that opens up different ways forward. It is somewhat ironic that the business of WV is community development, and yet the principles and practice of development theory had been largely overlooked as we considered staff trauma and stress. When individual trauma is placed in the context of community experience, perspective shifts and new ways to move forward appear.

The team was in Cambodia for nearly four weeks, interacting with local staff and families in a variety of different ways. Various psychological tests were administered, and group sessions were held. The results of these measures are still being assessed.[22] However, the particular results may not be as important as the process that framed the team's time in Cambodia.

As mental health practitioners, the team behaved in accordance with the predictions noted by Summerfield. Thus, the programme began with a mental health perspective, based on the assumption that trauma would most likely be present in the Cambodian staff. This assumption restricted our intervention options to therapeutic practices, and ultimately we could only proceed by ignoring the wider social and political contexts and by simply moving forward and defining the debriefing environment as post-traumatic.

However, an assessment from a community-development perspective opened up a whole new range of tools and options. First, our focus moved from the individual to the community. When we did this in Cambodia, more 'sense' began to emerge. With a defined population (the staff of World Vision Cambodia), we were able to ask the question, What impact has this event had on the lives of the local staff?, which led to, What assistance could WV offer to ameliorate these effects?

While a mental health focus offers options for treatment within the mental health field, this more open-ended process led away from the cul-de-sac of individual trauma treatment. In effect, the team began to behave much more like social anthropologists than psychologists. Even though the team followed through with the initial plan to apply psychological measures to individuals, this may have been more to reassure the team than to lead to firm conclusions of a traumatic nature.

A step-wise process was developed to explore some very broad issues. This was done by asking groups of staff a number of more specific questions.

1. *What constitutes stress and trauma in Cambodian lives?* Is there a concept of individual stress in Cambodian culture? If so, what are the indicators? How do Cambodians identify stress in others? What other words or phrases are used to describe trauma? Is there a psychological component to a Cambodian definition of stress? If not, how is stress experienced?

2. *Traditionally and historically, what have Cambodians done to deal with stress and trauma?* What is the individual role in managing stress? What is the community role? What role do community institutions such as the church or the Buddhist *wat* (temple) play in such management?

3. *What is the nature of stress and trauma today?* What specifically causes stress and trauma? Are these stressors the same as or different from past stressors? What, if anything, has changed during the past 20 years?

4. *What mechanisms do Cambodians use today to cope with stress and trauma?* Are today's coping methods any different from past techniques? How?

5. *Do these present methods provide sufficient power to relieve stress and trauma?* Are the present methods inadequate or have historical methods been lost to the present generation? Have present circumstances overpowered past cultural mechanisms, or have these methods been lost as a result of Pol Pot's genocide?

6. *What resources, skills or knowledge do Cambodians require to address any shortfall between perceived need and identifi-*

able resources? Is it a recovery of cultural memory that is required? Is it a matter of re-building social institutions such as
the temples and monasteries? Or is there a need to create new
social institutions to meet completely new situations?

7. *In what way would Cambodians see that an international relief and development agency such as World Vision might assist in the support of this objective?* Is there a role for an NGO
   or is it a community response? Is it effective to limit organisational responses to local staff or should the provision of services be community wide?

The shift in adopting this approach is not at all subtle, and the
effects are potentially wide-ranging. Rather than prescribing a treatment after a professional (external) diagnosis, the assessment team
is there to learn. The basic assumption is that there already exists
within the local community much wisdom, maturity and the capacity to meet both individual and community challenges. It is the
team's task, on behalf of the NGO, to discover and reveal these
strengths and to follow the lead of the local staff in developing any
organisational intervention. Psychological skills are still important,
but this is not a psychological assessment. A psychologist seeks to
determine which psychological intervention is appropriate, working from an assumption that the framework of psychology is the
correct viewpoint for analysis. A community assessment team, alternatively, seeks to bridge the gap between two cultures: one being
the international NGO, with all its beliefs, structures and values;
the other, the pre-existing local culture, with its long history and
complexity. The skill required is not that of a clinical psychologist
but more of a "weaver"; the need is to pick up all the threads of
multicultural experience and weave them into a fabric that will
hold the community together and support the growth and healing
of the people. In doing so, of course, a new culture is designed and
built, one that has components of both new and old and has the
resilience and internal integrity to be self-sustainable and not reli-
ant on external "aid and advice."

The result of utilising this type of approach is to acknowledge
that the intervention is not yet over. Indeed, it has hardly begun.
Community development projects often take years to design and
decades to run their course. But the more a development focus is

applied to matters of trauma and local staff care, the less appropriate pure psychological paradigms appear to be. Indeed, it may be possible to argue in the future that the individual psychological approach to trauma work in populations affected by war and civil violence is not only inappropriate but counter-productive. By its very nature, the individual focus makes it unlikely that issues of justice, reconciliation, peacebuilding and social reconstruction will be addressed. But, as the present day Truth and Reconciliation Tribunal in South Africa and the Nuremberg Trials of World War II should tell us, community matters such as war require community interventions such as tribunals and courts to bring healing. In *Rethinking the Trauma of War*, Patrick Bracken and Celia Petty conclude, "Communities recovering from war are increasingly faced by unresolved problems caused by the absence of justice. Establishing a sense of justice within society is a multi-layered task."[23] Justice, the authors assert, is an essential component of the healing of trauma, maybe even more so than therapy.

Further, the assumption that communities and cultures do not have the internal capacity to deal effectively with the effects of community-wide disruption is disconcerting. The involvement and promotion of external specialists may have a tendency to disempower pre-existing cultural wisdom and marginalise the traditional cultural locations of such wisdom and potential healing. In Cambodia, for instance, the roles of the monk and the *Kru Khmer* (traditional healer) appear to be critical for healing. By supplanting these roles with the psychologist ("Western mind wizard"), the society is affected both on a structural level (what happens to unemployed *Kru Khmer?*) and on a cultural level (historically important themes are negated and may be lost). The impact on cultural values and cultural independence can be profound, especially if training programmes in psychology and therapy become part of the intervention. In societies torn apart by war, employment and income are critical to survival. Adopting a new profession, such as psychologist, may open doors for young people to wealth, security and status, maybe even a ticket out of the environment. The power of the NGO to confer this kind of patronage either directly or through modelling behaviour is greater than often accepted in the NGO community. A community development approach to issues of mental health could prevent some of the excesses presently being seen in the international relief and development fields.

PROGRAMME 2:
THE CARE AND SUPPORT
OF INTERNATIONAL RELIEF AND DEVELOPMENT STAFF

As with other international NGOs, WV has long pursued a policy of providing support services to expatriate staff and families. Over the years, this support has become more sophisticated and effective. Of course, much remains to be achieved. However, the international community of humanitarian agencies, in the past few years, has increasingly sought to identify appropriate support mechanisms in an increasingly complex world. International relief and aid workers are prone to trauma and stress as a result of their employment. The difficulties of their working environment are often no surprise. Indeed, many people deliberately choose these dangerous and challenging working environments. Those living in the most difficult of situations, such as Rwanda and Bosnia, are there by choice, and they remain as long as they wish. The reasons people do this are complex and varied. Within the NGO community there is a common appreciation of the concept of service. Actions of staff are often in response to a call to care or love, a desire to see healing. This "higher" world view provides both an intellectual and an emotional framework within which to process personal experiences and events of the wider world.

The employment of people to deliver service in complex humanitarian environments is the concern of NGOs and agencies. Support and care of such staff is widely recognised as essential, although there are huge variations in the nature and extent of support structures within organisations. Some have well-developed institutional services; others, unfortunately, abandon staff and families to their fate with no support at all.

WV responds to complex disasters worldwide. A significant component of its present work is in relief and disaster response. Staff working in these environments expect to be personally challenged by their experiences in the field. This expectation goes a long way towards developing personal resilience and capacity to survive difficult events. However, as described earlier, the last 10 years have been extremely difficult for World Vision staff, as it has for most international aid agencies.

The Critical Incident Stress Debriefing model developed by Jeffrey Mitchell has been found effective for emergency services personnel and for survivors of major traumatic events.[24] However, as Mitchell indicates, the debriefing component of post-incident care is most effective when deployed as part of an overall process of support, one which includes attention to such issues as shelter, clothing, finances, medical attention and, if necessary, transportation to a safer location. Obviously, this is difficult to plan for in crisis situations, but for people who intend to be located in places where violence and death are expected, full-care programmes potentially can be developed.

One of the complexities of disaster work is that staff are often exposed to a series of traumatic events over the length of their careers. The combination of specific traumatic events and the ongoing background of chronic stress, both present and remembered, creates an individual psychological dynamic that requires considerable personal resilience and organisational support. Jonathan Shay concludes that the ability to survive emotionally the most challenging violent environments is directly related to the strength of the relationships between colleagues and with supervisors.[25] The nature of the external event itself is not as much an indicator of the likely development of a trauma-related condition as the strength of interpersonal relationships. Where supportive work relationships are absent, stressed employees quickly develop cynicism and bitterness, and an increasingly demoralising paranoia where secrecy becomes common practice and communication breaks down. Individual staff burnout occurs with the inevitable failure of programmes with all the public consequences associated with such events. On the other hand, where staff feel free to discuss and address issues of personal stress and where collegial support is available, severe trauma can often be avoided, staff morale remains high and programme objectives are met. It appears that the ability of individuals to survive the most complex and dangerous of situations is as much an organisational matter as an individual one. Given a sound and supportive collegial environment, individuals will deal with the most violent and complex environments with minimal traumatic stress reactions.[26]

A factor that many organisations find too challenging to address, but which is key to the creation of a sound work environment, is that of leadership. Shay has argued convincingly that the quality of leadership in a field situation may be the single most significant factor in reducing the likelihood of staff developing post-traumatic stress disorder. Shay's considerable experience with military units has led him to state that "the most effective way of preventing stress injury is the all-round excellence of leadership—leadership that strengthens staff in this way also creates trust, mutual respect and positive enjoyment of the field community."[27] Further, he asserts that the prevention of stress injuries lies mainly in the hands of management professionals, not in the hands of health professionals.

It appears that the internal stress created by inadequate management ability significantly affects workers' capacity to cope with severe work-related stress. The structure of an organisation and how decisions are made and passed on to staff are also significant sources of stress that directly lead to increased symptoms of traumatic-stress disorders. Many organisations deny these factors, preferring instead to focus on individual staff resilience, security preparedness and personal stress-management planning to address what are really corporate management shortcomings. An over-emphasis on the mental health aspects of stress and trauma can be an indication of a refusal by organisations to address critical management issues.

Unless managers are prepared to focus equally on organisational issues in the prevention and treatment of traumatic-stress disorders, then we will spend our time essentially developing excellent ambulance services (therapy and other psychological interventions) while doing little to address one of the root causes of damage in the first place. Unfortunately, many managers are themselves in a state of denial of their own stress reactions and, without assistance and courage, will find it difficult to allow their organisations to focus on these root causes.

One aspect of stress and trauma that asks for more examination is religious or spiritual belief. Traumatised staff display, along with the recognised psychological symptoms, profound spiritual trauma. Recent conferences on stress and trauma matters (for example, the European Society for Traumatic Stress Studies Conference held in Istanbul, Turkey, June 1999) have included discussions on the centrality of faith and belief and even spirituality as important factors to consider when designing support initiatives. Indeed, compelling arguments can be raised for including all humanitarian workers, regardless of culture, race or employer, in this discussion, as most workers enter a career in such work with quite strong faith-based world views. While it is normal to raise questions about the nature of God following a traumatic event (and staff need to be reassured that it is quite normal to do this), this matter is of profound importance to Christian and faith-based agencies and missions. The existence of a statement of faith is a pre-existing requirement for employment with many Christian relief and aid agencies. This faith is a belief structure based on both intellectual and experiential history. A faith-based or religious frame of reference legitimises the individual and corporate involvement in CHE work and provides a structure within which interventions and programmes can be designed and implemented.

When a worker raises issues relating to this faith, there needs to be both an emotional and an intellectual aspect to a trauma and health-care intervention. While it is normal to refine a world view and a theology (a God view) during the course of life, a faith-based organisation has a responsibility to provide an environment where the deep spiritual questions raised by such experiences as genocide can be addressed and discussed, if not answered. In military experience, a soldier who has lost his belief in the purpose of the war is a danger to both self and colleagues. Such soldiers may become deserters or traitors. In the Christian community, particularly the conservative evangelical community, such individuals may be accused of being sinful or faithless.[28] The appropriate organisational response is not to silence or fire the individual who raises these questions, but to allow these questions to inform and expand the wider organisational vision for ministry. The nature of suffering is a complex matter, and answers are often ambiguous. Evangelical traditions are generally uncomfortable with ambiguity and will have a struggle in creating environments where such issues can be raised. But for healing to occur, such processes must be encouraged.

There are indications in the research literature that faith may have some impact on overall resilience and coping with extreme circumstances[29]. However, this type of faith is not restricted and, indeed, may be opposed to religious faith. Gina O'Connell Higgins postulates that faith or belief in oneself or one's world view (which incorporates a religious view) may be the key to understanding the impact of faith on resilience. The author is aware of no studies that support the thesis that a religious faith (whether Christian or not) is, in itself, a strong indicator of resilience or reduces the impact of trauma.

Emergence of a model for expatriate staff care and support in crisis situations

In Cambodia in July 1997, the situation was volatile and dangerous for all. The expatriate community in the city was deeply affected by events of the weekend of 5–6 July. Staff had been caught in the crossfire, had witnessed death in the streets, or had been terrified that they might not be able to escape. Even a year later, many had not returned to Cambodia.

Members of the local community, on the other hand, often had no option but to remain. Apart from those Khmer holding foreign passports, they could not escape either the street fighting or the aftermath. This was true as well for local staff of international NGOs and foreign businesses. While expatriate staff exited the city, local staff either continued to manage the operations or retreated to the few places of safety remaining.

For a brief moment during the weekend of 5–6 July, the primary occupation of *all* people was survival—but this convergence was only for a moment in history. Our examination and involvement with the people of Cambodia led to the conclusion that there are two distinct communities who experience the same events in markedly different ways—so different, in fact, that the experiences should not be compared in terms of magnitude or degree, but more in terms of kind. Expatriate staff experienced an abnormal event that broke into their normal lives. The magnitude and suddenness of this event was shocking and traumatic. After having fled, expatriates found themselves working through emotional, psychological and spiritual issues in a safe physical location. The expatriate experience fits readily into a broad psychosocial category where well-designed mental health programmes are appropriate interventions. The rapidly developing field of traumatic-stress studies forms a suitable framework for organisations to plan sound support and follow-up strategies for expatriate staff.

A psychosocial model for expatriate humanitarian staff

The model I propose comprises a number of stages as it attempts to address many of the issues of staffing CHE responses. Some of these stages appear in most organisations in one form or another, often the responsibility of human resources or recruiting staff. This model proposes, however, that consideration of all stages in this process from a viewpoint of stress-and-trauma management would pay handsome dividends for all humanitarian organisations.

Pre-employment
1. Provide applicants with accurate information regarding the programme, country, political, cultural and current events, especially as they might relate to stress and potential critical incident stress.
2. Provide general information regarding stress, stress management education, critical event and critical incident interventions in relation to complex humanitarian work.
3. Provide newly hired staff with specific, up-to-date country and security profiles. Provide new employees with organisational stress-management resources and ensure they are aware of organisational staff support mechanisms and how to access such resources if required.

In-country occupational stress-management services
1. Each field office will have a complete country security plan for all staff in accord with established security practices.[30]
2. Field offices will have clear policies regarding occupational stress management and will provide access to appropriate services both local and international.
3. Each field office will have a trauma and emergency support service (TESS) plan in place.
4. On arrival in the country, each new employee is to be thoroughly briefed on the country environment with special reference to security and military issues.
5. Senior or experienced staff are responsible for on-site orientations for new staff.

6. With assistance and on-going support, staff encourages the new employee to develop and initiate his or her own stress-management programme.

Trauma emergency support services (TESS)

World Vision's experience in attempting to provide critical incident stress debriefing for staff involved in major incidents (full-country evacuations) in Sierra Leone, Chad, Liberia and Cambodia showed us that debriefing itself is not sufficient to meet the needs of traumatised and stressed staff. The practical and logistical needs of people escaping war are immense, and the support services available in the locality of evacuated personnel generally so limited, that it is essential that the employing NGO provide these along with psychological debriefing. This has led us to the development of the TESS model.

1. *Sideline support services:* When a critical event occurs, the objective of sideline support is to move staff involved in a critical event safely and quickly away from the event site, providing brief services that will assist this process. A TESS team will be on site or as close as possible to provide these immediate support services. Interventions may include determining whether someone is injured; providing minor medical assistance; providing water and food; providing emotional, physical and spiritual support; providing transportation away from immediate danger; providing "defusing" services (brief information on stress reactions and what can be done to prevent severe trauma reactions or how best to manage such reactions).

2. *Logistic support services:* For persons affected by a critical event, TESS will organise and provide direct assistance through short-term respite care at a previously designated "retreat style" location; communication services; emergency personal finances; local and international travel assistance for those needing to leave the field location or travel to a home destination.

3. *Trauma debriefing services:* A critical event debriefing is a structured, confidential, psychoeducational group meeting that emphasises expression of reactions after an acutely stressful

event and education on how best to promote prevention or management of any post-traumatic stress reactions. Anecdotal findings suggest that such a process is most helpful when provided 24 to 72 hours after the critical event. Debriefing services will include group, individual and special cases (children, families).

4. *Brief counselling services:* After the debriefing services, especially when individuals and families are still in transit or after arrival at a final destination, brief counselling services will be made available.

5. *Follow-up services:* After the critical event TESS team members will continue to track and communicate with individuals and families involved with the critical event. Through tracking, it may be seen that certain other types of services are required. These services could include psychological and social support services or referrals; spiritual guidance or support services; health services; employment services; relocation assistance; insurance claims for personal or property-related matters. It needs to be emphasised that the above is, at the time of writing, a theoretical model guiding the planning of international staff care and support within WV. Only parts of this model are presently operating and will require alteration as our knowledge and understanding increases.

CONCLUSIONS

The explosion of knowledge about trauma and stress in the last two decades has added much to our understanding. The connection between events and individual trauma is well documented, and intervention methods have been widely tested in the Western world. These methods are useful in the care and support of expatriate staff who have experienced trauma in their work. However, even for expatriates, these methods are most helpful when packaged with practical logistical and corporate measures taken to enhance staff members' ability to survive in CHEs. Additionally, it is important in faith-based organisations to support and encourage traumatised staff as they work through the inevitable questions they will face about the nature of God and God's goodness. There is doubt, however, regarding the applicability of individual psychological definitions of trauma and psychological methods to provide adequate support and care for local staff or community members who experience societal events such as civil war.

International relief and development agencies wishing to become involved in CHE environments should consider the following points:

1. The huge investment by international relief and development agencies, and other international organisations, in community psychological support programmes in CHEs appears to be based on largely untested assumptions and may be self-serving for the Western psychological community.

2. International relief and development agencies urgently need to develop and institute effective and comprehensive measures of support and care for staff who are exposed extensively to extreme CHE conditions. A significant number of staff are expatriate, coming from an increasingly wide cultural base, and while these people are experienced, skilled and dedicated, the evidence to date suggests that long-term involvement in extreme situations does not necessarily lead to increased resilience to stress. In fact, chronic stress, burnout and even post-traumatic stress disorder may be hidden beneath excessive psychological dissociation and camouflaged by a lifestyle characterised by frequent relocation and a reduced social network. International agencies that ignore the wealth of evidence as to the organisational costs and personal impact of long-term CHE assignments will inherit a staff with the complete range of stress and trauma-related conditions and the consequent diminishment of productivity. International staff-support programmes need to include considerations of recruiting and employment behaviour as well as individual resilience, stress-management capacity and psychological/spiritual maturity. Such programmes should not be confined to phrases in corporate mission statements but need to be clearly measurable components of a complete human resource management structure.

3. Local staff-support interventions during or after CHEs should not be based on assumptions of depth of trauma or purely psychological paradigms. In particular, the critical-incident debriefing model appears to have serious shortcomings when applied to the complex, on-going reality of most local staff in field locations. Talk therapy may not be the most appropriate process in many cultures.

4. Partnership with local communities in determining the existence and levels of traumatic stress will, it is theorised, produce more long-term and sustainable intervention plans and will enhance the local communities' abilities to incorporate any new learning into pre-existing strategies for both individual and group support and care. International relief and development staff should endeavour to establish long-term relationships with key community people in order to gain a full understanding of the strengths and resources available to provide support. These people should aid the local leadership in programme design and implementation, in line with established community development principles. Issues of justice, morality, financial recompense and reconciliation need to be included in any design programme. The public nature of such processes needs to be affirmed, and mental health professionals will need to struggle with Western concepts of privacy and client confidentiality.

5. The resolution of trauma is an intensely spiritual process for an individual. The journey to wellness is conducted in the context of a belief in the nature of suffering and pain. This belief is founded on a spiritual world view. Persons who believe that suffering is either inevitable or deserved will have a significantly different path towards healing from those who believe that all pain will be wiped away. In Cambodia, for example, outside helpers need an understanding of the prevailing Buddhist spirituality if trauma and stress are to be managed in a healthy manner. There are very strong beliefs in Cambodia concerning a series of prophecies that appear to have been partially fulfilled by the Khmer Rouge years, but the suffering, according to the prophecies, is not yet over. If the general population believes it is "cursed" to experience profound trauma, then interventions will need to take this into account. Given that Christianity is intimately related to employment by WV (as well as some other aid organisations) and that employment of local staff is directly related to avoiding poverty in Cambodia, the raising of spiritual aspects of trauma work requires much thought and study. All staff, both local and international, employed by faith-based or secular agencies will benefit from an open examination of the spiritual base of relief and development work, and organisations need to create opportunities for individual changes in such world views to be discussed and incorporated into agency activity.

6. Local staff trauma-support teams should include psychological expertise, but the broad perspective needs to be sociological and developmental rather than psychotherapeutic. Public health and community institutions need to be partnered with in order to ensure local sustainability of staff care and support services.

7. Finally, although this was, ironically, the very first thing we learned in Cambodia (even though the full implications did not become apparent to us for a long time), local staff need to be involved in the selection of the personnel purporting to aid the community in dealing with trauma and stress. Organisations need to retain management control of the process, but not at the expense of or counter to local staff wishes. Effective outcomes will be attained only where there is a sound partnership between management, both in-country and out, and the staff being assisted. In Cambodia, the local staff were not totally supportive of the membership of the first team proposed by the organisation and recommended a different team. This was partly based on personal relationships with the people they recommended. Although the team still had a very strong psychological background, the key team members had lived and worked in Cambodia previously and had an understanding of Cambodian culture and history. In the end, it appeared that the professional background of the team was of less interest to the local staff than previous relationships and personal credibility. It could be postulated that the team recommended by the local staff had previously demonstrated an acceptance of Cambodian society and a respect of Cambodian capacity. This seems to bear out Flannery's contention that social context may be critical in how individuals react to war and adds to Summerfield's thesis that war is experienced as a public and community event. The team members had, to some extent, become identified with the local wounded community through their own experiences while living in Cambodia previously. This experience appeared to be very important to the local staff as they worked through the process of identifying stress and trauma within a Cambodian context.

It is not only what we do but how we do it that is important. I recall a conversation with a colleague who is heading up reconciliation ministries in Rwanda. He told me that many people had been to many workshops and seminars on reconciliation, but few reported reconciliation with their neighbours.[31] Not until more culturally appropriate methods of meeting together and sharing experiences were adopted did group reconciliation begin. It is likely that cultures outside the West have developed excellent ways to meet and to cope with trauma and stress that do not involve group work or talk therapy. It may be most effective for international NGOs to seek to discover what these processes are as we attempt to provide the very best care and support for our local staff working in the most challenging of environments.

NOTES

[1] Mary Anderson, *Do No Harm—Supporting Local Capacities for Peace Through Aid* (Cambridge, Mass.: Collaborative for Development Action, 1996); People in Aid, "People in Aid Code of Best Practices in the Management and Support of Aid Personnel," Relief and Rehabilitation network paper 20 (February 1996); available at www.peopleinaid.org/codemain.htm.

[2] "Staff Stress and Security: A Management Challenge for UNHCR," UN (EC/47/SC/CRP 49), 1.

[3] *The Los Angeles Times*, 2 August 1998, A8.

[4] "Room for Improvement: The Management and Support of Relief and Development Workers," a report by the Overseas Development Institute (ODI) (London, 1995), 1.

[5] Overseas Development Institute (London), "Code of Conduct for the International Red Cross and Red Crescent Movement and NGOs in Disaster Relief," Relief and Rehabilitation network paper 7 (September 1994); available at www.odi.org.uk/hpn/pubs/net-ab7.html.

[6] Gill Eagle, workshop presentation, European Conference on Traumatic Stress, Istanbul (June 1999).

[7] Gina O'Connell Higgins, *Resilient Adults: Overcoming a Cruel Past* (San Francisco: Jossey-Bass, 1994), 174.

[8] UN, *Staff Stress and Security*, 3.

[9] Derek Summerfield, "Assisting Survivors of War and Atrocity: Notes on 'Psychosocial' Issues for NGO Workers," *Development in Practice* 5/4 (1995).

[10] Yoav Lavee and Amith Ben-David, "Families Under War: Stresses and Strains of Israeli Families During the Gulf War," *Journal of Traumatic Stress* 2/6 (1993), 240.

[11] Raymond B. Flannery, "Social Support and Psychological Trauma: A Methodological Review," *Journal of Traumatic Stress* 3/4 (1990), 594.

[12] Derek Summerfield, "The Impact of War and Atrocity on Civilian Populations: Basic Principles for NGO Interventions and a Critique of Psychosocial Trauma Projects," Overseas Development Institute network paper 14 (London: ODI/RNN, 1996).

[13] I Agger, S Vuk, and J Mimica, "Theory and Practice of Psychosocial Projects Under War Conditions in Bosnia-Herzegovina and Croatia" (Zagreb: ECHO/ECTF, 1995).

[14] Gillian Straker and Fathima Moosa, "Interacting with Trauma Survivors in Contexts of Continuing Trauma" *Journal of Traumatic Stress* 7/3 (1994), 457.

[15] Gillian Straker "Exploring the Effects of Interacting with Survivors of Trauma," *Journal of Social Development in Africa* 8/2 (1993), 37.

[16] Jeffrey Jay, "Walls for Wailing," *Common Boundary* (May/June 1994), 31.

[17] Summerfield, "The Impact of War and Atrocity on Civilian Populations."

[18] D Somasudaram et al., *Community Mental Health in Cambodia* (Phnom Penh: Transcultural Psychosocial Organization, 1997), iii, italics added. The work of TPO is highly recommended to the reader. Further information can be obtained directly from TPO in Cambodia at P.O. Box 1124, Phnom Penh, Cambodia, or at www.bigpond.com.kh/users/tpo/default.htm#below.

[19] The team consisted of two external WV staff, one local staff and a clinical researcher from the School of Psychology at Fuller Seminary, Pasadena, California.

[20] Perpetrators of violence or trauma are not included in this group. This is not a reconciliation process but a survivor intervention.

[21] R J Ursano, B G McCaughey, C S Fullerton, *Individual and Community Responses to Trauma and Disaster: The Structure of Human Chaos* (Great Britain: Cambridge University Press 1994), 48–50.

[22] The School of Psychology at Fuller Theological Seminary, Pasadena, California, USA, has provided a research assistant to analyze test scores and other measures used in Cambodia. WV wishes to acknowledge the collaboration with Fuller Theological Seminary, and the outstanding work provided by Dr Cynthia Eriksson, the research assistant.

[23] Patrick J Bracken and Celia Petty, eds. *Rethinking the Trauma of War* (London: Free Association Books Ltd., 1998), 191.

[24] J T Mitchell and G S Everly, *Critical Incident Stress Debriefing: An Operations Manual for the Prevention of Traumatic Stress Among Emergency Services and Disaster Workers*, 2d ed., rev. (Ellicott City, Md.: Chevron Publishing Company, 1996).

[25] Jonathan Shay, *Achilles in Vietnam: Combat Trauma and the Undoing of Character* (New York: Atheneum, 1994).

[26] Military research shows that combat units with strong inter-personal relationships and high trust in unit leaders have significantly lower incidence of stress and trauma symptoms, and are also more likely to obtain the identified objectives of the mission. For a fuller discussion on this matter, see Shay's publications.

[27] Jonathan Shay, workshop presentation, International Society for Trauma Stress Studies, San Francisco (1997).

[28] It is possible that this is similar in other faith-based organizations. However, the author is not experienced enough to write authoritatively on religious agencies other than Christian.

[29] O'Connell Higgins, *Resilient Adults*, 171ff.

[30] See, for example, Charles Rogers and Brian Sytsma, *A Shield About Me: Safety Awareness for World Vision Staff* (Geneva: World Vision International, 1998).

[31] Tekle Selassie, The Rouner Center for Reconciliation, personal communication.

5.

Agricultural Recovery

Achieving Post-CHE Food Security

JON WHITE, JAMES CHAPMAN, CLAUDE NANKAM, AYO ABIFARIN AND JOHNSON OLUFOWOTE

INTRODUCTION

The Universal Declaration of Human Rights recognises freedom from hunger as one of the "inalienable and inviolable rights of all members of the human family."[1] In practice, millions of people are *not* free from hunger. This is true for developing countries, especially in Sub-Saharan Africa, where the Food and Agriculture Organisation of the UN (FAO) estimate that 43 percent of the population (about 215 million people) are chronically undernourished.

Household food security can be defined as the ability of household members to ensure themselves sustained access to sufficient quantity and quality of food to lead healthy and active lives, both now and in the future. This concept was first advanced in 1974 at the World Food Conference in Rome in response to the growing number of people affected by hunger in the early 1970s.[2] In 1986, the World Bank defined food security as "access by all people at all times to enough food for an active and healthy life."[3] International convention has adopted this definition. In 1992, the United States Agency for International Development (USAID) defined food security as "when all people at all times have both physical and economic access to sufficient food to meet their dietary needs for a productive and healthy life."[4] The recent World Vision Food Security Program, Africa Region strategy adopted the following definition: "the integration of food production, income generation, food use and asset creation."[5] This forms the framework of food security efforts. This definition engages a variety of disciplines including agronomy, agricultural economics, botany, nutrition, medicine, geography, anthropology and political science. The sectors involved by such definition include agricultural production, marketing, enterprise development, health, nutrition, water and sanitation.

Factors that result in food insecurity include detrimental land tenure systems and smallholdings (small plot farming), low labour productivity (lack of technology, knowledge and skills), limited supply of labour in essential agricultural periods, declining soil fertility, drought, lack of access to inputs, consumption of stock and seed originally meant for planting, debt, lack of assets, weak market integration, limited or absence of governmental resources, poor government policies leading to disincentives, overburdened women, rapid population growth, increased rates of urbanisation, income inequality, displacement of people due to war and conflict, changing demography due to HIV/AIDS, disease and insect infestation of crops.

WV works throughout Sub-Saharan Africa to improve both current and future food security, thereby reducing levels of malnutrition and hunger among children as the more vulnerable members of society and increasing the economic well-being of their families. WV's resources directly address the food security of households in rural areas through improving availability of, access to and utilisation of food at the regional, household and individual levels. The nature of these activities within the context of a CHE is discussed in this chapter following experiences in countries such as Mozambique, Angola, Rwanda, Ethiopia, Liberia and Sierra Leone.

FOOD INSECURITY IN EMERGENCY SITUATIONS

Two basic emergency situations can be identified as disrupting farming systems and negatively affecting food security—armed conflict and natural disasters. The environment in CHEs can vary—from conditions of large-scale military action, through on-going chronic wars of attrition, to lulls between military actions and cessation of hostilities following a signed peace agreement. In each situation there are different levels of tension, insecurity and uncertainty. These environments often force people to leave their homes, frequently destroyed or now unsafe. The displaced population attempts to congregate in relatively secure areas. Farming families who are internally displaced or who have become refugees as a result of armed conflict or guerrilla warfare have lost access to land, the means to work land, their agricultural inputs and their livestock. Even when farmers affected by war do not flee their land, the following problems are commonly apparent: loss of food and seed stocks and productive infrastructure, loss of livestock, difficulty in marketing agricultural produce, and disruption to agricultural production activities. Production of agricultural crops and income from farming are drastically reduced or non-existent. In both situations, civilians are additionally subjected to the trauma of war, and human rights abuses are often committed against women and children.

F. C. Cuny and V. Tanner state that the socioeconomic disintegration of a population leaves it far more vulnerable to the next crisis, whether another bout of fighting or a natural disaster.[6] Households are impoverished; capital and savings (often invested in livestock, machinery, hand tools) are destroyed, stolen or sold; and social solidarity mechanisms are dissolved. The destruction of natural coping mechanisms in times of emergency is a particular feature of the disruption to food security created by armed conflict.

In many cases, little can be done to prevent drought, flooding or other natural calamities. However, in on-going, disaster-prone CHEs, active measures can be taken for disaster preparedness, such as those WV took in southern Africa to prepare communities for El Niño:

- *Promote public awareness:* Alert communities about the potential impact of possible natural disaster so that they can take measures to deal with it.
- *Network:* Establish and maintain contacts with government ministries (particularly health and agriculture) and other NGOs and community organisations in order to advise them of strategies and activities and to listen to what others are planning. It is important that one NGO's actions not be taken in isolation but become part of a consolidated effort to deal effectively with the impending situation.

• *Be continuously informed:* Maintain contacts with the national meteorological services and others involved in weather prediction and similar forecasting.

WV developed a list of specific actions that could be suggested to or discussed with clients regarding maintenance of adequate agriculture and health, and made this list accessible to the public.[7] Some measures, in a peaceful environment, can be taken through agricultural recovery programmes to minimise the impact of such disasters. These include strengthening farming practices to mitigate the effects of drought or flood conditions; diversification of farming systems over time and location; improvement of traditional storage structures to protect harvests; adopting improved water management techniques and irrigation; holding onto food stocks in excess of those required until the next harvest; use of early maturing, drought-tolerant crop types and varieties; and integrating farming systems with livestock.

Adoption of some or all of these measures contributes to alleviating the impact of CHEs and reducing the vulnerability of individual households. Just as important, they allow emergency response to act as a vehicle for widespread introduction of the most appropriate crop varieties and other improved technologies during recapitalisation of farming systems disrupted by a CHE.

THE DEVELOPMENT OPPORTUNITY

Agricultural recovery may be defined as the activity of regaining and renewing agricultural inputs and capital for the purposes of agricultural production and marketing. During CHEs, farmers lose their seeds, tools, other inputs and livestock. Productive infrastructures are lost or in a state of disrepair. Affected communities cannot recover these facilities without external aids, which NGOs usually supply in CHE environments.

The overall objective of WV's agricultural recovery programmes can be stated as improved household food security, health status and well-being of children and their families through broad-based, sustainable improvements in agricultural productivity, market access and enterprise development within targeted areas.

Agricultural recovery contributes to the process of participatory development by creating rural stability through improved food security and economic growth and through the empowering of grassroots communities by pursuing development activities. Agricultural recovery activities restore hope among traumatised populations and can facilitate social reintegration and the process of reconciliation.

In a simplistic analysis, the following table summarises key interventions during three major phases in the development process to restore food security in response to a more stable operating environment following a CHE. The sequence between each programming period does not necessarily flow smoothly and can be complex, reflecting the dynamics of a constantly changing operating environment. More than one programming phase may be run concurrently in distinct geographical areas.

Programming Period	Strategic Interventions
I. On-going armed conflict/population displacement	• Targeted distribution of critical inputs to meet acute survival and immediate food security needs of displaced and disoriented populations. • Food and survival aid, agricultural production support and health/nutrition interventions restore hope and confidence in the future. • On-going injection of support as long as security remains a constraint.
II. Resettlement/ recovery after peace agreement	• Infusion of inputs to allow rapid recovery of a sustainable level of household food security and re-establishment of community life. Large-scale multi-sectoral programmes in agriculture, including marketing, food for work, child and maternal health, nutritional education, de-mining and rehabilitation of infrastructure. • Increased household cash income, self-reliance and marketing activity. • Move away from free distributions and downsizing of emergency response capability.

III. Stability/sustain-able development/ disaster mitigation	• Establishment of development programmes to address longer-term issues related to food security, household income, health status, education and micro-enterprise development.
	• Enhancement of civil society, social reintegration.
	• A move towards facilitation through partnerships with local civil society organisations with less direct programme implementation and greater emphasis on sustainability.

Table 5-1. Basic programming phases to restore food security following a CHE.

Agricultural recovery interventions can be conceptualised as falling into three groups according to their objectives. The first two include

1. Those aimed at assisting families through the process of "recapitalisation," such as obtaining sufficient hand tools; stocks of seeds, roots and tubers; livestock of different species.
2. Interventions designed to increase productivity, such as introducing improved crop varieties, quality of planting materials and crop diversification.

These two kinds of interventions are closely linked and predominate throughout the initial phase of restoring food security (mainly phases I and II in Table 5-1), although they continue in phase III with increasing emphasis on cost recovery and sustainable mechanisms for delivery. For example, the introduction of perennial tree crops and restocking with animals requires a more stable environment than that required for production of annual crops or vegetables.

The third group of interventions occurs during the final phase of agricultural recovery, to restore food security in the longer term in a more stable environment.

3. Marketing, post-harvest storage, food processing and micro-enterprise development. These activities are predominantly programmed during phase III in Table 5-1.

All of these interventions facilitate the transition into long-term, broad-based agricultural development to improve food security. They are described in more detail in the following sections.

Recapitalisation

Farming families in war-torn rural areas or families displaced from their homelands for prolonged periods of time return to their land with very few possessions. With basic foodstuffs at a premium, providing hand tools to open up and prepare land along with replacing seed stocks are priority needs. Seed packs containing seeds of either grain crops or horticultural crops are an effective response to this demand and, providing open-pollinated varieties are distributed, farmers can save their own seed at harvest time.[8] As security permits, the local multiplication of perennial crops such as sweet potato and cassava also allows for strategically located areas to produce replanting material lost during armed conflict or natural disasters.

Later, recapitalisation activities include rebuilding livestock populations and propagating and distributing tree crops. Hand tool and seed distributions that were formerly free during the emergency/disaster and immediate resettlement period—a practice made necessary due to the destitute situation of rural families—must later be offered for sale (subsidised or at full cost) or repaid with similar in-kind contribution. In this way, market demand is created for involvement of the private sector. Animals provide a natural coping mechanism in areas where erratic rainfall makes crop production unreliable. The restocking of small animals (such as goats) on a loan basis will improve nutritional status, represent an additional source of income and reintroduce coping mechanisms in insecure regions. Repayment can be in-kind, and the animals received in repayment will be redistributed to other interested farmers' groups.

Distribution of tools, seeds, livestock and seedlings is thought of as an activity to accelerate the process of recapitalisation in order to restore the stock of basic productive assets needed by rural households. Providing assistance to accelerate this process in itself is an important contribution. However, WV also views this process as a unique opportunity to introduce new technology, including improved varieties and new crops to further increase and diversify food-crop production.

Transfer of appropriate production technology

Lack of availability of high-quality seeds of improved and farmer-selected varieties is often a constraint to agricultural recovery. This problem has two root causes: First, extended conditions of war and displacement have contributed to low technology development and, consequently, lack of knowledge about which new crop varieties are suitable to the various agro-ecological conditions affected by the CHE. Second, there is often minimal capacity for local seed production at this time, even when appropriate varieties have been identified. In a chronic emergency situation, the majority of farmers may be unaware of the potential of this improved production technology.

WV has encountered various problems at the beginning of the agricultural recovery process:

- Stocks of seed and planting material were lost or in short supply. This required an emergency injection of planting materials from external sources;
- Lack of information on adapted varieties led to large-scale imports of mostly inappropriate varieties that were later replaced by low-yielding local varieties. Several seasons were required to identify suitable varieties and multiply seed, slowing the pace of agricultural recovery.[9]

Farmer-selected seed

These problems pointed to the need to conduct field trials with farmer participation to evaluate the performance of different crop varieties under farmers' conditions over a range of agro-ecological situations. To improve the quality and availability of seed, promising varieties had to be identified from germplasm stocks maintained by the International Agricultural Research Centres (IARCs),[10] national seed programmes, private seed companies in the region, and from farmers' existing seed stocks where available.

Based on knowledge of agro-climatic conditions and farmers' preferences in the target areas, WV screened the most promising germplasm in participatory field station trials.[11] Crop varieties evaluated included cereals (maize, rice, sorghum and millet), legumes (groundnut, pigeon pea, cowpea, Phaseolus bean), oilseeds (sunflower, sesame), tubers and roots (cassava, sweet potato), vegetables (onion, tomato, green pepper, Portuguese kale) and tree crops (cashew).

After initial testing, one or two of the most promising varieties then underwent multiplication and were rapidly sent into thousands of on-farm trials for exposure to a wider range of conditions and regional farmer preferences. WV, in close partnership with the National Institute for Agronomic Investigation, conducted thousands of on-farm trials each year throughout five agro-ecological zones in central and northern Mozambique.[12] In Angola, the Seeds of Freedom Project used a network of seven NGOs and the extension department of the Ministry of Agriculture to allow smallholder farmers in 13 of the 18 provinces of the country to establish 2,950 on-farm trials.[13] The varieties preferred and selected by farmers through this participatory methodology were called farmer-selected varieties (FSVs).

In a chronic CHE, where conventional seed supply systems do not exist, farmers in "pilot villages" can be organised in groups and trained in seed-production technology to fill the gap. Foundation seeds of FSVs are produced by WV and, through its extension network, are distributed to farmers and farmers' groups for multiplication. This approach promotes the development of a farmer-to-farmer seed movement, which accounts for about 90 percent of seed supply in developing countries.[14]

Decentralised sites for the local multiplication of perennial crops such as sweet potato and cassava can be established at strategic locations for further community-based dissemination.[15] Through this process it has been possible to transfer farmer-selected, improved germplasm to remote rural areas over a period of two to three years.

Varieties are tested not only for their yield under local farming systems but also for other characteristics that can be important to small-scale farmers. The following varietal characteristics, beside yield, are considered to be generally important in responding to

CHEs. They also provide for the mitigation of ensuing natural calamities.

- *Drought tolerance:* Crops such as sorghum, millet, groundnut, cowpea, pigeon pea, sweet potato and cassava are considered to be more tolerant of drought. Quantity of seed and planting material distributed should allow for re-sowing failed planting under dry conditions.
- *Early maturity:* Early maturing varieties serve to close the hunger gap between harvests and can be sown late or out of season. These characteristics are of immense importance in an emergency situation when rapid food production is at a premium. These crops often escape the effects of end-of-season drought stress, offering greater flexibility in time of planting. Early maturity can also serve as a protection against pests, as such crops mature before the pests attack.
- *Pest and disease resistance:* In the absence of crop-protection chemicals, crops must have resistance or tolerance mechanisms to pests and diseases. For example, leaf sheath cob coverage and grain characteristics in maize are determinants of post-harvest storage losses to weevils.
- *Palatability and other characteristics:* Smallholder farmers may not adopt new varieties unless characteristics such as taste and aroma (as quantified by palatability tests), cooking time, seed size and colour are acceptable to the local populace.

Varieties identified as acceptable to the family sector and significantly superior to traditional varieties in yield or other desirable characteristics are further tested together with cropping techniques designed to improve productivity and make more effective use of labour. The development of farmer-selected varieties—varieties grown and evaluated by farmers in conjunction with agricultural technicians—has resulted in the identification of varieties which offer substantial yield benefits under low-input farming systems while combining the other characteristics important to smallholder farmers.[16] Varieties known to be highly acceptable to farmers and with yields exceeding the local traditional variety by 50 percent to 200 percent have been promoted and made available through a "Farm Family First" extension network that operates semi-informally with farmer groups and associations. This approach includes on-farm or farmers' trials where the farmers verify the performance of crop varieties under their own farming practices and condition. Evaluation criteria are defined by the farmer rather than by the technician. Beneficiaries of seed distributions continue to replant seeds of the new farmer-selected varieties of food crops—such as maize, rice, cowpea, sweet potato, cassava, millet, sorghum, and groundnut— plus seeds of new crops such as sunflower, finger millet and mungbean. Beneficiaries frequently distribute seed to neighbouring farmers as well.

Encouraging results from WV's agricultural recovery programmes continue to be obtained through activities which rapidly improve the quality of and access to planting materials. Originally applied in Mozambique during the late 1980s and early 1990s, these strategies have resulted in positive appraisals from concerted, NGO-promoted crop improvement programmes in Rwanda, Eritrea, Sudan, Angola, Somalia, Zaire, Liberia and Sierra Leone.

Most of WV's intensive seed-based programmes have been conducted in countries which have recently experienced humanitarian disasters. Success in those countries has led to speculation within the organisation and from the outside that the situations in these countries were not representative of the potential in other African countries. Data from a wide geographic area of the continent constitute overwhelming evidence that high returns to investment are possible in large parts, if not all, of Sub-Saharan Africa. By evaluating seed of improved, adapted varieties from international and national agricultural research centres and testing them both on-station and on-farm in rural areas which were experiencing food shortages and where farmers lacked access to quality, adapted seed, WV's results include the following:

Country	Crop	Increase in yield
Angola[1]	Beans	26%
	Maize	14%
Mali[2]	Sorghum	24%
Mozambique[3]	Sweet Potato	61%
Mozambique[3]	Maize	71%
Mozambique[3]	Sorghum	133%

Senegal[4]	Cowpea	100%
Senegal[5]	Maize	53%
Sudan[5]	Cowpea	108%
Zaire[6]	Maize	18%

1. C. Nankam and C. Magorokosho, "World Vision Angola Agriculture Program Technical Report: 1997/1998 Growing Seasons" (1998).

2. P. Dembele, J. Sogoba, and J. Darra, *Rapport sur resultats tests sorgho resistant au Striga* (Bamako, Mali: World Vision International, 1997).

3. J. White and L. Sitch, "Report of the 1993/94 Yield Trials: Tete, Zambezia, Sofala and Nampula Provinces" (Maputo, Mozambique: World Vision International and Instituto Nacional de Investigacao Agronomica, 1994).

4. University of California—Riverside, "1993 Executive Summary: A Program to Develop Improved Cowpea Cultivars, Management Methods, and Storage Practices for Semi-arid Zones" (Riverside, Calif.: University of California, 1994).

5. G. Janson and P. Kapukha, "Southern Sudan Agricultural Recovery Program Annual Report" (Nairobi, Kenya: World Vision Sudan, 1995).

6. C. Asanzi and J. D. DeVries, "End of Season Report: Zaire Agricultural Recovery Program" (Kinshasa, Zaire: World Vision International, 1995).

Table 5-2. Increases in crop yields.

Although the scope for extension support in an emergency context is somewhat limited, it is clearly important to involve community leaders and leader farmers in seed distributions and the local multiplication of perennial crops such as sweet potato and cassava. A practical approach that relies on field demonstrations with a high degree of involvement by participants allows for evaluation of crop varieties on the criteria considered to be important by smallholder farmers. A series of on-farm field trials where analysis of performance is based on replication over a large number of sites (at least 30 trials in any one agro-ecological environment) also serves as demonstration plots where farmer groups can verify crop variety performance under their own farming practices and conditions, and in many instances the trials also serve as multiplication areas (for self-pollinated or vegetatively propagated crops).

A highly cost-effective intervention in emergency situations is the promotion of vegetable crops to produce rapidly available sources of highly nutritious food from a limited area of land. Extensionists can raise awareness of the importance of vegetables as a food source with a high concentration of vitamins and minerals.

Appropriate farming practices

Improved farming practices such as timely sowing and weeding, optimum plant spacing, and natural methods of pest control are demonstrated and discussed during farmer field days at substations and/or demonstration plots located throughout the project area. Identification and widespread demonstration of farmer-selected varieties and improved cultural practices maximise adoption rates by smallholder farmers.

Extension activities focus mainly on farmers' groups or producer organisations, as technicians can reach more farmers through farmers' groups. Also, participation of women is higher in community-based groups. Working with groups provides a mechanism for sustainability through self-help and interdependence. Salaried extension staff receive regular training to help them identify and successfully work with farmers' groups and develop activities appropriate to farmers' needs. The ratio of extension agents to farmers is typically in the range of 1:400 (Mozambique), but 600–800 farmers per extension agent has also been used (Angola). The gender of the extension agents may be a sensitive issue, according to the particular social context (see "Programme design" below). The number of farmers assigned to each extension agent is usually based on a compromise between effective extension support and a disproportionate and unsustainable cost of providing such a service. Factors considered include logistical constraints, levels of education, farmer school methodology and rural population density. Delivery of extension messages over the radio is a very cost-effective supplement to extension visits. Participating farmers receive technical on-the-job training through a series of field days designed to identify problems and demonstrate and discuss topics such as improved techniques for seed saving. This focus on providing extension assistance to farmers' groups helps to strengthen the social fabric of newly reformed communities that have been torn apart by war or natural disaster.

Marketing, post-harvest storage and micro-enterprise development

In an environment with greater stability, contributions to agricultural marketing can be made through the formation of rural group enterprises. Food security is enhanced when rural families have access to additional sources of income. Households are able to retain more of their income if the costs of food production and processing are reduced. In addition to promoting an increased supply of food, WV focuses on improving individuals' access to food by creating employment and cash-for-work opportunities to permit cash purchases of appropriate foods for an adequate, nutritious diet. Cash-for-work opportunities include the rehabilitation of rural roads and large-scale multiplication of improved crop varieties, while more sustainable employment opportunities occur through facilitation of access to markets to promote trading, small-scale processing of crops, asset creation and provision of credit to establish rural enterprises. Introducing small-scale food processing equipment, particularly oil presses and hammer mills, improves rural access to processed agricultural products.

Opening up market access to isolated communities through the repair of roads—to connect farmers to distant markets for the marketing of their agricultural production and to link farmers' groups, markets and transporters of agricultural produce improves the sale of cash cropping and surplus production. Improving on-farm storage techniques and preservation practices reduces losses, extends the period of time over which produce can be consumed and allows marketing at higher prices.

WV promotes more intensive and diversified methods of agricultural production, enabling the targeted farming families to increase their participation in local markets, thereby increasing household income while improving household nutrition. The stimulation of livestock restocking and animal health within target communities is a means of restoring an important coping mechanism. These initiatives will accelerate progress towards food security in its broadest sense, including improvements in household income and quality of the household diet.

PROGRAMME DESIGN

If a programme is to use a food-security conceptual framework for organising its programme activities, it will need to establish priorities and choose those activities that are most appropriate to the relative circumstances and potential of any particular community. For this, the most constraining vulnerabilities to meeting community food needs must be clearly identified. Initial field assessment should be completed by a multi-disciplinary team. A rapid food-security assessment (RFSA) provides timely information in a cost-effective manner to determine causes, dimensions and characteristics of a food insecurity situation in a given area through a dynamic and interactive data-collection process. A team of four to six people should represent the host government, a range of technical backgrounds and experiences, as well as local knowledge and expertise. Appropriate co-ordination should be made with other aid agencies and organisations of the UN. Site inspection, direct observation, and group household and key informant interviews with the affected population are used to evaluate the disruption to food supply, seed stocks and farming systems. Considerable importance is given to expressed needs of the intended beneficiaries, and sensitivity is shown to the issue of gender, particularly since women often bear the major responsibility for food production and child nutrition. Accuracy and reliability of information depends upon the relationship between interviewer and interviewee; women in WV's programmes have tended to be more open when talking to other women. Unfortunately, it is often difficult to recruit trained women who will live and work in rural areas; often marriage and family commitments include spouses working in urban areas. Also, within communities, almost all the women are housewives and cannot take full-time jobs to the detriment of their farm activities.

The RFSA should result in characterisation of the food-vulnerable population and identification of the most appropriate responses. Timely implementation in relation to the agricultural season is essential to the success of any response. Key general principles found to ensure an appropriate response to both short-term and longer term restoration of food security include:

Security risk

The environment must be conducive to recovery activities. The level of risk must be determined before initiation of the programme; financial, political and personal risks should be assessed. Guidelines can be issued, but the ultimate decisions in relation to security risk have to be made at a decentralised level.

Appropriate scale

Design should be on a scale sufficiently large to make a real difference in selected areas. When applied in an emergency situation, this concept naturally allows for transition to developmental programmes as well. The capacity installed and created during emergency efforts can provide a base for developmental activities.

Developmental relief

Emergency funding should be used to initiate activities that are a continuation of, or precursor to, a sound development process. The volatile environment created by emergencies should be considered as a window of opportunity to change behavioural paradigms, including introduction of new ideas and technology. Distribution of seed is not only a means of recapitalisation but also an opportunity to introduce improved germplasm capable of providing farmers with higher yields under local conditions. Providing that characteristics of the improved varieties are acceptable to farmers, this yield increase will be repeated in subsequent years as farmers select and save their own seed. Emergency situations help break down pre-existing institutional barriers to technology transfer. Farmers short of seed are far more receptive to receiving, sowing and adopting new varieties on a large scale. In a development context, when farmers already have adequate quantities of planting material, more conservative attitudes to adoption of new technology prevail. Therefore, if implemented appropriately, emergency seed distributions can be an important opportunity for introduction of improved varieties over a wide geographical area and can have a significant impact on levels of agricultural production. Conversely, due to low germination rates, distribution of grain as seed causes quality control and low-productivity problems. This cheap and quick option is actually quite expensive when the high logistical costs of distribution and the value of missed yield benefits through replanting over a number of years are taken into account. In Mozambique, distribution of high-yielding maize varieties without suitable participatory farmer evaluation resulted in failure. Within a few seasons, farmers resorted to their traditional varieties due to preferences in grain characteristic and storage ability.

The increasing occurrences of chronic and continuing conflict highlight the need for development skills among specialists in emergency response. Maintaining a development perspective while operating in an emergency context, as developmental as the emergency situation allows, ensures a smooth transition to sustainable development programmes and maximises benefit to the targeted populations.

Holistic integrated approach

There is a clear need to integrate food aid, infrastructure, water, health and nutrition activities with the provision of basic agricultural inputs in order to maximise complementarity and rapidly restore food security. This multi-sectoral approach with programmes working closely together can ensure that the complete needs of affected populations are addressed. WV first carries out what Cuny and Tanner called the "first objective"—to alleviate suffering by reducing abnormally high morbidity and mortality rates during the acute phase of the emergency.[17] This acute emergency phase is characterised by on-going conflict; massive population movements; and associated problems of malnutrition, dehydration, poor sanitation, epidemic diseases and exposure. During the CHE, food aid and emergency health and nutrition interventions are the immediate actions. This first stage of assistance is vital to save lives and to help people gain access to the most basic rights to shelter, water, and enough to eat.[18] Distribution of seeds and tools follows subsequently, depending mainly on the timing of the agricultural seasons, access by the displaced and affected to land, along with health status and capacity to cultivate land, and the likelihood of eating seeds intended for cultivation. This second phase of assistance, which Cuny and Tanner called "spot reconstruction," is defined as "those activities that are undertaken to provide comprehensive, integrated reconstruction and development assistance to communities where conflict is relatively low." A holistic approach can be achieved by effective co-ordination with other emergency response agencies, some of which operate sectoral-specific programmes. This co-ordination should normally take place under the auspices of the host country government.

Sequencing of interventions

It is important to ensure appropriate combining and sequencing of interventions in target areas. For example, malnourished farmers have difficulty preparing land for farming, and hungry populations will eat seeds rather than plant them. Therefore, adequate food distributions should always come before seed distributions.

Planning for transition

Donors' need for a "result" channels attention towards certain kinds of operations and encourages short-term vision. High-profile disaster relief programmes, with their dramatic public appeals, rapid assessments, and special funding procedures convey the unspoken message that the appropriate NGO response to conflict is an emergency programme. Although such interventions have saved lives and played a significant role in removing or reducing human suffering, in some cases they have made little impact on the underlying problems and causes of the conflict or emergencies. Steve Commins underscores this, stating that there have been major shifts in thinking about operations in emergencies during the 1980s. There has been a new emphasis on famine early warning systems and a greater emphasis on links between relief programmes and development programmes. Many institutions and organisations have invested considerable resources in building up both the theoretical framework for and operational requirements of the emergency-to-development transitions. Valuable changes were made in NGO operations, with the introduction of technical packages that could enable both stable communities and resettled refugees to return quickly to food-producing activities.[19] After a major expansion in efforts to meet the many challenges in an emergency, there is a need to withdraw just as rapidly from emergency activities and change to a developmental mode, although the two modes can occur concurrently where there are geographical differences in security levels.

Reaching the target population

To ensure impact, the logistical means to reach the target population and ensure effective distribution must be available. When adequate results cannot be attained by working through the current institutional and logistical structure, implementation of a new structure may ensure an effective delivery system.

Gender sensitivity

Women traditionally perform the most important tasks relating to household food supply, and they are encouraged to participate fully in the development process in order to promote their empowerment in the community, to ensure long-term sustainability and to expose them to the benefits of labour-saving technologies. Women are often considered to be the heads of households and as such are the direct recipients of the distribution of agricultural inputs. Countries like Angola and Mozambique are characterised by a high rate of single-parent households headed by women, due to deaths of men in the battlefields.

Accountability with government donors

An initial significant level of response may be guaranteed through emergency funding, but a sustained response requires the injection of additional resources through government donors. Use of flexible funding needs to be optimised for maximum impact throughout the period of crisis and during the transition into development to allow for leveraging and matching government-donor grants. There is a need for more flexible, long-term and innovative programmes. Relationships between government funding agencies and NGOs will continue to be crucial in the operating environment of CHEs to ensure the scale and holism of the programme, maintain the best balance between the menu of varied agricultural activities, and facilitate an on-going series of seamless transitions in response to an evolving operating environment. Administrative and financial systems must be in place to support programme activities and provide a high degree of accountability to donors.

Partnerships

A key feature of WV's success stories in Angola and Mozambique has been partnership among different organisations, each playing the role to which it is best suited. The international agricultural research centres (IARCs) and national agricultural research centres provide sources of potential new varieties for evaluation; farmers help screen varieties and provide feedback on adaptability and acceptability; seed companies provide seed and packaging services; and NGOs provide capacity to implement and facilitate the overall process. These partnerships allow for rapid transfer of technology from the IARCs to the grassroots farmer within a two- to three-year time frame (as opposed to the traditional 10–15 years). At the national level, partnerships also allow for rapid dissemination of FSVs and promotion of best practices between provinces. One example of such a partnership is the Seeds of Freedom Project in Angola, which involved five IARCs, seven NGOs, four institutions of the Ministry of Agriculture, and farmers. The project not only supplied quality seeds to farmers for increased production, but also provided information to build up a database on variety adaptability and acceptability in different agro-ecological zones of the country in preparedness for any future calamity.

The CHE context often constitutes a more laissez-faire government structure that allows NGOs to forge effective alliances with government for joint planning and co-ordination of activities. Operation on a large scale confers the privilege of active participation at the national level in the formulation of host government and international donor community emergency-response strategies. This participation allows on-going dialogue and strategic positioning during the transition phase to development.

APPROPRIATE RESPONSE

Seed supply and harvest-pack design

Use of hybrid varieties and reliance on external inputs such as fertiliser have in general been avoided due to some or all of the following factors: farmers' ability to save their own seed, limited resources to access external inputs, lack of availability of inputs, lack of understanding of appropriate use of inputs, logistical constraints and traditional mixed cropping with legume crops. Soil fertility after many years of civil war was relatively high in Mozambique and Angola, and with a relatively low population density, good crop production was possible without use of fertiliser.

However, appropriate technology is dependent upon context, and where there is more pressure on land and soil fertility is low, fertiliser has been distributed in conjunction with seeds (for example, in the Democratic Republic of Congo and Liberia).

The amount of seed and type of crops required in individual farmer packs vary with agro-ecological conditions and other factors. At an early stage of an emergency, appropriateness of the crop varieties commercially available for large-scale distribution requires verification (as described earlier in this chapter). This is a modified participatory rural appraisal technique, in that the expressed opinions of the farmers are taken into consideration for selection of the potential varieties that should be evaluated. In many countries, lack of information has necessitated field trials with farmer participation to evaluate performance of different crop varieties, including locally available material, under farmer conditions over a number of seasons. Seed should only be purchased from reputable international seed companies. WV has entered into contracts with several regional and national private seed companies to multiply and package seed of farmer-selected varieties for distribution. Local grain should not be purchased as seed, with its concomitant problems of poor quality and substandard production. The goal of agricultural recovery programmes is to create food security in former famine and food deficit areas. Ag-Paks containing seed of staple cereal crops and legumes are designed to reflect the most commonly grown and appropriate crops for each agro-ecological zone in the area affected by the CHE. The amount of seed is determined by the amount of land available and any seed stocks that may already be with farmers.

These strategies have allowed newly settled families to achieve a high degree of food self-sufficiency during their first crop season, and the level of production from 1.5 hectares can be expected to support a family of five for 6 to 12 months. Training and incentives are provided to encourage beneficiaries to save their own seed to supplement seeds provided from Ag-Paks during a second year of recuperation and to plant an increased size of *machamba* (farm). After a second harvest, provided that sufficient land is available and there are no natural disasters, food self-sufficiency with a surplus for trading is normally achieved. After a good season, every family will normally save its own seeds, but hunger and post-harvest pest infestations can reduce availability of seeds, particularly those of legumes, after the first harvest.

Farmers' food production is carefully evaluated through interviews, examination of stocks and yield evaluations in the field, with random sample crop cuts at harvest time to determine the timing and amount of any food aid that may be required before the next harvest. A high percentage of the target population will save enough seed at the end of the season to achieve self-sufficiency in future seed needs. A WV baseline survey in Angola in 1997 indicated that 21 percent of farmers saved their own seed and 48 percent bought seed from the local market. In Mozambique, a 1998 smallholder farmer survey in four provinces of central and northern Mozambique showed that 62 percent of households obtained seed from their own stocks, and 14 percent obtained seed from neighbours and friends.[20] During the 1997/98 planting season, almost 50 percent of farmers interviewed sold, bartered or gave seed to their neighbours. Virtually all farmers know of larger or better-than-average farmers from whom they can obtain seed.

In addition to this quantitative impact on agricultural production, certain crops, particularly vegetables, can provide a valuable nutritional supplement to food aid. Veg-Paks containing seeds of 10 vegetable crops and legumes selected for their nutritional value and potential as cash crops are distributed with hand tools and a 15-litre watering bucket for planting during the dry, cool season. Vegetable production also helps farmers generate some cash income.

Targeting beneficiaries and impact

Targeted beneficiaries will be people who have suffered the effects of war and natural disasters or for some other reason are presently incapable of obtaining by themselves the basic inputs for their food-production recovery. An emphasis on women recognises them as the prime movers in the agricultural activities of farming families and strengthens the organisational capacity of rural communities.

Within the context of neutrality and positioning in CHEs, careful identification and targeting of beneficiaries (geographically and within communities) in conjunction with government or controlling faction, military and UN agencies will be an increasingly complex challenge. Identification of the most appropriate response to CHEs and timely delivery of emergency goods and services to the targeted population involve increasingly sophisticated requirements in terms of co-ordination, personal security, logistics and monitoring.

In the case of free distribution of seed packs, women are considered to be the heads of the household, except in the case of single-male-parent families and demobilised soldiers. In order to be registered, the head of the household is required to be present at the registration. Seed packs are distributed through a public roll call, in the presence of a representative of the local leadership structure or government official. Recipients are requested formally to acknowledge receipt of packs during the distribution to avoid duplicate distributions. This is done by signature or by registering the recipient's fingerprint on the distribution lists. Distribution is made only to beneficiaries who are physically present at the time of the distribution. Four types of selection criteria are used for identification of various beneficiary groups:

1. *Selection based on time of arrival:* This group is selected according to when the people return to their place of origin, in recognition that the majority of persons will be suffering from a similar set of circumstances (for example, returning refugees).

2. *Selection based on physical location:* This group is selected according to a geographic location that has suffered from a similar set of circumstances to the extent that the majority of families are in need of assistance (for example, acts of war or a drought-affected area).

3. *Individual selection:* People who meet certain criteria can be identified on an individual basis. This is the most complex, time-consuming and costly selection process and is applied only if the need is not a general one and cannot be dealt with by other selection procedures (for example, outpatients at WV feeding centres for the acutely malnourished). Demobilisation packs (D-Paks) containing seeds, tools, watering buckets and clothing were provided by WV for distribution by the UN to 94,000 demobilised soldiers in exchange for arms at the time of de-mobilisation in Mozambique (1994).

4. *Additional selection criteria:* Other criteria could include those with access to suitable land for dry-season vegetable

production, or families identified by health programmes or social services as having problems with crop production. Once families have been identified as meeting certain primary criteria, this additional screen can be applied.

EXAMPLES OF AGRICULTURAL RECOVERY: MOZAMBIQUE AND ANGOLA

Both Mozambique and Angola historically have been characterised by long-term chronic emergency situations, with significant resources for emergency response made available by the international donor community. WV has provided large-scale assistance for resettlement and rehabilitation programmes in both countries. These programmes, described earlier in the chapter, are cited as examples of similarly successful agricultural interventions in such countries as the Democratic Republic of Congo, Rwanda and Liberia.

Within World Vision Mozambique's programme area, for example, the value of agricultural production after post-war resettlement has shown a mean annual 25 percent increase in household income from an average US$186 per household in 1995 to US$279 per household in 1997. This is the result of increased land in cultivation and increased yield.

Immediately following the peace agreement of 1992 in Mozambique and 1994 in Angola, WV's health programme operated emergency feeding centres in the most needy zones. Acute malnutrition reached the highest levels in central Mozambique and northern Angola. The number of admissions into these therapeutic feeding centres decreased significantly during the period from 1993 to 1996, from hundreds of monthly admissions to single figures. This decrease reflects the success of integrated interventions of WV's agriculture, commodities and health programmes. Outpatients from the therapeutic feeding centres were targeted to receive Ag-Paks and Veg-Paks. At most of the feeding centres, mothers of malnourished children received training in the cultivation of vegetables and farmer-selected varieties of staple food crops, with practical participation at demonstration sites and in nutritional education. With health education and follow-up extension support, our strategic intention was to prevent the return of the same young mothers and children to the feeding centres.

The overall level of acute malnutrition fell from 4–5 percent in 1993/94 to less than 2 percent in 1994 in Mozambique, and was stabilised at that level in northern Angola till November 1998. In both countries, improved access to maternal and child health services combined with increased agricultural productivity was reflected in an increase in children who gained or maintained their weight in the 0–3 year age group. Growth monitoring of 142,955 children in Mozambique showed that, overall, 87 percent of children gained weight in 1997 as compared to 83 percent in 1996.

LESSONS LEARNED

Positive aspects of the experience in Sub-Saharan Africa in the past decade include the following:

- Emergency situations break down institutional barriers to agricultural technology transfer. However, if a suitable participatory methodology is not used to identify appropriate technology for this opportunity, farming-systems research and development clearly demonstrate that inappropriate technology will be quickly rejected by farmers.
- An integrated approach to emergency response, with a developmental vision from day one and transition to more sustainable activities as quickly as the operating environment allows, is an effective strategy to restore food security rapidly and re-establish smallholder family productivity and livelihood in former food deficit areas.
- A participatory approach, with farmers heavily involved in the process from the beginning, helps ensure high rates of adoption of new technology, programme efficiency and a transition to longer-term development.
- There are lower barriers to seed-embedded technology adoption, providing that suitable evaluation methodology and evaluation criteria are used.
- Agricultural recovery is highly cost-effective and inherently sustainable because it shortens the time that food aid and supplementary feeding are needed. There is a need to "gear up" quickly to take advantage of the critical moment, at peace or post-disaster, when significant donor funding is available for introduction of adapted germplasm.

- Partnership among different organisations, each playing the role to which it is best suited, adds value: the host country government provides for overall co-ordination, IARCs/NARs provide candidate varieties, seed companies provide seed and packaging services, farmers screen varieties and provide feedback on which are best, NGOs facilitate the process.

Some issues and constraints identified in responding to CHEs include the following:

- Initial unavailability of adapted seeds implies that any emergency response is not as effective as it could be if improved varieties were tested and readily available. This problem is aggravated when operating in emergency situations where little or no information is available on local farming systems. Early initiation of a suitable participatory variety evaluation programme is essential.
- The practice of distributing grain as seed (used by some relief organisations) represents a lost opportunity and the "cheap and quick" is in reality less cost-effective.
- The market for emergency seed distribution is temporary, as farmers begin to save seed of open-pollinated varieties. There are negative implications for seed market development with the commercial sector but large social gains from this investment.
- A regional strategy for disaster mitigation should assure supplies of appropriate seed adapted to prevalent agro-climatic conditions and farmer preferences in the region.
- There is a need for funding to support creation of regional integrated development projects with strong extension components. Government policies should facilitate the development of agricultural sector partnerships of NGOs with government research and extension services.

CONCLUSIONS

WV has responded effectively to different types of need for agricultural recovery in CHEs. Currently more than 200 qualified staff are working to address food-security needs in 22 countries throughout

Africa. Distribution of seeds of farmer-selected varieties, basic hand tools and other inputs has proven a highly appropriate and cost-effective strategy for promoting rapid recovery of local food-production systems in CHE environments. This approach has successfully transformed famine-stricken areas into communities with a high degree of self-sufficiency. An associated package of extension assistance offers encouragement in the struggle to grow food and to market surplus production in rural areas. WV's focus in this area centres on supplying the best adapted and most productive crop varieties possible through its contacts with national and international research centres and commercial seed companies. Follow-up activities in crop improvement, extension, seed multiplication, animal restocking and participatory evaluation of new technologies with farmer groups can rapidly improve productivity of farmers across broad geographical areas. This transition maximises the impact of re-capitalisation of farming systems and provides for sustainable availability of self-targeted food for needy children and their families. WV uses the momentum generated by emergency response and improved farmer productivity to broaden agricultural recovery into marketing, food processing and other activities that promote sustainable economic development in rural communities.

NOTES

[1] UN, Food and Agriculture Organisation (FAO), *Fighting Hunger and Malnutrition*, World Summit, Rome (13–17 November 1996).

[2] United Nations, "Assessment of World Food Situation, Present and Future," World Food Conference document E/CONF.65/3 (New York: United Nations, 1974).

[3] World Bank, *Poverty and Hunger: Issues and Options for Food Security in Developing Countries* (Washington, D.C.: World Bank, 1986).

[4] USAID, "Food Aid and Food Security: USAID Policy Paper," unpublished report (February 1995); and USAID, "U.S. International Food Assistance Report, 1998" (January 1999).

[5] Ayo Abifarin and Johnson Olufowote, eds., "Africa Region Strategic Plan, FY 1999–2004" (Accra, Ghana: Food Security Program, Africa Region, 1998).

[6] F. C. Cuny, and V. Tanner, "Working with Communities to Reduce Levels of Conflict: Spot Reconstruction," *Disaster Prevention and Management* 4/1 (1995), 12–20.

[7] Specific measures developed for the southern Africa El Niño situation are contained in James Chapman, "El Niño and Drought in Southern Africa: A Suggested Mitigative Response," an unpublished WV document (SARO/ARRO, 1998).

[8] Improved-variety, open-pollinated seed is important to use in development situations. Unlike hybrid seed, open-pollinated seed can be multiplied and saved by farmers for use as seed, achieving excellent results for multiple planting cycles. Hybrid seed can only be used one time and will not achieve good results when replanting.

[9] J. Chapman, J. White, and C. Nankam, "World Vision's Experience with Seed Supply During Emergency and Resettlement Programs in Mozambique and Angola: Implications for the Future," International Crops Research Institute for the Semi-Arid Tropics (ICRISAT) workshop entitled Enhancing Research Impact Through Improved Seed Supply: Options for Strengthening National and Regional Seed Supply Systems, Harare, Zimbabwe (10–14 March 1997).

[10] International Agricultural Research Centres (IARCs) are a network of agricultural research centres located around the globe focused on developing improved-variety, high-production and disease-resistant types of crops such as legumes, tubers, maize, vegetables, potatoes, tropical agricultural crops, etc. These centres work closely with agricultural universities globally and are funded by government donors, the World Bank and foundations such as Ford and Rockefeller. IARCs such as the International Institute for Tropical Agriculture (IITA) in Nigeria work with NGOs and governments to test, develop and multiply improved variety crops and improved methods in field locations in many developing countries.

[11] C. Bias et al., "Variation in Grain Yield Among Early Flowering Varieties in Mozambique," *Developing Drought and Low N-Tolerant Maize*, proceedings of International Maize and Wheat Improvement Center (CIMMYT) conference, Mexico (March 25–29, 1996); Claude Nankam, "World Vision Angola Agriculture Program Technical Report: 1996/97 Growing Seasons" (1997); C. Nankam and C. Magorokosho, "World Vision Angola Agriculture Program Technical Report: 1997/98 Growing Seasons" (1998).

[12] L. Sitch et al., "Multi-location Testing of Improved Varieties of Maize on Farmers' Fields in Northern and Central Mozambique," *CIMMYT Proceedings of the Fifth Eastern and Southern Africa Regional Maize Conference*, Arusha, Tanzania (3–7 June 1996), 18–27.

[13] Claude Nankam, "Agriculture Recovery and Emergency Seed Restoration in the Post Disaster Situation of Angola: A Case Study," paper presented at the FAO International Conference on Developing Institutional Agreements and Capacity to Assist Farmers in Disaster Situations

to Restore Agricultural Systems and Seed Security Activities, Rome (3–5 November 1998).

[14] C. J. M. Almekinder, et al., "Local Seed Systems and Their Importance for an Improved Seed Supply in Developing Countries," *Euphytica* 78 (1994), 207–11.

[15] S. A. Henderson, et al. "Multi-location Trials of Sweet Potato Varieties in Northern and Central Mozambique," *ROOTS* 4/1 (June 1997); Nankam, "Agriculture Recovery and Emergency Seed Restoration in the Post Disaster Situation of Angola. A Case Study."

[16] D. Sperling, et al., "The Evaluation of Open-Pollinated Maize Varieties Under a Range of Zero Input Farming Systems in Central Mozambique," in *CIMMYT Proceedings of the Fourth Eastern and Southern Africa Regional Maize Conference*, Harare, Zimbabwe, Maize Research for Stress Environments (28 March–1 April 1994), 101–5; Nankam, "Agriculture Recovery and Emergency Seed Restoration in the Post Disaster Situation of Angola: A Case Study."

[17] Cuny and Tanner, "Working with Communities to Reduce Levels of Conflict."

[18] D. Bryer and E. Cairns, "For Better? For Worse? Humanitarian Aid in Conflict," based on "Providing Humanitarian Assistance During Internal Conflicts: Dilemmas and Prospects," an address given by David Bryer at an International Peace Academy Seminar in Vienna (23 July 1996); "The Sphere Project: Humanitarian Charter and Minimum Standards in Disaster Response" (Oxford: Oxfam Publishing, 2000).

[19] Steve Commins, "What NGOs Can Bring to the Food Security Table," *Together* 53 (January-March 1997), 1–3.

[20] This survey was conducted by World Vision—in collaboration with the International Crops Research Institute for the Semi-Arid Tropics (ICRISAT), the provincial department of agriculture and the National Institute for Agronomic Investigation.

6.

Building on Local Capacities for Peace in a Complex War

The South Sudan Challenge

WOLFGANG JAMANN

This chapter analyses the link between WV's humanitarian-aid programme and the various layers of the conflict environment in South Sudan. The context is the dramatic humanitarian crisis in 1998 and 1999. To improve its programmes in the context of conflict, WV used methodological tools developed by the Local Capacities for Peace project (LCP) and identified some potentially harmful aspects of its projects in Sudan. At the same time, alternative programme options were developed that would contribute to reconciliation and reduction of local conflict. A case study is described, in which the LCP method contributed to redesign of a humanitarian-aid intervention. The end of the chapter provides a critical review of opportunities and limitations of the LCP concept.

INTRODUCTION

Does humanitarian aid cause more harm than good? Does it increase and prolong, or even cause, wars and armed conflicts? Such questions are being asked by the public, by the international aid community and by the media. In different conflict environments, there have been several examples of relief food feeding soldiers or relief goods becoming the target of looting and raiding. Aid might also have more subtle effects, like freeing resources for wars or legitimising misdeeds of warlords and criminals. And can aid do the opposite—help to decrease tensions and conflicts, which are often enough caused or exacerbated by lack of resources?

The link between aid and conflict has become a subject of recent debates, mainly instigated by negative effects of humanitarian interventions in Somalia and Rwanda. In both cases, aid may have contributed to the outbreak or continuation of the conflicts: in Somalia, through the manipulation of food aid by Siad Barre's regime from the early 1980s, and the subsequent failure of the international community to stabilise the humanitarian situation; in Rwanda, by the misuse of humanitarian aid by the Hutu militia, which was enabled to attack and invade Rwanda after the first phase of the genocide partly through aid provided in refugee camps outside Rwanda.[1]

Since then, the link between aid and conflict is being questioned more systematically. The international community has become tired of having its well-intentioned aid fail to produce substantial improvement in most conflict areas around the world. It is dismayed that in some cases aid may even prolong wars and increase suffering. Books with titles like *Famine Crimes* and *The Road to Hell* focus on suspected evils and dangers of humanitarian aid. However, other sources try to build on the good which humanitarian aid can produce and suggest means and methods to limit unintentional negative effects.

WV's response to South Sudan's humanitarian crisis in the late 1990s is an example of how the link between aid and conflict can be reviewed and programmes re-designed to do as much good as possible, while limiting potential negative effects of aid. The case study will demonstrate the potential for using a particular model of humanitarian aid in conflict situations, LCP, as part of project planning and implementation.

"DO NO HARM": THE LCP INITIATIVE

In the mid 1990s, a group of researchers and aid practitioners led by Mary Anderson, head of a relief and development NGO named Collaborative for Development Action (CDA), started a global initiative called the Local Capacities for Peace Project. The project's objective is to understand how humanitarian aid might worsen conflict and how it might fail to build on local capacities for peace. It then seeks alternative strategies and methods of delivering aid so it will have a more positive impact on conflict environments.

CDA has collected a number of case studies from international NGOs working in conflict areas and compiled them in two publications.[2] The lessons learned from these cases have been widely shared in feedback workshops with both practitioners in humanitarian aid and academics. During these feedback workshops an analytical framework was developed that can be used as a tool to analyse the relation of humanitarian aid and conflict and to improve and refine aid programmes.

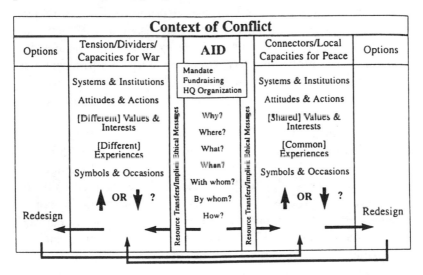

Figure 6-1. Do no harm.
(From "Do No Harm: How Aid Can Support Peace—or War," by Mary B Anderson.
Copyright © 1999 by Lynne Rienner Publishers, Inc.
Reprinted with permission of the publisher.)

In short, the analytical framework tries to identify the right questions regarding the impact of aid on locally observable tensions and groups in conflict; it provides a different perspective on needs-oriented aid programmes; and it helps to identify alternative programme options on how, where, what, when and with whom to deliver aid.[3]

LCP is not meant primarily as a peacebuilding project, but it seeks to improve delivery of aid in ways that do not fuel conflicts.

Recognising that NGO interventions are often targeted at the community level, the focus is on identifying *local* capacities for peace, as well as local potential for conflicts. Systems, motivations, institutions and actions that bring people together, even in times of war or conflict, are dubbed LCPs or "connectors." Where these connectors are not fully explored (or are undermined), and where tensions are increased through an aid programme, alternative programme options are necessary.

Some problematic areas identified so far include working with (and legitimising) authorities; relationship with local counterparts, beneficiaries, warlords and armies; impact on peace or war economies (through prices, wages, benefits); and handling of commodities and resources in resource-scarce environments. On a more political level, expression of particular (religious, political) identities or lack of neutrality and impartiality are to be carefully addressed.

Since 1997, a number of international NGOs have formed a loose collaboration in a pilot implementation phase of the LCP project, during which methodology is being tested in several conflict areas around the world; WV Sudan has been a partner since the end of 1997.[4] In October 1998, WV also initiated an LCP project in Kosovo; this project was interrupted by the war in early 1999.

The results of WV Sudan's effort to utilise the LCP framework are still being processed, and the analysis is being refined continuously. So far, the process has led to some re-adjustment of project strategies and project implementation (see the case study below). The analysis has found additional issues worth discussing, such as the relationship between rebel movements and their humanitarian wings, and WV's organisational identity. As a Christian NGO with a strong support and funding base in the USA, this identity has the potential to interplay with the war in Sudan in both positive and harmful ways. Those issues are being documented elsewhere, especially as the position of WV and other NGOs has changed seriously recently.[5]

CONTEXT OF WV LCP PROJECTS IN SOUTH SUDAN

CHE in Sudan

South Sudan became one of the most dramatic CHEs of the 1990s. A combination of natural climatic catastrophes and a 15-year-old civil war brought the country into a famine comparable only to the Ethiopian famine of the mid-1980s. Civil war in Sudan began as a contest between the North and South, between Arab and African, between Muslim and Christians or animists. In the last few years the war has grown even more complex, with the South's military forces splitting into more than one faction. The factions not only fight the North but also each other. By mid-1999, at the time this chapter was written, the crisis had eased, but South Sudan remained a fragile and desperate place for its people, despite all efforts by the international aid community to ease the suffering.

The complexity of the situation has led to resignation creeping into the hearts of many aid workers. It is true that lives are being saved and people are being helped. But no major, long-term change seems in sight. Sudan has become the never-ending war, interrupted only by periodic natural disasters and subsequent mass starvation.

Many layers of difficulties make the South Sudan CHE unique. The high vulnerability of local communities, very harsh climatic and geographical conditions, a multifaceted war with changing factions and different causes, and involvement of numerous neighbouring countries in the conflict are just a few aspects that keep disasters occurring regularly. The extreme isolation of South Sudan has also meant that the world knows little about the conditions and plight of the Sudanese people.

The international community has sought traditional and innovative ways of responding to the crisis of South Sudan. A UN/NGO consortium, Operation Lifeline Sudan (OLS), co-ordinates humanitarian assistance with the support of humanitarian wings of local rebel factions (SRRA and RASS) and with the permission of the Government of Sudan (GoS). Interventions of the UN and NGOs are focused on relief and rehabilitation response but include accompanying measures like peace-and-reconciliation initiatives, support of humanitarian principles and formation of civil society in the South.

Despite a continuous and rather multifaceted response to crises in Sudan, 1998 brought another setback. Three million people were threatened by death through hunger, and a major trigger for this disaster was the combination of a worsening war and crop failure through droughts (caused by the 1997 El Niño). Considering this development, and after 10 years of combined humanitarian response by over 50 NGOs and the UN, one has to ask what could have or should have been done better to prevent this part of the country from sliding into another disaster.

Successes and failures of aid in South Sudan

After the formation of OLS in the late 1980s, a consortium of over 40 NGOs has sought to deliver multiple aid interventions into Sudan in a largely co-operative and participatory manner. OLS initially was hailed as an innovative and co-operative way of delivering aid in a complex war environment but eventually came under criticism for lack of outreach and lack of finding sustainable solutions to the Sudan problems.[6] In the past, interventions ranged from emergency relief aid in the late 1980s to mid-1990s to more recent efforts to support the formation of a civil society, lobbying for human rights, and offering peace-and-reconciliation initiatives. The initiatives targeted the Intergovernmental Authority for Development (IGAD) peace process[7] and supported grassroots organization which contributed to peace and reconciliation between warring parties.

Peace initiatives were not always co-ordinated in a systematic manner, and many actors chose various approaches towards the creation of peace in Sudan. For example, ex-US president Jimmy Carter brokered a cease-fire between North Sudan and South Sudan in 1995; the New Sudan Council of Churches (NSCC) managed to start a dialogue between the Nuer and the Dinka in Bahr el Ghazal, between the churches and the rebel movements, and between churches in the North and the South; the UN pursued implementation of human rights and humanitarian principles through a special unit/programme. The UN had also been successful in developing "OLS ground rules," which have been accepted by warring parties. These aim at ensuring the peaceful, impartial, accountable, transparent and secure delivery of humanitarian aid.[8] Large international NGOs have chosen either to participate in the above efforts or to start their own programmes to promote peace and reconciliation in Sudan.

The intent here is not to give a comprehensive overview of the initiatives and approaches chosen so far but to point to the fact that, despite huge and varying efforts, peace in South Sudan seems further away than ever. If anything, the relations between warring parties have deteriorated, and there are even more warring parties. Besides the split and re-unification of South Sudan factions, neighbouring countries like Ethiopia and Uganda have become more involved in this conflict, increasing the complexity of the situation.

A similarly sobering picture emerges when one looks at the overall impact of the billions of dollars that have been spent on relieving, rehabilitating and developing South Sudan. During the mid-1990s, it seemed that South Sudan was developing in small steps towards self-sustenance, that the combined efforts of the international aid community were bearing fruit. Peoples' livelihoods became more stable in a number of regions, a civil administration was being established, some slow transformations were observable, and local communities appeared to develop (or re-establish) coping mechanisms for their survival. But in early 1998, a combination of factors turned this optimistic picture into the grim reality of mass starvation; assumed successes seemed but an illusion. The interplay of the El Niño drought in 1997 and the faction shift of a single warlord and the subsequent increase of fighting in Bahr el Ghazal caused mass migration and the internal displacement of hundreds of thousands of Sudanese. These already vulnerable people were not able to cope with the additional stress, and thousands died of hunger and disease.

World Vision in South Sudan

WV began its commitment to Sudan in 1972, at first working through partner organisations. Later, in the early 1980s, WV began an operational presence in Sudan, working on road and infrastructure rehabilitation, providing food aid and emergency primary health care in Eastern and Western Equatoria. In 1988, the GoS declared several Christian NGOs, including WV, as *persona non grata* in the predominantly Muslim north. As a response, WV recommitted its efforts to Sudan by concentrating operations in the South Sudan. WV started its work in South Sudan prior to the formation of OLS, and became a founding member of OLS in 1989. Since then, WV has provided numerous forms of emergency assistance to the people of South Sudan, such as food aid, survival kits and agricultural inputs.

By 1999, WV was working in three areas of South Sudan: Tonj County in the Bahr el Ghazal Lakes region, neighbouring Gogrial County (Bahr el Ghazal) and Yambio County in the Western Equatoria region. Tonj County has a total estimated beneficiary population of 150,000 individuals. The population of Yambio County is approximately 100,000 individuals. Toch and Pathuon *payams* (districts), Gogrial, host up to 110,000 people, of which up to 50 percent could be internally displaced at any given time due to insecurities caused by militia leader Kerubino, by the neighbouring Nuer cattle raiders, or by the GoS. Most of the communities in South Sudan, especially in Bahr el Ghazal, lack regular access to markets, essential commodities, income and health services. The condition of chronic need makes these communities all the more vulnerable to the caprices of war, drought, flooding and disease.

The famine in 1998 prompted WV to initiate a new emergency-relief programme, which included opening four feeding centres, overland delivery of some 1,200 metric tons of food to Tonj, and distribution of seeds, tools and other non-food relief items. In 1999, the food distribution programme was expanded, and approximately 10,000 metric tons of food were being delivered to food-deficit areas in Bahr el Ghazal.

WV, like other NGOs, has started questioning the effectiveness of relief interventions which do not include follow-up rehabilitation and development aid. As a matter of principle, WV Sudan seeks to accompany relief aid with longer lasting interventions and tries to build local capacities to cope with potential disasters. Capacity building is a particularly important approach to link relief and development and to ensure that aid reduces local vulnerabilities to the regular emergencies and disasters in the country.

Part of these local vulnerabilities include the regular upsurges in fighting and the on-going war. The question of what can be done to reduce conflicts and foster peace processes became increasingly important for WV staff, who wish to improve the general livelihood of the people in Sudan in a sustainable manner. In addition, the presence of a huge aid organization like WV in the midst of a local war over a long period of time brings certain dangers. For instance, a huge commodities programme can bring the potential for diversions, for misappropriations, and for transferring resources to warring parties without intending to do so.[9]

In mid-1998, World Food Program (WFP) food meant for the starving population was diverted from the beneficiaries, and suspicion mounted that humanitarian aid was being used to feed armies and continue the war. The UN/OLS established a task force to look into these diversions and to suggest strategies to ensure that humanitarian aid reaches the most vulnerable beneficiaries. The task force came to a few conclusions about improving distribution mechanisms but generally conceded that little means were available to avoid these negative events. WV tries to go beyond the task forces' recommendations to address such harmful developments. It is not only the misdirected targeting of aid that concerns WV Sudan. The potential contribution of several layers of WV's aid, emergency or rehabilitation, to the on-going conflict prompted WV to take up a pilot implementation of the LCP project, also known as the "do no harm" initiative. The preliminary results are the subject of the following, exemplified through a case study of relief aid in Western Equatoria.

Environment of conflict

The contrasts among WV's project sites are marked. The people in Bahr el Ghazal are mostly agro-pastoralists whose lifestyle and economic activities revolve around cattle herding. Located within raiding distance of government-held areas, Tonj and Gogrial both have suffered incursions from GoS forces and occasional bombing by government aircraft. Even more destructive in the past several years have been attacks by forces loyal to Kerubino Kuanyin Bol, one of the initial Sudanese Peoples Liberation Army (SPLA) commanders, who broke with the rebel movement several years ago. In the beginning of 1998, Kerubino and his forces switched allegiances again, leaving the GoS to return to the SPLA. Later in 1999, he returned to become an ally of the GoS again.

Parts of the two counties have also suffered from cattle raiding between rival Dinka groups and between local Dinka and Nuer from neighbouring counties. While the cattle raiding is a long-standing part of intergroup relations, this activity has become increasingly violent and destructive as traditional restraints and mechanisms for resolution have waned in the face of the war. In fact, the formation of the South Sudanese Independence Movement (SSIM) has transformed this traditional conflict into a war between two factions, which are now identified through the mentioned ethnic groups.[10]

Yambio County, in contrast, has seen little or no fighting since the area was taken by the SPLA in 1990. The population in the area is agricultural and is capable of producing large grain surpluses, although the lack of storage and trade capabilities have served to limit production. Cattle are not held in Yambio County because of the tsetse fly infestation of the area.

Tonj, Gogrial	• Marauding warlord Kerubino Kuanyin Bol • Cattle raiding between Dinka and Nuer (increased in violence through interfactional fighting between SSIM and the SPLA) • Fighting between SPLA and GoS, including bomb raids • Raids by Arab PDF (Peoples Defense Force) militia (GoS backed) • Culture of war and violence • Competition over scarce resources
Tonj, Gogrial, *vs.* Yambio	• Suspicion against "occupying" Dinka soldiers from Bahr el Ghazal in Yambio • Different economic livelihoods, religions (Christian *vs.* animists) and lifestyles (migratory *vs.* settled) • Some history of raids
Yambio	• Military takeover by SPLA from GoS in 1990 • History of tension among Western Equatorian ethnic groups • Bad governance

Table 6-1. Some sources of local tensions.

Despite the long-lasting issues that appear in the above table, local conflicts change. South Sudan has become a place of shifting alliances, political manipulation and surprise splits and reunions. Warlord Kerubino, one of the major causes for conflict, was killed 15 September 1999. And although the Nuer and the Dinka have initiated a very promising peace process, it leaves out some subclans and causes suspicion among other ethnic groups, mainly from Equatoria. It is extremely difficult to form a valid picture of a conflict which is so fluent and changing.

Potential for a South-South war

"The next war will be between Dinka and Zande." This was a sobering statement of a Yambio resident who spoke openly about animosities between the ethnic groups and about the political and power struggle that might arise once the war with the North ends (or before). As a matter of fact, even the so-called North-South conflict is increasingly fought either between southern factions or between armies composed of African Sudanese recruited to the GoS forces or paid and armed by the GoS but acting independently. Therefore, the likelihood of one or several South-South conflicts following whatever end to the North-South conflict can be expected is rather high.

LCP approach

WV and the LCP project decided to concentrate initially on WV programmes in Yambio, Western Equatoria, because of the more troublesome security situation in Tonj. This decision was later justified when WV was forced to evacuate its staff from Tonj County just before the start of the implementation phase of the pilot project in early 1998.

The focus on Yambio was also chosen because of the fact that dormant or potential conflicts seem to characterize this region. These are relatively often ignored in the analyses of South Sudan's war and have partly to do with the SPLA conquest of Equatoria in 1990, the subsequent occupation by Dinka soldiers, and the domination of the SPLA by an ethnic group which is not well received in Equatoria. Further sources of conflict are related to problematic relationships with the authorities, both for international NGOs and the local population.

The WV LCP assessment team identified three main areas of conflict as potential sources of violent or destructive discord related to Yambio County:

* the North-South war;
* ethnic tensions (Dinka-Zande, tensions among various Equatorian groups); and
* problems of governance.

The war in Sudan is usually referred to as a conflict between North and South, between Arabs and Africans, or between Muslims and Christians or animists. It is also a war over power and resources, particularly oil, water and the vast agricultural production capacity in the South. However, there are more complex relations to be observed in analyzing conflicts, especially in a local context. As indicated above, different southern factions are now adversaries in the war, and political or power interests are being mixed with ethnic or religious diversities.[11] The Yambio, Western Equatoria, case is also interesting because a hidden conflict among ethnic groups in the area (mainly Zande and Dinka) might be exacerbated by the aid that is delivered to the area. A first benefit of the LCP analysis was therefore the demystification and clarification of the conflict layers and the inclusion of inter-ethnic and political problems in the conflict analysis. Although WV staff had some vague notion of inter-ethnic tensions in Yambio prior to the LCP analysis, it was only during the assessment exercises that these could be systematically described. Subsequently it became possible to adjust projects so they decrease such tension.

Tensions between Zande and Dinka result partly from the invasion of Equatoria by the SPLA in 1990 (officially referred to as the liberation) and is reinforced by the subsequent presence of Dinka soldiers who have developed all the attitudes that characterize an occupying force—looting, random harassment, road blocks, diversion of resources, etc. While over the years this attitude has been controlled slightly by the authorities, the fact remains that the Dinka represent a very different ethnic group from the resident Zande and have so far failed to integrate or even achieve good levels of mutual understanding. Some kind of living alongside one another has developed, but there is suspicion and a significant difference in lifestyle, social position and access to power and resources.

Other conflicts concern the unclear levels of authority in the area. While the military administration has partly been replaced by a civil administration (formed as a result of efforts to support civil society formation in the early 1990s), there are still at least four potentially competing authority structures:

1. The military (SPLA/M), represented by the governor as the highest authority in the Equatoria region and by local or

regional commanders. Authority over civil affairs is limited, but in fact, the soldiers form the most powerful authority in the county.

2. The civil administration, with a county commissioner, *payam* (district) administrators and several civil institutions, like the police, law courts, and so on. The civil administration is by law the highest authority at county and *payam* (district) level.

3. The traditional administration—chiefs, sub-chiefs, village headmen. These are the power in the countryside and theoretically are subject to the civil administration. However, traditional mechanisms like courts are fairly autonomous and independent of the newly formed civil structures.

4. The SRRA, formed as the humanitarian wing of the SPLM in the early 1990s. It has the mandate to serve as counterpart to humanitarian-aid interventions. Formally, reporting lines are to the civil administration and through SRRA headquarters to the SPLM. Because of its direct access to resources through international NGOs, the SRRA is in permanent conflict with other authorities.

Relations among the above mentioned institutions are often unclear and characterized by competing interests and/or authority levels. NGOs on the ground are often caught between the different authority levels and have to develop strategies to avoid increasing conflict (or ending up in the middle of it).

Such relations are made more complicated by ethnic differences: SRRA and SPLM are—at least at HQ levels—dominated by Dinka, and civil and traditional administrations by Zande or Equatorian minority tribes. The danger of ethnic conflicts even within areas under SPLM control is significant. The following case demonstrates this. In mid-1998 a group of displaced Dinka migrated into Yambio County, causing anxiety and disagreements between local and central authorities over the best way to deal with them. The displaced Dinka in Nadiangere provided an insightful case of how (or how not) an aid agency might increase or avoid exacerbating conflicts in a CHE.

CASE STUDY: DISPLACED PEOPLE IN NADIANGERE

Background

In May 1998, a significant number of Dinka people from various parts of Bahr el Ghazal walked to Nadiangere, a small town in northern Yambio County, in search for food. The number of the displaced was estimated between 800 and 2,000 people (200–400 households). Due to fighting and two years of drought, Bahr el Ghazal was experiencing a famine situation, while the food security in Yambio, Western Equatoria, had been relatively stable. In 1998, the international humanitarian aid focused on Bahr el Ghazal, but not all needs had been met and people were starving to death in this area.

The migration of Dinka (a Nilotic tribe) into Yambio (which is populated by Zande, Balanda, Bongo, and Jurubeir tribes) is very unusual. This is because the Dinka are agro-pastoralists, and due to the tsetse fly in Yambio, they cannot bring their cattle to this area. The last "visit" of Dinka into Nadiangere happened in 1987–88 and was accompanied by raids and fighting. While the majority of the displaced people were Dinka, there was a considerable portion of Bongo and Jurubeir among them, minority groups in both Bahr el Ghazal and Yambio counties. The Jurubeir form a sort of buffer zone between Dinka land and Zande land, and intermarry with both tribes. The Bongo are found mainly north of Nadiangere but also in Bahr el Ghazal.

The prime reason for the migration was hunger, but some statements by the displaced hinted at further problems in their home area: poor organization of food distributions, selling of relief food by the authorities, little NGO effort to serve Bahr el Ghazal, and lastly, instructions from Bahr el Ghazal authorities to move south. None of these explanations could be verified, and the local community suspected hidden agendas: that the people were sent to "invade" Yambio County, that they were soldiers in disguise, that they were criminals or some other kind of outcasts.

The needs

Two quick assessments by SRRA, WFP and the NGOs on the ground identified food assistance as required most urgently. Some moderately and severely malnourished children needed supplementary feeding and medical assistance. Potable water was not available, and the displaced people lacked essential household items as well as seeds and tools for cultivation. In order to provide the proposed assistance, a road from Yambio to Nadiangere needed to be cleared and some bridges needed reinforcement.

Overriding concerns: Potential conflicts

As mentioned, the displaced had come not only because of hunger, but also because of some political problems in their home communities. They could not easily move back to their areas of origin. SRRA officials from HQ and from Bahr el Ghazal area confirmed that these people had little chance of benefiting from the food distributions, but they were not willing to clarify this further.

At the same time, the host community of Nadiangere and the civil administration were not enthusiastic about the displaced settling in this area. Two very different tribes had met in a time of need and were forced to share scarce resources like land, food and shelter. There was potential for conflict. In addition, if substantial aid for this group of displaced people was given, NGOs and authorities feared this might attract further migration from Bahr el Ghazal. More Dinka had already moved from Wau into Tambura County, next to Yambio.

LCP analysis

In order to address both humanitarian needs and the potential for conflict, a quick analysis of "connectors" and "dividers" (using the categories of the LCP framework) between the two groups was done. After that, the food-aid intervention was to be tailored in a way that would avoid increasing the dividers and reduce the potential for conflict.

Dividers—Local capacities for conflict

 * *Different attitudes and systems of economic and social support:* The two groups speak different languages and can hardly communicate with each other. They have different economic

(agro- *vs.* agro-pastoralists) and social behavioural patterns. The Dinka have a system of sharing (and taking) that has caused a lot of irritation in the host community. They have taken food, space and other resources, often without asking. For example, a wooden table construction at the clinic was dismantled by the Dinka to use the sticks for mango collection. This caused anger and frustration among the residents who use the clinic and who use mangos as supplementary food. The mangos, traditional coping food during cultivation times, were almost exhausted at the time of the assessment due to the increased demand by the displaced.

• *Different value system (witchcraft):* The Dinka chiefs have not tried to meet the chiefs of the host community. Little communication was going on, and Dinka were being regarded with suspicion and lack of understanding. A local resident suspected that they had started eating their children during the long walk to Yambio County. A major reason they were not welcome was their perceived ability to perform witchcraft, mainly for rainmaking. This conflicts with the strong Christian belief of the local residents (and possibly causes anxiety).

• *History of war:* As mentioned above, the Dinka had raided the area some 10 years earlier. They also dominate the SPLA/M, who took over Yambio County from the Government of Sudan (Khartoum) in 1990.

Connectors—Local capacities for peace

• *Friendly attitude and action:* The displaced people in dire need were received with some hospitality. The local communities shared space, food, cooking facilities and some shelter with the newly arrived. The Dinka were perceived as "human beings who need to survive, just like us."

• *Common experience:* Both local and displaced people face some (differing) level of food insecurity because of the shared burden. A Zande chief said, "We are now displaced together with the Dinka." The two groups face the same problem with lack of water and share the same health facilities (WV clinic).

• *Common value system (religion):* Some Dinka are Christians and have joined the local communities in the Sunday church

(ECS). Although they do not understand the local language, members translate the preaching for them.

* *Common economic actions and systems:* Both Dinka and the resident population are capable of agricultural production. The local community is giving some agricultural work to Dinka men and women and providing them with food (or money) in return. Both men and women seem to connect easily with the other tribe when working together in such food-for-work schemes. Also, Dinka from Bahr el Ghazal have some history of trade with Yambio County. There is a small but constant supply of meat (cattle) from Bahr el Ghazal to Yambio markets. This is mostly exchanged for money, and sometimes for grain.

* *Common occasion:* A recent common festival (liberation day) was being prepared by both groups through food collection. Unfortunately, this food was taken by the SPLA for mobilization, and the festival did not take place.

Programming options

In light of the above, and considering the immediate needs to ensure survival of the displaced, programme options were identified to deliver humanitarian aid without enforcing dividers or undermining existing connectors. The proposed food-aid assistance was broken down according to the following questions:

Where should aid be delivered?

The Dinka refused to return home, even after being promised assistance at their place of origin. After some initial hospitality, the local communities refused to host them any longer. The local authorities did not want them to migrate further into Yambio County. Hence, it was suggested that the displaced move to Menze, a sparsely populated place near the river, some 18 kilometres north of Nadiangere. The chiefs of the neighbouring areas objected to this for security reasons but were overruled by the local authorities. Despite the above-mentioned connectors, the geographical separation of the two groups seemed to be inevitable. All further aspects of assistance were only acceptable to the local community on the basis of this separation.

When should aid be given?

While some assistance needed to be given immediately to ensure survival, an important question was, For how long? The assessment team followed the recommendation of the local community that a one-time food distribution be done and the displaced people supplied with some tools and (short-maturing) seeds. This would prevent the internally displaced persons (IDPs) from staying longer than desired by the local population; the locals expected them to move back to Bahr el Ghazal by December or January at the latest.

Who was to benefit?

Initially, the host community suggested that it also be provided with food, because it had shared and exhausted its food reserves with the displaced. This opinion changed after some discussions, and the priority needs of the IDPs were communicated and generally accepted by everyone. A single distribution of food (and some seeds and tools) to the IDPs was accepted by the local Zande. However, if non-food assistance were to be provided, the Zande wanted to benefit too. Through the involvement of local chiefs in this decision, it was hoped that envy could be minimized.

How was aid to be provided?

The NGOs and WFP suggested providing the food assistance through general free distributions. However, the roads had to be cleared, and local brigades were paid to do this work.

What?

A one-time distribution of food for two months and limited amounts of seeds and tools, plus some accelerated nutritional/health intervention, was planned. It was unclear whether this would suffice, as first harvests might come later than August.

By October 1998, the initial 800 IDPs had been assisted according to the above recommendations, which were made by the interagency assessment team including the SRRA secretaries from both Yambio and Bahr el Ghazal. During the assistance, heavy criticism came from SRRA HQ on the grounds that the IDPs needed much more assistance than suggested. At the same time, the assistance provided by WV to the IDPs was repeatedly hindered by local authorities and SRRA, who demanded that some of the resources go to the local Zande population. A follow-up assessment in October 1998 resulted in the following observations:

Change of humanitarian situation

Since July 1998, WV and WFP had provided 10 metric tons of food and some locally procured seeds and tools. WV accelerated the primary health-care programme in the area, including supplementary feeding to children under five and to breast-feeding and pregnant women among the displaced population. The road from Yambio was cleared by local brigades to facilitate transportation of relief items. At the same time, the displaced people moved to Menze, where they constructed huts and started planting.

Meanwhile, migration from Bahr el Ghazal continued, and an additional 5,000 people moved into Yambio County in July and August. These people, like the earlier group, cited hunger as the main reason for migration. But again, there were some uncertainties about the reasons they could not benefit from relief assistance in their home areas. They moved further south from Nadiangere and reached Lirangu, Yambio, and even far places like Bangasu.

Sometime in August and September, the IDPs in Menze left their newly constructed camp and moved southwards too. After having planted maize, there were no further activities possible in Menze which could have helped them to survive, and the Dinka moved looking for employment and economic opportunities. The area around Menze is now almost uninhabited, and no infrastructure is to be found. Maize has now grown half high.

Over the previous months few additional displaced people came to Yambio. This was partly due to the heavily swollen river which separates Yambio and Tonj counties, and partly to the harvesting season in Bahr el Ghazal. There were rumours that people were camping on the banks of the river, and as the harvest in Bahr el Ghazal was less than sufficient, it was feared that more people would come into Yambio towards the end of the year.

Changed survival strategies

Between July and October, the IDPs had turned to seeking food and income through piecework, that is, clearing, weeding and other assistance in cultivation to the local resident community. The IDPs had scattered all over the county and added some root-collecting, hunting and selling of firewood to their survival strategies. The piecework does not give them long-lasting income or food provision, so their source of livelihood remains very fragile. As most resident farmers are rather poor and without large resources themselves, the IDPs have to move frequently to find new opportunities. Only a few chiefs and headmen keep migrating IDPs at their places for longer periods.

Local communities and local authorities alike treated the visitors with understanding and some sympathy. They tried to accommodate their needs by sharing resources but had limits. A few instances led to conflict; for example, when the IDPs settled in public places like in the clinic in Bangazagino and made it un-operational. This particular conflict had the potential of turning violent, as the IDPs were "ready to fight in order to stay at the unit" (Bangazagino health worker).

The Yambio authorities had accommodated some 160 IDPs in a SPLM office near the WV compound. This place was otherwise inhabited by a few soldiers and kept available for possible visits by SPLM headquarters to Yambio.

Improving intergroup relations

In places around and north of Nadiangere, there seemed to be some comfort in hosting the IDPs from Bahr el Ghazal. This was because common ethnic identities of IDPs and residents (mainly the Bongos and Jurubeiris) may have caused some ease in intergroup relations in and around Nadiangere. Children from the different groups were found playing with each other, and the local headman talked about his ancestors' migration from Bahr el Ghazal into Yambio.

The situation was a bit different in the rest of Yambio County. Here, the displaced people were not necessarily understood and not so easily accepted by the local population. However, there is a considerable Dinka resident population, mostly soldiers and their families, and there were some visible interactions between them and the IDPs in Yambio town. The Dinka IDPs were also developing some relation to the few Dinka traders in the area.

Competing interests and potential for a new conflict level

The local population had agreed not to benefit from relief assistance given to the IDPs. However, in another development, large numbers of Zande started returning from the Democratic Republic of Congo (DRC) into Yambio County (due to the deteriorating security situation in the DRC). At the time of the follow-up assessment, over 12,000 returnees had already been counted, and up to 40,000 additional people were expected in Yambio, Maridi, and Tambura counties.

While these returnees were not in a very bad shape, there clearly was some need for transport, food, and medical assistance. The returnees were likely to be absorbed by their former home communities (which they had left during the SPLA occupation of Yambio eight years before), and they could benefit from the food production in Yambio County. However, there was a potential for conflict between the returnees and the IDPs if one group were being served before or without the other being considered. By sheer number, the returnees formed a much more visible group and might take priority over the displaced, who had developed some coping strategies over the last three months but were less visible because of their scattering into the countryside.

Fear was expressed by members of the assessment team that local Dinka communities and soldiers might retaliate if only the returnees were given assistance without considering the Dinka IDPs.

On a higher political level, there had been pressure from different sides in the SPLM. Dinka in influential positions had pushed for assistance to the IDPs, while the Equatoria governor and local commanders were pressing for quick response to the returnees.

Programme options

During inter-agency discussions, and debates with the local authorities, the fear of more displacements was expressed repeatedly. An influx of more Dinka into the area might exhaust the resources of the county and could cause serious friction between the local and visiting communities. The most viable economic connector, the day labour of IDPs for local households, was not expected to last beyond cultivation season (November-December). In addition, it might not be possible for too many people in the long term. Yambio has only 80,000 residents, and these were already sharing resources with returnees from DRC.

Nonetheless, the failure of the Menze IDP settlement called for more integrative ways of assistance. Food-for-work schemes—

rehabilitation of roads, construction of communal projects like the primary health care centre in Nadiangere or the Lirangu sleeping-sickness hospital—were suggested. While these might not be sufficient for tens of thousands of people, at least they would build on the initiatives which had already been taken by the IDPs themselves. In any case, the assistance to the IDPs would have to be co-ordinated with assistance given to returnees from DRC.

So far, the conflicts observable between the groups had been limited, and the humanitarian-aid intervention, which was chosen carefully, had had no significant negative impact on the potential tensions in this situation. But the aid had not succeeded in building on or increasing local connectors between the displaced and the resident communities, and therefore failed to a certain extent to exploit its peacebuilding potential.

Lessons learned from the case study

Despite the fact that the above case reflects a rather moderate humanitarian need, it was felt by NGOs and the Sudanese authorities that the potential for conflict in this case was very high and that careful interventions had to be chosen. The situation was therefore approached with great caution, and the LCP analysis provided a good tool to approach the complexities of the situation systematically. The analysis enabled WV to respond appropriately to the dilemmas that were faced in ensuring the survival of the IDPs while minimizing the tensions among people groups.

The analysis of the dividers and connectors that determined the conflict environment enabled the NGOs and their counterparts to go beyond the needs analysis, and plan a humanitarian response that would "do no harm." Decisive factors were the open debate and the inclusion of local authorities and chiefs in some of the decision-making processes, along with the inclusion of local residents in part of the actual response (brigades clearing the roads). This helped ease some suspicions and reduced the potential for bitter feelings against strangers who received assistance when locals did not.

The particular situation posed a serious challenge to WV Sudan and its partners. The LCP analysis, through a detailed discussion of the conflict environment and the planned humanitarian aid, provided the agency with a clearer picture of how to deliver aid and how to prevent deterioration in relations among the groups. In that way, the LCP analysis proved a helpful and useful tool.

It also had some very practical limitations. The assessment was done under time pressure and lacked the depth needed for a comprehensive understanding of the situation. It was, for instance, not possible to verify causes for migration and to seek programme options at the places of the origin of the IDPs. The assessment team could reach out to only a limited number of IDPs and representatives of the host community due to the extremely difficult logistics and limited road access to the hinterland of Nadiangere. This might have caused contradicting views on issues such as the degree of hostility *vs.* hospitality shown by the resident community.

The fact that the migration surely had political aspects and reflected some problems among the various communities of the SPLM-administered parts of South Sudan made a clean and thorough assessment difficult. In such a situation, the findings and statements of the external assessment teams were possibly challenged, altered, or even manipulated by counterparts to suit the interests of the political stakeholders involved.

Lastly, the returnees of neighbouring DRC into Yambio County at almost the same time of the influx of IDPs from Bahr el Ghazal quickly changed the focus of WV, SRRA and other aid agencies. The returnees were ten times the number of the IDPs, and they formed a very visible (because easily accessible) and "international" phenomenon; thus, more resources of the aid agencies were directed towards addressing the humanitarian need of the returnees. This fact does, however, reflect a reality that LCP, or any other new methodology, has to face: it may be brushed aside by other factors, like publicity, sheer humanitarian needs and the urge to respond to human suffering. The LCP strategy of averting misery *and* laying the foundation for sustained peace through combined interventions may need to be promoted more actively to bring about longer-lasting successes.

In spite of these limitations, the case is an example of how WV Sudan tried to deal with the potential impact of aid interventions on conflicts. To a certain extent, the LCP analysis was made easier because WV was dealing with a "limited" (in time and location) situation and with a moderate humanitarian need. Such an analysis could be more difficult when interlinking sectors, longer-term interventions, and more complex conflict environments are to be considered. LCP analysis also relies on a good understanding of the conflict environment and therefore will be more difficult in situations where the NGO has little or no understanding of the situation in which it is working in (for example, in quick responses in areas where there has been no prior presence). Another obvious limitation is (in)security: In the heat of an on-going war, or in highly politicized environments, an analysis of the conflict might be too dangerous to conduct. Even simple questions might pose a danger to the one who asks them.

However, a generally positive feeling among WV Sudan staff, local or international, has developed towards the usefulness of the LCP tool, even if it is not sufficient to solve or address all aspects of the relationships between aid and conflict. Its limitations are primarily of a practical nature, and some of those will be mentioned in the following section.

OPPORTUNITIES AND LIMITATIONS

The LCP analysis in South Sudan has so far been a very practical effort to improve planning and delivery of aid in a conflict environment. WV Sudan is still in the early stages of this process, but it has seen the potential benefits as well as some limitations. In particular, the use of a practical methodological tool (the LCP framework) in assessment and planning processes has created some comfort in dealing with a rather challenging and unpredictable environment. Besides the actual results of the analysis (and some recommended programme changes), the following opportunities have occurred:

- The assessment teams (including the HQ-based programme staff) have been able to reflect on their work environment in a systematic manner. Sudanese and non-Sudanese have been able to share and discuss the layers of conflict and the impacts upon their work.
- Security threats and their underlying reasons were reflected upon and were demystified. Sometimes misperceptions that WV was

the immediate cause for a conflict could be clarified (in reality, the causes were much deeper), and it became clear that individuals or the organization were merely caught in the middle of local troubles due to their rather exposed and prominent role.

* "Low key" conflicts, especially those with a potential for turning violent and damaging, could be verbalized and discussed easier. The LCP process provides opportunities to act in a preventive manner rather than simply to react to a situation after violence erupts.
* The staff developed greater comfort in dealing with experimental or innovative project aspects (like supporting a finance centre or introducing foreign exchange salary payments in a relief and war situation).
* Changes in programme planning and implementation (like targeting, participatory approaches, recruitment procedures and partnering) were facilitated and enriched by the LCP analysis. A practical assessment tool is at hand to complement needs analyses.
* Dialogue across management lines, including planners, policy makers, and implementing project staff, was made possible. Particular interventions could be screened for their usefulness and dangers in a more participatory way than before.

To date, WV Sudan has found the LCP analysis most helpful in dealing with pieces or aspects of the programme. Some specific, tangible results have been possible. Larger issues, however, have been more difficult. One example of this is the symbolism (the Christian and seemingly American identity of WV) and the perceived, or real, lack of impartiality and neutrality of WV Sudan in the Sudan war. While this has been identified as potentially harmful or at least worth discussing, the LCP analysis could only help to identify some options, not to work through their possible implications. The organizational identity of WV and its impact on the conflict have certainly become more difficult "nuts to crack" in the LCP process.

Another difficult limitation of the LCP process has to do with practicalities. Why do recommendations and analytical conclusions not always bring about the desired results? Why is it so difficult to reach those conclusions in the first place? It was amazing to observe during the assessment process how many of the issues had been discussed previously among programme staff, but how few opportunities had been found to include such analyses into programme decisions.

THE REALITY TRAP: WHY DO WE STRUGGLE?

The issues at hand seem pertinent; a discussion about the harmful impact of aid is necessary; and conflicts during project implementation should be dealt with more systematically. However, there is also some reluctance observable in applying the LCP framework to the daily work of the programme staff. A number of reasons could be found for this, including a misperception of the LCP-process and the demands of the reality of project implementation in relief and conflict environments.

Traditional gap between sectoral projects and advocacy work

A relief or rehabilitation intervention is often managed and administered according to technical sectors like health, food security or water. Advocacy, conflict prevention, or security concerns are either treated as a cross-sectoral "appendix" (which comes as an additional burden) or as a separate sector, which is administered separately. Lack of integrative planning and programming, and lack of cross-sectoral collaboration (especially in NGOs with a particular-sector specialization), might reinforce this gap. This is true both for individual staff perception and for organizational mandates; humanitarian NGOs rarely have conflict management written into their core values, policy statements, or primary mandates, assuming that there are more specialized and qualified organizations active in this area.

Workload and delivery pressure

A relief staff as well as a humanitarian organization has a primary objective to fulfil. This usually entails saving lives and averting disaster, and is a full-time job. A notion exists that conflict management (just like gender issues, environmental protection, or capacity building) is the bonus, that the work can be done when there is extra time—though there is hardly any of that in emergencies. The rapid project cycle of a CHE is determined by needs, not by opportunities or threats. Starting with assessments, the needs (and not the potential dangers) usually override other considerations, and this approach is difficult to change. NGOs also have pressures to deliver during highly publicized emergencies, and programme options which call for cautious proceedings might not be acceptable in times of haste, when the public (or the donor, or the marketing department) asks for quick action. To a certain extent this issue limited the thoroughness of discussions during the Nadiangere case, though the humanitarian need was moderate, hence more time seemed available for consideration of the conflict environment. This changed, though, when 50,000 returnees from DRC poured into South Sudan, and the NGO mode switched to "urgent action."

Lack of indicators and ability to monitor

The success of a conflict-prevention programme can only be verified by its contribution to the lack (or end) of conflict, which is almost impossible to prove through direct causal links. So far, little work has been conducted on developing indicators for the effectiveness and validity of peacebuilding (or harm preventing) programmes. In times of increasing pressure for impact, accountability and rates of return, this shortfall might limit the acceptance of such efforts. The willingness of the humanitarian-aid community, including local counterparts, to engage in LCP and similar ventures will depend on the usefulness of the tool and processes, which is difficult to prove with tangible outputs.

Lack of exposure, knowledge, and training

The availability of a practical analytical tool to assess harmful programme options in conflict environments is not known to many actors in the humanitarian-aid community. As long as there is no minimal common standard or language for dealing with the relation of aid and conflict, there will be disagreements or at least reluctance to deal with the issues at hand in a co-ordinated manner.

Common languages have been found in assessment methodologies and or planning, where they certainly contribute to necessary co-operation. Technical sector specialists have been and are being exposed to assessment and planning standards, but sometimes lack the skills (and commitment) to add yet another facet to their work—the management of conflicts. This may be the simplest hurdle to overcome but also the most time- and resource-consuming one.

Threats to those benefiting from CHEs

A methodology which aims at reducing conflict is likely to collide with the interests of warlords, warring parties, profiteers and possibly corrupt authorities. Such collisions may be harmful for those using the methodology. Thus the limits to the use and efficiency of LCP are being set by the potential of physical danger to those who implement it. Even greater resistance might come from those who misperceive the "do no harm" approach as an appeal to "do no aid." In recent publications, some suspicions have been raised about the "new relief agenda," to the effect that humanitarian aid will (or should) be reduced as a response to analysis as performed under LCP.[12] The danger of this debate is that it focuses on the protection of mandates and resources but overlooks the positive effects that a critical review of some aspects of the humanitarian aid can have.

The LCP project and the utilized methodology, as the author understands it (and as it has been applied in the Sudan context), is not meant to reduce aid or even slow it down. It is meant, rather, to facilitate a better and more thoughtful implementation of aid in conflict environments, and should provide opportunities for reducing the likelihood of fuelling wars. It is also helpful in supporting the argument that aid agencies should remain involved despite dangers and harmful effects, because it gives the tool to overcome shortcomings.

CONCLUSIONS

The above aimed to share experiences from dealing with potential harmful impacts of aid in (and on) a conflict environment. WV

Sudan has, in collaboration with other international NGOs around the world, started a pilot implementation project which is being observed and analyzed over three years. The project has already shown some encouraging results in learning and improving programme quality. This quality has not least been found in the fact that the project collaborators are developing increased consciousness about their environment and about the role that they, as relief staff, play within a conflict.

So far, the "side effects" of the assessment tool have almost been as important as the actual results of the assessments—like the facilitation of conscious debates about the conflicts, the inclusion of Sudanese counterparts in programming decisions, the improvement of security situations for WV staff, and the improved comfort level in assessing and planning complex situations. In addition, the first results of the conflict (and aid) analyses have been encouraging and show the potential for more qualitative improvement of WV's aid programme in South Sudan. "Success" might lie in the actual impact that LCP can provide to lessening tensions and conflicts in WV project areas. This does not mean that solutions to the war and conflicts in Sudan can be found through applying the LCP methodology, but that incremental positive changes should happen and can be attributed to changed programme strategies. We promise a revisit of the LCP project after completion of the pilot phase.

NOTES

[1] See Michael Maren, *The Road to Hell—The Ravaging Effects of Foreign Aid and International Charity* (New York: Free Press, 1997). More balanced yet still critical assessments are found in a number of publications, such as Africa Rights, "Humanitarianism Unbound? Current Dilemmas Facing Multi-Mandate Relief Operations in Political Emergencies," discussion paper no. 5 (November 1994); Alex de Waal, *Famine Crimes* (Oxford: James Curry; Bloomington, Ind.: Indiana University Press, 1997 [in association with the International Africa Institute]).

[2] Mary B Anderson and Peter J Woodrow, *Rising from the Ashes: Development Strategies in Times of Disaster*, 2d ed. (Boulder, Colo.: Lynne Rienner Publishers, 1998); Mary B Anderson, *Do No Harm: How International Aid Can Support Peace, Not War* (Boulder, Colo.: Lynne Rienner Publishers, 1999).

[3] Details on the methodology, which has been disseminated in dozens of training workshops around the world, can be found in Anderson, *Do No Harm*.

[4] The LCP project in South Sudan was funded by the International Humanitarian Assistance of the Canadian International Development Agency (CIDA).

[5] First results of the Sudan LCP analysis have been collected and compiled in confidential progress reports and are yet to be evaluated comprehensively. To ensure protection of the process and actors, only selected results will be discussed and shared in this article. The analysis is focused on the situation during the years 1998 and 1999, when a humanitarian crisis characterized by a major famine was at its peak. It was also written prior to the events in early 2000, when 12 international NGOs temporarily relocated from South Sudan after political controversies with the southern movement could not be resolved.

[6] One major OLS problem is that it lacks access to those needy areas which are not approved by the GoS to receive OLS assistance. This includes places like the Nuba mountains, or parts of northern Bahr-el-Ghazal, which are served only insufficiently by NGOs outside the OLS consortium (see J Millard Burr and Robert O Collins, *Requiem for the Sudan: War, Drought, and Disaster Relief on the Nile* [Boulder, Colo.: Westview Press, 1995]).

[7] The IGAD consists of the nations from the Greater Horn Region and has been the most regular forum, so far, to facilitate dialogue between the GoS and the South Sudan rebel factions.

[8] A good overview over the mechanisms and objectives of the UN humanitarian principles programme in South Sudan is given by I. Levine, "Promoting Humanitarian Principles: The South Sudan Experience," RRN paper no. 21 (London: ODI, 1997).

[9] John Prendergast and Colin Scott have described a variety of mechanisms in which resources are transferred other than through direct theft and diversions, for example, through fees, taxation, manipulation of beneficiary figures, bribes, etc. ("Aid and Integrity: Avoiding the Potential of Humanitarian Aid to Sustain Conflict: A Strategy for USAID/BHR/OFDA in Complex Emergencies" [Washington, D.C.: USAID, 1996]). Mary Anderson has further refined such mechanisms into six sub-categories (see Anderson, *Do No Harm*).

[10] SSIM is a southern military faction which has split from the SPLA; it became an ally of the GoS in 1996. This alliance was terminated early in 2000, when Riak Machar officially withdrew his support to the Karthoum peace charter from 1996.

[11] For example, a bizarre alliance has been formed by the Islamist Government of Sudan and the cult leader and warlord Joseph Kony, whose

Ugandan LRA (Lord's Resistance Army) commits atrocities in North Uganda, operating out of Juba and other GoS-held bases in South Sudan.

[12] D Hendrickson gives an overview about recent discussion papers presented at an ODI seminar examining international responses to humanitarian tragedies ("Humanitarian Action in Protracted Crises: The New Relief Agenda and Its Limits," RRN paper [London: ODI, 1998]). The general tone of these papers is reflected by titles like "The Death of Humanitarianism—The Anatomy of the Attack," "Military Humanitarianism—Trends and Issues," and "Origins of the Assault on Relief Aid."

7.

Rwanda:
Telling a Different Story

WARREN NYAMUGASIRA,
LINCOLN NDOGONI
AND SOLOMON NSABIYERA

THE RWANDA CRISIS: AN UNPRECEDENTED CHE

The root causes of the Rwandan genocide and war lie in its history,
in the pain that its citizens have carried for years. This culminated
in the 1990–94 war and the genocide and the consequent movement abroad of about three million people, the majority of whom

---

This chapter describes two workshops that are healing deeply wounded
people in Rwanda. The authors argue that this healing is essential before
development activities can lead to sustainable social transformation.

The authors are grateful to all participants in the two workshops and
to those who shared their testimonies with us. We also acknowledge the
contributions of Nigel Marsh, who compiled the reconciliation stories
from Ruhengeri; John Steward, who dared to believe in, steered and documented the work of reconciliation and peacebuilding in WV Rwanda during 1997 and 1998; Frank Cookingham, who read through the draft and
made valuable suggestions; Josephine Munyeri and Regine Uwibereyeho
of WV's PDW team and Anastase Sabamungu and Joseph Nyamutera of
African Evangelistic Enterprise, who shared their experience in the facilitation of the two workshops. We also thank the following donors for the
financial support: AusAID; WV Australia, United States, Canada and
Taiwan; and the Netherlands Government.

have since returned. The experience of chronic traumatic situations during the pre-genocide, the genocide, and the post-genocide readjustment phase has had an overwhelming effect on the Rwandan psyche.

The country we call Rwanda is no ordinary African country. It is a small, with an area of 26,338 square kilometres and an estimated population density of 290 people per square kilometre, making it the most densely populated country in Africa. Because of its landscape, it is generally described as the land of a thousand hills—the physical terrain is mountainous and astonishingly beautiful. Yet Rwanda has received more than its share of problems. The one still fresh in many people's mind is the 1994 genocide.

That crisis is not easy to comprehend, particularly the brutality that accompanied the killings. However, to make some sense of this, it is important to look back and try to understand what has shaped the minds of the people of this country. It is clear that each ethnic group has been a creator as well as a product of the ideas concerning it, and these ideas are entrenched in the minds of its members. As Lipson points out, such ideas are "an integral part of the life of the group, since they embody the hopes and aspirations of its members, expressing their conception of the group's purpose, and understanding about process."[1]

This chapter describes two workshops which have had a significant healing effect on wounded people in Rwanda. The chapter starts by describing the uniqueness and complexity of the Rwanda CHE, and the need for beginning the journey of individual and community healing as a necessary condition for effective emergency intervention, rehabilitation and sustained socioeconomic transformation. This is necessary not only for the community but also for the staff of the agencies providing the assistance. The chapter then gives the WV approach, outlines and discusses the methodology and content of the two workshops, and concludes by drawing lessons learned from them.

Rwanda having experienced repeated violence in most of its colonial and post-colonial history, and much of the bias, ethnically construed, being passed on from generation to generation by adults, the only way to break the cycle of violence is to "tell a different story" than the one inherited. This chapter argues that it is only people who have taken steps toward healing who are able to tell and live out such a story.

Uniqueness of the Rwandan CHE

The case of Rwanda was extreme even for a CHE. This was not a war where one group fought another for a purely political cause. It was a genocide. A total of 800,000–1,000,000 people are thought to have been killed within a period of 100 days. Another 3,000,000, slightly under half of the entire population, fled their homes to become refugees in neighbouring countries. And another 1,000,000 became internally displaced persons (IDPs). First estimates put the number of orphaned children at 500,000–600,000.

Men and women killed their own relatives, sometimes including members of their immediate family, particularly in cases of mixed marriages. Innocent children were caught up and some were forced to participate in the killings. People in positions of authority, who should have provided safety to those who were fleeing for their lives, often represented additional threats. Teachers, law enforcement officials, even church members could not necessarily be relied upon for help. As Danielle de Lame put it, "Children have been killed by their teachers, (while) other children have seen their teachers kill the pupils they were supposed to protect and guide. The same can be said about bourgomestres [mayors], church people and even parents."[2]

All this violence also shattered Rwanda's culture and society. Therefore, Rwanda's physical, psychological and cultural integrity has been grossly undermined.

It seems that every person in Rwanda has been wounded in one way or another. This wounding has taken place at all levels: physically, psychologically and economically. Events surrounding the genocide were traumatising to all groups, including the perpetrators. In addition, the country received back about 1,000,000 people, commonly referred to as the "old caseload," from different parts of the world, each coming with different wounds and cultures (see Table 7-1).

For restoration to be effective, interventions in CHEs need to have strong peacebuilding, conflict-transformation and reconciliation components. Incorporating such components is neither easy nor even attempted by many NGOs. Those agencies which have attempted to address some of these components do so from a very specialised and localised approach.[3]

Group	Expressed Needs	Challenges
Survivors Up to 200,000 people who were targeted but escaped death in the genocide. This includes many children (60,000 of whom now care for siblings) and some adult wounded.	Justice, social and legal protection (as witnesses of the genocide), housing, reparation, a means of livelihood, food and healing.	Many are widowed, some were raped and infected with AIDS. Children under 18 are heads of households. Orphans need to be integrated into society. All live under the fear of death and have been targets of extremist attacks.
Stayers Over 4,000,000 Rwandese, of whom some 1,000,000 were internally displaced during 1994-95.	To be cleared of suspicion and guilt by association (the innocent); fear of reprisals; release for those unjustly imprisoned; protection against false accusations or threats.	Separate the innocent from criminals. Encourage the guilty to take responsibility, apologize for crimes committed and return any goods wrongly acquired; trauma recovery; self-esteem.
Old Caseload Over 1,000,000 fromer long-term refugees from 1960s and 1970s who returned after 1994. Some were born in exile, coming to Rwanda for the first time. Many are highly educated.	Adjusting to the new situation and circumstances; bonding, acceptance, integration; desire to see the guilty punished; employment; recovery of ancestral lands; safeguard of their right to be Rwandese; an end to cultural impunity.	To resettle them and make them feel accepted. To help them overcome their desire for revenge. To integrate them into the common culture. To come to terms with the loss of their relatives and to deal with entrenched fear and hatred, long-term pain and betrayal. To ensure that former victims do not become future victimizers.

Table 7-1. The post-war Rwandan population mix.

(Continued on page 190)

Group	Expressed Needs	Challenges
New Caseload Around 3,000,000 who fled into refugee camps in Congo and Tanzania, lost some of their relatives there and returned to Rwanda between December 1996 and May 1997.	Identify and punish the planners and implementers of genocide; clear others of suspicion and reintegrate them into society.	Fragmented families; 130,000 in prison, mostly men. Need to deal with guilt or its lack. Fear of apprehension, of mob justice. Some were trained to fight, may be armed, hard to recognize as genocide participants because active in other communes.
Extremists (a) Over 300,000 actual and potential infiltrators, returnees, ex-inerahamwe, ex-FAR members.	Power sharing and integration for intellectuals; victory over RPA; regain power in Rwanda; continue "ethnic cleansing."	To help them change their mentality, accept responsibility for the genocide and channel their energies into more positive and productive activities.
Extremists (b) Unknown number unable to reconcile, their sympathizers, some of them in the army, survivors, some "old case" returnees.	Revenge; "ethnic cleansing"; justice	To help them to make a just society, to heal their pain and anger.
Permanent refugees Over 50,000 still dispersed.	Stable, safe, open society with political participation; good economic prospects; possibility of general amnesty for suspects.	Accountability, reintegration, or ability to contribute in other ways to the reconstruction and development of Rwanda.

Table 7-1. The post-war Rwandan population mix.
(Modified from the *Reconciliation Commission Report* [September 1998], 95–97.)
This division of the population is a generalisation, of course. The needs expressed
by each group are based on anecdotal evidence gathered from workshops and
conversations with different groups of people and individuals. Some groups overlap.

In the case of Rwanda, the extent of the crisis and its visibility in the international media attracted a large number of international and local NGOs. The need for reconciliation and peacebuilding was so overwhelmingly obvious immediately after the end of the war and genocide that for a time reconciliation seminars and workshops mushroomed around the country. However, the effectiveness of these workshops, in terms of healing, is not always evident, despite the enormous efforts and funds put into them. This failure may have been at least in part because the staffs of these NGOs did not have a personal experience of the healing they were trying to promote. The intentions of the interveners were good, but the outcome was ineffective or, at best, a short-lived palliative.

This may have contributed to the backlash against the notion of peacebuilding by the government and also the survivors, who often contend that those promoting reconciliation dodge issues of justice and trivialise the extent of the victims' pain. For example, a common question asked whenever reconciliation is mentioned is, Reconciliation between whom? The public execution of twelve of the genocide convicts in April 1998 was viewed by many as justice served. And the release of prisoners for whom there was not sufficient incriminating evidence was received with hostility and feelings of betrayal, just as the activities of the international tribunal trying Rwanda genocide suspects in Arusha are viewed.

Some NGOs argued that to get involved in the area of peace and reconciliation was premature; the people of Rwanda needed time to grieve. As evidenced by two programmes WV is implementing, this assertion is true. However, a method, an approach, or even a time frame for this grieving was needed—but not provided. In the meantime, many agencies preferred to concentrate on physical reconstruction, such as building houses, in the hope that such activity would bring about reconciliation. But many inside and outside Rwanda believe that without reconciliation, physical reconstruction is like building with straw. When the next cycle of violence comes, the physical reconstruction efforts will "go up in smoke."

World Vision Rwanda's approach

In the process of delivering emergency relief and rehabilitation programmes, it became apparent, first among children in the unaccompanied children centres, then among our staff and within the community of beneficiaries, that there was a great need to address individuals' inner wounds and trauma. The dysfunctionality of our own staff, each of whom has his or her own story of the psychosocial impact of the events that have occurred, and conflicts in churches and other institutions provide clear evidence that there is a need to encourage grieving and healing. But there is little scope for individual psychological treatment of any sort, the numbers of potential patients being too high and the number of Rwandan psychologists and mental health workers inadequate to cope with the demand. WV Rwanda also observed that in attending to the need for physical rehabilitation, inner healing must be given priority, otherwise wounded people are not able effectively to utilise the infrastructure or to contribute to the development effort. In fact, such intervention can easily become irrelevant or a source of more conflict.

In April 1994, as the camera's eye focused on Rwanda, WV's president, Graeme Irvine, declared the need for a high-level response to the CHE. WV delivered food to the displaced and suffering people, as did many other agencies. It also provided medical care and temporary shelter materials; assisted the displaced; and distributed seeds, tools and essential household items such as blankets, pots and pans, water containers and soaps.

In 1995, as the relief mode ended, WV became involved in rehabilitation. Many damaged health centres, schools and houses were fixed, and new ones built. Farmers were helped to obtain and multiply improved varieties of seed that had been wiped out by the war. New agricultural technologies were introduced, enabling farmers to produce more than twice as much food as before. An ambitious programme to terrace unproductive steep hills was started in an effort to increase cultivable land.[4] Farmer associations have been restored or formed, and micro-enterprises promoted. Current changes are shifting WV more towards an integrated development programme, which involves more community participation.

In the process of delivering these programmes WV Rwanda's planners became less confident that purely practical development activities could contribute to a lasting peace and development, a goal all aid agencies work to achieve in their programmes. Indeed, practical development interventions alone could be just an unintended step toward helping prepare the community for the next cycle of violence. Humanitarian aid can be used as a source of negative energy for conflict or as a source of positive energy for peace—and local staff are critical in this energy mix.[5] For example, local staff who survived the genocide in Rwanda perceived the feeding of the Rwanda refugees in the Congo and Tanzania camps as strengthening the refugees in order to continue the genocidal atrocities. On the other hand, denying them food would have been perceived as a form of punishment or even revenge. Such perceptions by national staff may have been due to the state of shock, anger and unprocessed trauma. Also, mutual suspicion exists among many NGO national staff where trauma has not been processed.

THE PERSONAL DEVELOPMENT WORKSHOPS (PDFS)

Of every 20 staff members in international NGOs in Rwanda, 19 are Rwandan nationals. In places like this, where involvement in the conflict is virtually universal, national staff will be variously victims, agents and witnesses of all the violence that has gone before or may still be going on. Individuals may be shocked and traumatised, bitter and vengeful, fatalistic and apathetic, paralysed by unexpressed grief. These are people who have to explain clearly the situation in which they work to donors and partners outside the country. They have to prove they have the integrity to design and implement programmes that introduce peacebuilding "connectors" into the community-based projects while resisting pressure which may be put on them by community leaders and others to use development aid negatively.[6]

How can staff who are themselves products of the conflict be assisted so that they can engage in humanitarian work without prejudice or bias and with a peacebuilding perspective? To help answer this question, WV Rwanda decided to provide a workshop, the Personal Development Workshop (PDW), for its 350 staff. This was based on methodologies researched by Dr Simon Gasibirege of the University of Butare, field tested by his team, and refined by WV's former trauma co-ordinator, Evelyne Burkhard.

The PDW was initially greeted with scepticism and even fear by the staff. Some resented the implication that they had a problem. Others feared that examining deeply buried emotions might cause them to lose control and slide into madness. As early groups went through the course, however, many showed visible signs of improved mental and emotional health, with positive repercussions in work and at home. The progress led to acceptance for the course, which became a priority for managers, some of whom had previously objected to the time commitment it required of their staff.

The aim of the PDW is that each member of staff can speak not just for his or her own group, but on behalf of the people he or she used to consider enemies, as well as for third parties, demonstrating the willingness and ability to see other people's points of view. In that way, development genuinely becomes more comprehensive and all encompassing, rather than being just the pursuit of whatever is best for one's own group. Connectors in projects cease to be theoretical but actually emerge from among the people themselves.

PDW structure and content

These voluntary workshops are carried out in 11 one-day sessions over four months.

Introductory session

The workshops start with an introductory session referred to as the information day. The aim is to create an understanding of the workshop and solidarity among the participants, and to build trust and a willingness to share among the group members. The participants begin by viewing a video tape entitled "Rwanda—A Country That Went Mad." The film helps the participants to understand the historical context of the conflict in the pre-colonial, colonial and post-colonial periods.

The rules of protection for small-group discussions are established, putting the responsibility for protection of the process on the individual and the group. The rules are then discussed and the participants are requested to commit themselves to them and to the process.

At the end of the day, participants choose either to continue the process or to opt out. This is a healing process in itself, because people are given a choice to participate only when they feel ready. Once people have committed themselves to participation in the workshops, it is highly desirable and impressed upon the participants to complete all the sessions. It is not considered helpful, and can even lead to more difficulties, if people do not complete the process (half a dose is worse than none).

Module I: Bereavement and loss

This three-day module is aimed at providing a safe and trusted environment where people can express their pain, grieve their losses and begin to heal. The whole group receives information in a lecture on the theory of the grieving process and bereavement pathology. Thereafter, they are divided into small groups of six to eight people to share experiences in confidence with the help of guide questions and facilitators.

The following are examples of the guide questions:

Take a moment and think about how you lived and the way you organized your time before the 1994 war and genocide. Share your past individual story with others in your group. You may use the following questions to help in sharing your story:

- Where did you live?
- What was your status?
- How did you spend your time?
- Before the war and genocide, did you experience significant changes concerning your standard of living and time structure?
- What do you remember concerning those changes?
- Compare those changes with the ones caused by war and genocide(for non-Rwandans, those changes caused by major crises in your life).
- What were your feeling then?
- What are your feelings today?
- Think about any bereavement experienced in your life before 1994. Share with each other in turn.
- Think about the people and property you lost during the genocide and massacres. Share with members of your group. Share the qualities and memories which made the people special to you.
- Are there any feelings you suppress concerning the people you lost? Are there any you allow yourself to feel?
- What feelings would you like to adopt today concerning your deceased loved ones?

Module II: Dealing with emotions and feelings

The second three-day module takes place one month after the first. The time lapse is important to allow participants to integrate what was learned and felt in the first module. The aim of the second module is to understand the value and role of emotions and feelings in one's life. It also helps the participants to get in touch with their own emotions and begin to express them, as well as relate them to various levels of maturity and immaturity within themselves. Feelings and emotions of anger, sadness, fear, guilt, hurt, joy and others are explored and discussed through the eyes of the "parent," the "adult" and the "child" within each person. Then, in their original small groups, participants discuss their feelings and how they express them in the context of their experiences of loss.

Think about your life in the past few days. Write down any thoughts, feelings and behaviours you have had during this period. Allow yourself to listen to your inner dialogue, especially in regard to the emotions you felt. In your small groups, share what you have written down.

- What feelings concerning the people who died or disappeared during the war and genocide do you not allow yourself to feel?
- What feelings do you allow yourself to feel?
- What feelings would you like to adopt today in regard to the people who died or disappeared during the war and genocide?

Module III: Forgiveness and justice

This is another three-day course, again taking place one month after the last. This workshop looks at the theoretical and practical bases of forgiveness and how forgiveness relates to legal justice. Emphasis is given to forgiveness as a process, and that as an end product of a wider process of healing and empowering victims to look at the whole issue of justice from a position of emotional and psychological strength. Social violence, injustice and the bases for personal and community forgiveness are discussed together and in small groups.

Think about any accusations that you make or hear around you related to the war, the genocide and massacres in Rwanda.

◆ Can you separate those accusations into those concerning you, those concerning others, and those concerning nonhuman factors?
◆ In what ways are you concerned by your inner, social, political and ethical conscience?

Evaluation and feedback

The last day of the workshops takes place a month after module III. This is a time for reflection and celebration. All the participants give feedback on the impact of the process they have been undergoing, first as it affects themselves, then as it affects participating colleagues, and finally, as it affects relatives, friends and family members. This feedback is both oral and written. Participants also celebrate personal achievements (in terms of having successfully passed through a painful process) and the creation of new group solidarity and friendship.

These workshops were not readily accepted when they started running; neither participants nor facilitators knew what to expect from the process. But as more people participated, the level of acceptance and confidence in the process increased significantly. With experience, the original discussion questions, which had focused exclusively on people's experiences and loss during the genocide, were broadened to include the experiences before and after the genocide. The need for flexibility on the part of the facilitators to follow the process as it unfolded rather than being too strict with the format was also another adjustment that had to be made. Facilitators needed to be sensitive to participants' needs and emotions provoked by the process.

Outcomes

It may be still too early to draw precise conclusions and to discuss the long-term impact of the PDFs on participants, but it is clear, based on observations, feedback and testimonies from participants, that the process has already achieved significant benefits. The 200 participants who have completed the full course are nearly unanimous in their statements that every Rwandese, especially those holding responsibility for and authority over others, could benefit from this process. This is all the more significant because some of those making this recommendation were highly sceptical of the value of such a course when they started.

In a situation like that of Rwanda, which is easily dismissed as hopeless, the PDFs provide a very important sign of hope. Wounds need to be revisited and appropriately addressed; they are deeper than observers normally assume, reaching into people's emotions and subconscious as well as their personal and ancestral history. This realisation is itself a beginning to the healing process, personally and for the community. As far as work is concerned, there has been a marked improvement of functionality among the staff, as reported by their managers and supervisors, increasing their productivity, re-establishing meaningful relationships across the ethnic divide and creating a more conducive working atmosphere than existed before the workshops began. To do their work gives meaning to their lives. Time and again they may be reminded of their own still unprocessed experiences, but they know how to overcome such difficulties. There are reports of improved relationships at the family level between spouses and in the way parents treat their children.

As a result of this process, some participants decided to contact people they previously considered to be enemies and start on the process of reconciliation. Some have decided to give up their desire for revenge and their "right" to hate. The attitude that justice is a prerequisite for reconciliation, and that the offender must ask for forgiveness before it can be given, has changed. People have become more concerned with how they can connect with the former enemy across the social boundary; they strategize on ways to "get through" to them, rather than planning how justice can be meted out to the offender. Priorities have been reversed. Justice has not become any less important, but connection to others, including former enemies, has gained a higher priority.

A TESTIMONY FROM THE PDW

I was widowed in the 1994 genocide. Two of my children were killed, one disappeared, and four survived.

Since childhood, I have experienced oppression because of my ethnic group, and the culmination came in the genocide. Before the workshops I had many difficulties in my relationships with people who do not belong to my ethnic group; I could not even go to the market.

I carried a lot of inner pain. I had lost peace of mind and suffered from constant headache. I hated my life. I lived on from day to day, asking, Why me? I always felt angry and bitter.

Often, I would sit and think about the events that had taken place in my life since 1959, when the first major ethnic violence broke out: my mother was beaten, I slept in the bushes several times after running away from boarding school between 1959 and 1965; my father was thrown into a pit (from which he escaped); my father-in-law and his sons died in 1963; we escaped the machetes and the sticks in 1973. I remembered the killings, looting and burning of houses in 1993, and how we ran away, only to come back in time for the fatal day that made me an orphan, a widow and a rootless person.

There were 11 sisters and brothers in my family. Today we are only three. In the genocide, my father and mother were killed with machetes, along with more than 50 grandchildren. Now, nothing is left but memories. Hundreds of close relatives have disappeared. Among my in-laws, only my surviving children remain; apart from them there is not a single relative alive.

The Personal Development Workshops enabled me to mourn my relatives and to grieve. I never understood before that I can mourn my deceased relatives without burying their dead bodies. After some time I felt relieved of my strong inner pain.

Every night, after a day of the workshop, I thought deeply about my deceased relatives—their good deeds for me that I now miss; the physical contact; and their good wishes that would strengthen me and help me plan my future life.

Through the workshops, I came to understand myself and the causes of my different behaviours. This gave me the strength to deal with my anger. I know that we will all die one day, but *gupfa uhagaze* (to die a gradual death through revenge, unresolved anger, guilt, hatred and so on) is the worst that could happen to me. For this reason I decided not to retaliate against those who have committed atrocities against me and my family, not to inflict on them the same wrong they did to me. Rather, I chose to try to help my offenders realize their wickedness, repent and turn from their wrong deeds.

With this in mind, I approached one family that was among the perpetrators of genocide. I met with the head of the family, but when he saw me approaching he ran away. Some days later, my children told me they had met with the children of this man. I asked my children to trace his home. After some days I met his wife, and I asked to accompany her to her home. She looked fearful, but I tried to show her I did not plan revenge by chatting politely with her. I told her that those who died are gone, it was their time to leave this world, but we have to live in this world as human beings, created in God's image, endowed with wisdom to distinguish evil and good.

Slowly, I saw her changing, and she told me of their difficult life in the refugee camps, how they returned and the kind of life they are living. Eventually she asked me how my relatives died, among them my brother, who her family is suspected of having killed. When I explained, she became sad and cried. She started to curse the devil who deceived people and led them to "devour" each other. She told me many other things that betrayed her shame.

Later, I was able to meet her husband. We talked for a long time. He talked repeatedly about the repercussions of wickedness. Now this couple is relaxed enough to tell me about some of their plans, such as devoting themselves "to helping orphans and vulnerable people."

I used to live in deep loneliness. The PDWs have helped me to love my life again. I sleep with peace, and I remember my deceased relatives with joy. I relate to my children without venting my anger on them, as I used to do. I no longer have a negative attitude towards the other ethnic group. I can even go to the market. Even when they belong to an ethnic group different from mine, I see them as fellow Rwandans.[7]

Clearly, some staff have been helped more than others. There are some, however small the number, for whom there has been no noticeable change. A few others, one or two in a group of forty, do drop out of the process. There have been a few transformed over-night. Yet for most, these workshops set them on a journey of im-provement which will take time to complete. All in all, the out-come has been such a success that WV Rwanda is convinced that this should be integrated in its overall approach to emergency relief and transformational development in conflict situations and complex emergencies.

PDW: Replication among wounded communities

As a result of the positive and encouraging results from this phase of the workshop, WV Rwanda has embarked on the process of providing the PDW to communities where it has projects. Special attention will be given to those who tend to be out of reach for such programmes due to the language barrier. These include peasants, and within them women and children, who have to comply to demands of different kinds in order to have access to therapies where they exist. With careful planning, we have identified the "communities" for this next phase. These communities will have to include children, for their own sake, but also because they are the men and women of tomorrow. One method, already being used in Uganda and to some extent Rwanda, is the use of artwork to help children step back into their traumatic experiences, process them, and be able to look into and be part of creating a more hopeful future.[8] This will require that "healed" children be trained to help their peers. Mechanisms to handle consequences of the process, such as confessions that can have legal implications, have been put in place.

In addition, another phase of the PDW, designed to facilitate people who attended the first phase to move deeper in the process, will encourage, it is hoped, more people to take practical steps towards actual reconciliation and peacebuilding. Support mechanisms to enable this to be effective include making the workshops available to staff family members willing to attend, as experience has shown that there can be strained relations when one party has not gone through the process. The next phase of PDW will equip staff to deal with vicarious traumatisation—the lasting negative results in one's world view due to exposure to a variety of intense traumatic situations over a period of time.

Attention will be given to increasing cultural anthropological insights through study group encounters and to providing ongoing external supervision for all staff involved in leading or facilitating these workshops. Clearly, there is a need for anthropological information regarding such cultural issues as the stages of development of trauma in children in Rwanda; stages of grieving as practised in the local culture; and community coping mechanisms (and which of them can be energised by new applications of existing rituals as well as the growing of "new" rituals which fit the culture). There is need to investigate, document and integrate the positive cultural healing methods and rituals in both the trauma healing and reconciliation efforts administered by teachers, clergy, health workers, and those born in and still living in the areas where they work and enjoy a good reputation in the community. These will help their communities to build a future on the basis of mutual acceptance, thus building new social ties.

THE AFRICAN EVANGELISTIC ENTERPRISE (AEE) HEALING AND RECONCILIATION WORKSHOPS

The church and reconciliation

It is ironic that the horrors of the genocide and all of its consequences took place in a very religious country. As many as 90 percent of Rwandans claim to be adherents of the Christian faith and some 8 percent of Islam. Rwanda was the most Christian country in Africa when genocide struck.[9] But much of the church's credibility and its sacred image of glory and grace have been tarnished by the complicity of some of its members, including clergy, in the killings. "Not only were 'Christian' members of the congregations of every single denomination in Rwanda responsible for the most appalling atrocities, but so many massacres took place in the parishes where the targets of the genocide sought sanctuary."[10] Some were involved directly, while others sided with the regime that planned and carried out the genocide. The church is accused also for its silence, for its reluctance to denounce the planning and implementation of the genocide. "Many Church leaders have acknowledged that the Church in Rwanda failed as an institution, although individual clergy showed immense courage, risking their lives to save those of others. [But] they have been less willing to comment upon the specific accusations against certain clergymen."[11]

Consequently, many Christians had their faith in God seriously undermined. They questioned the existence of the love of God—if God is the loving Father, why did he allow the genocide to happen?

How did the power of the Evil One overcome God's mighty protecting power? Some even came to the conclusion that perhaps "God was an *interahamwe*, a killer," who could allow the innocent to be killed so atrociously.[12]

The post-genocide church has been left in a difficult situation. Some of its leaders were killed in the genocide; others are imprisoned or have fled into exile. The new leadership is struggling to reconstruct ruined church buildings and set up new structures. Some church buildings have been turned into national genocide memorial sites. The church finds itself in a dilemma. On the one hand, it has the desire to rebuild; on the other, it has the temptation, the strong urge, to deny responsibility for the genocide. Doctrinal differences, denominational competition, accusations of favouritism and ethnic divisions conspire to make the situation for the church worse. This has made it virtually impossible for church leaders to build on ruined hopes, has led to mistrust and suspicion among Christians, and has caused the church to be dismissed by the authorities as a credible voice for reconstruction in the nation, at least until it has put its own house in order.

AEE workshop structure and content

It was in the search for approaches that produced real change and inter-ethnic fellowship in churches that WV Rwanda discovered the existence of healing and reconciliation workshops. These two-day workshops were developed by Dr Rhiannon Lloyd, a Welsh psychiatrist, and drew heavily from her personal experiences, professional training (medicine and psychiatry) and work in situations of ethnic conflicts.[13] The approach was tried and tested among Christian groups and reworked and refined as Dr Lloyd received feedback from participants. For example, terminology was modified to meet the needs of the different denominational backgrounds of the people who were attending the workshop or using the material. Dr Lloyd has since modified the workshop further for the South African context.

After assessing the situation of the church after the genocide and the possibility to help in trauma recovery, "the power of the cross to bring healing was realized afresh and God gave us the vision to gather church leaders from all denominations to look at healing, forgiveness and reconciliation."[14]

Since the first workshop in 1994 thousands of participants, including some local government leaders, have attended and experienced healing and forgiveness.

The metaphor of building a house is used to describe the progression of the workshops (see Table 7-2).

MODULE	FOCUS	CONTENT	EFFECTS
I. Understanding the heart of God	Laying a foundation	Understanding: •God's grace and love for all people; •God's promises and the power that God entrusted to the church to heal the nation; •human sinfulness and responsibility for the genocide; •the nature of loss, including loss of faith.	•Awareness of the love of God; •restoration of hope for change in and through the church; •awareness and regret for any personal responsibility for loss during the genocide.
II. Healing wounds	Building the walls	•Understanding the wounds; •writing memories; •sharing the wounds; praying for healing.	•Understanding personal wounds; •experiencing and expressing pain; •surrendering pain to Christ; •feeling deep release.
Forgiveness and repentance Acceptance of others	Setting the rafters and the ceiling	•Understanding forgiveness, justice and freedom; •personal repentance; •repentance on behalf of others; •moving toward reconciliation.	•Forgiveness given and received; •freedom and release; •hope for change •desire to bring others to freedom.

Table 7-2. Healing and reconciliation workshops.

The workshops are biblically based, ideal for church audiences, with psychological principles for healing past painful memories.

Day one
Biblical teaching focuses on love of God the Father, the fact of human sinfulness, faith in Jesus, the Cross, repentance and forgiveness.

Psychological principles taught and practised in the workshops include six ways of experiencing and expressing painful emotions:

- Writing the experience
- Sharing the memory (group processing and verbal expression)
- Praying for wounds, giving them to Jesus (acceptance, releasing one's pain)
- Nailing pains to the cross (separation between person and pain, release of memories)
- Confession, repentance and forgiveness (verbal expression, developing positive perception of the other group, restoration of fellowship)
- Embracing each other (body memory expression)

At the workshop, Christ is presented as the One who carries all our pain. Participants are encouraged to give the burden of their pain to him and begin to find healing. They are asked to write the five experiences for which they most need healing, and then go into ethnically diverse groups of three to share what they have written. The ground rules for these discussions have been laid ahead of time, ensuring that each participant is aware that these discussions are to be held in strictest confidence. Each person in the group has 15 or more minutes to share. Deep emotions are often expressed at such times, with many tears shed. After the entire group is reconvened, three things each small group feels most need to be healed are shared.

The participants are then encouraged to express their attitudes by telling God how they feel, not in "sweet" words but in real feelings. Following this, participants are invited to take the experiences and pains they have written and nail them to a wooden cross. The group sings as each participant hammers his or her paper to the cross. Then the paper-bearing cross is taken outside the room, and the papers are removed and burned as the participants look on. During that time, many weep. Healing takes place at the sharing of pain, at the nailing of pain, and when smoke rises to heaven to symbolize God receiving and wiping away pain. As one participant said, "As I saw the smoke rising up, I knew God was receiving my pain."[15]

After the burning ceremony, a discussion ensues about God's goodness in the midst of the darkness. The good things which God did through the suffering are written on green flip charts, green being a symbol of life. Steps towards healing are discussed, including various common misconceptions about healing and forgiveness.

Participants also discuss the relationship between forgiveness and justice. Other themes discussed include reconciliation and the free practice of "identification repentance," that is, recognition and acceptance of one's own responsibility and that of one's ethnic group and identifying with it in public repentance.

Day two
The impact of the first day on the individual, his or her family and community life is discussed. Then the group talks about how to deal with detailed issues such as counselling raped church members. Each workshop is facilitated by a mixed ethnic team, united for this effort.

Outcomes

Healing
Participants testify to new understanding of the extent of their wounds. They understand that the consequences of woundedness are normal, even for Christians. Contrary to their earlier beliefs, wounds or bad memories are not sins in themselves. Feelings of anger, fear and sorrow are natural human reactions to loss. There are remarkable stories of people who have experienced healing. The following two stories were gleaned from people testifying in public meetings in Ruhengeri, northwest Rwanda, in August 1998.

ENGINEER HELPS THOSE WHO RUINED HIM

Jean-Baptiste Nemeyabahizi's success was cut short when *interahamwe* rebels blew up his home with hand grenades. By a miracle, he survived, but he was forced to flee to Kigali and then to Zaire. "When I came back in 1994, I found the beautiful house I had built completely destroyed. Then I discovered some people in Kigali had stolen my buildings there and were claiming them as their own. The had even corrupted officials to put their names on the deeds."

Converted to Christianity during his exile in Zaire, Jean-Baptiste knew in theory that he should forgive those who had ruined him. But putting that into practice was another matter! He attended an AEE workshop but still struggled with the idea of forgiving people who were continuing to defraud him of his property.

"We were asked to write the things that hurt us on paper and to nail them on a cross. I did it only because everyone else was doing it. I didn't expect much. Then I was given the hammer. I wasn't really concentrating, and I hit myself hard on the thumb. I cried out, and as I did so, I heard a voice in my heart say, 'Why are you crying? You have hurt your finger, but don't you remember Christ was nailed on the cross because of you and your sins, and for your nation?'"

These words shook him, and at that moment his anger was finally defeated. His decision to forgive left him greatly relieved. He went on to become pastor of a church in Ruhengeri, and he makes a point of welcoming people from both sides of Rwanda's ethnic divide, Hutu and Tutsi, into fellowship.

LOOTERS' SON FINDS DEBT RELIEF

Leonard Hakizimana knows how it feels to have the debt burden removed. During the 1994 genocide, he was living with his grandmother. Taking advantage of the chaos surrounding the mass murders, his father's two new wives joined in the looting of properties that belonged to Tutsi neighbours in Ruhengeri.

As the Tutsi-led Rwanda Patriotic Front advanced across the country, the whole family fled with the mass Hutu exodus into Zaire. When they returned some months later, they had neither possessions nor money. One of the victims of the looting had survived. Antoine Karehe, a Tutsi who had earlier escaped into Zaire to avoid the genocide, tracked down Leonard's father and started a legal action against him to recover the value of the items his wives had taken. The father, realizing he could never raise an amount in excess of 60,000Frw (equivalent to US$200), committed suicide.

The legal burden now fell on Leonard, even though he had not taken part in the looting. "One of my father's wives has five children, the other has four, and I have four of my own," he explains. "How was I going to find this money? There were so many other problems to deal with, but for this one I could see no solution."

At this time he attended the first AEE workshop in Ruhengeri. Struck by messages which emphasized the importance of the Hutu community admitting its sins in the genocide as a prerequisite to national reconciliation, he stood to confess the wrong done by his family.

Leonard visited Antoine Karehe, who received him warmly and even agreed to release him from half the debt that was owed. However hard he tried, though, Leonard could not find money to pay back the rest. Morose and hopeless, he attended a follow-up workshop, where he explained his situation. The result was not at all what he expected. The other participants, Hutu and Tutsi alike, took up a collection. Together, they raised the sum he needed. Then they appointed a pastor from among themselves and sent him off with Leonard to give the money to Antoine.

Antoine now lives in a borrowed house with his wife, who was crippled in their escape to Zaire. He recalls, "After I found they had looted all my property, I was very angry. I vowed that if Leonard's father failed to repay what he owed me, I would put him in prison. But when Leonard came to apologise for his family, I knew that I should forgive him. If others could follow his example, I think all Rwandans could get back together and live in peace. I am really pleased that we can continue living here in Rwanda in harmony."

Leonard himself is overjoyed at what he sees as God's intervention through the help he received at the workshop and through Antoine's generosity. "I felt so relieved when the debt was gone, so full of happiness that I can't express it. I had no solution by myself, and while I had not come to the point of suicide like my father, I might have done if I had had no one to rescue me."

The church renewed as an agent of change

Stories like this put the church back on the road to being a credible agent of change. Some participants have recovered their faith in God. Weeping, one pastor confessed that he had not prayed in years because he was convinced that "God and the killers are one." Now he prays aloud and in his heart, believing God hears his prayer. Another pastor has said, "Before the workshop, my ethnic group was important to me. I did not pick up a machete [in 1994], I did not kill anyone. But in my heart I was a killer. When I was forced to flee to Zaire, I hated the Tutsi. After nailing things to the cross, my heart was relieved. Now I have been healed. I will try to help the Tutsi."[16]

Three salient truths can be drawn from these workshops (which, perchance, are also true for the PDW). First, people will recognize healing when it begins to take place, even if complete healing is a process that will take a lifetime. Second, after healing, people tend to become agents of healing. Third, a healing agent must also be on the road toward healing; healing is the start of reconciliation, not the other way round. People who wish for healing choose to do something about reconciling with their neighbour as a way of demonstrating what has taken place in their lives. They do not tend to get bogged down with ensuring justice has been done first or with who takes the initiative to seek forgiveness.

This is particularly true of pastors who are desperately looking for positive illustrations for sermons. When it is their own story, having gone through this workshop process, their example goes far in the community. Pastors have influence. The senior government officer in Ruhengeri, Rucagu Boniface, wryly observes, "I am sure that if church leaders work at it, we can bring peace to this country. The pastor doesn't need policemen or soldiers! I know a place where the prefet called people to come together and no one came to the stadium. The following day a preacher came and the stadium was packed!"

If the healing process is truly at work in one's life, it can be recognised as an increasing measure of inner peace, restored sleep, a sense of joy, deliverance from haunting memories, a feeling of relief from constant and energy-consuming emotions of fear, anger, hatred and desire for vengeance. Not only family members and neighbours but also the individual's assumed enemies notice and comment on changed attitudes and modified behaviour, and therefore the changes can be objectively identified.

Forgiveness

Perhaps the most important aspect of forgiveness is the willingness to surrender the desire to take revenge, voluntarily giving up the "right" to hate. These workshops demonstrate that this can be done—and that once it *is* done, the way for reconciliation is wide open. This leads to a wider acceptance of personal and common responsibility. It can be acted out by embracing the people representing the other ethnic group. Some participants have asked publicly for forgiveness on behalf of family members or members of their ethnic group who are not willing to do so themselves. In some instances this has even been done on behalf of the dead who committed crimes while alive. This is a powerful symbol of cutting the spell the dead can have on the living. When this is done in the workshops, it creates the will to do it outside as well.

Reconciliation

Through these workshops people adopt the concept, new in the culture, that all Rwandans belong to the same nation regardless of their ethnic and religious differences. They can treat people as individuals rather than assume they are "guilty by association" with their group. They begin to tell an alternative story as they take steps of rapprochement: seeking to interact and to fellowship (to use church terminology) with other groups, religious as well as ethnic. In Ruhengeri, until recently the most insecure place in the country, different church denominations have reactivated a committee for reconciliation and share the same platform to preach a message of unity.

Evaluation and feedback

AEE keeps records of testimonies and feedback from many participants concerning their healing experiences and the impact on their families and communities as they try to practice what they learn at the workshops. A tool has been developed and is being tested to evaluate the short-term and long-term effects of the workshops both at individual and community levels. In the meantime, AEE is training teams of facilitators to run the workshops in communities, prisons, schools and church parishes. The workshops have also been adopted for use by a number of Catholic clergy and religious.

SEVEN LESSONS LEARNED

The AEE workshops have been running for four years now, and PDW for two. There is a lot of similarity in methodology between the secular PDW approach and the Christian healing and reconciliation workshop, despite the fact that the two workshops have been developed independently. Both workshops start with loss; then talk of emotions, feeling and wounds; and both end with forgiveness and justice. Both use the methodology of group processing, writing out painful memories and telling stories in protected spaces. One major difference is on body-memory expression and the handling of written stories. Body-memory expression is less pronounced in the PDW, arising only occasionally when a participant expresses deep emotion; in the AEE workshops, embracing one another is an essential part of the methodology. In the PDW, people write a letter to a loved one, deceased or alive, or to God. They read out these letters to the small groups and keep their letters. In the AEE workshop, participants write out the most painful experiences, nail them on the cross and burn them. In both, the written materials indicate a decision to break with the painful past and start on the road to healing.

There are a number of lessons that can be drawn from these workshops. *The first is that the workshops confirm that nearly all Rwandans are wounded.* To promote meaningful reconciliation, one needs to provide a mechanism to deal with these wounds. Perhaps the most common pitfall of many interventions in CHEs has been to ignore this lesson. People need to grieve and process their traumatic experiences before they can start the journey to reconciliation and forgiveness. Thus there should be a deliberate mechanism to help them to do so. Without this, anything else is a mechanical reaction or simply an academic exercise that stands little chance of success.

The second lesson is that adults on a healing journey have a different story to tell, one that inspires others to build a more tolerant community. These two workshops reveal that the emotional wounds of the Rwandans are far greater than often assumed but not insurmountable. Once people can be moved from scepticism to hope, they are well on the way to healing and reconciliation. If a critical mass can be created of healed and healing people, societal reconciliation will almost inevitably follow. In addition, breaking the cycle of violence in Rwanda necessitates that more effort be given to addressing the trauma needs of children. As one of the most respected Christian leaders has argued, the current generation of adults are not all lost and can indeed be healed, but they perhaps may be too scarred to be the basis for such a new reality.

The third significant lesson arising from these workshops is that not only the Rwandans but the entire international community lost hope in Rwanda. Could this explain the lack of interest on the part of the international community to provide the necessary resources and technical assistance to support healing and reconciliation? Though there are honourable exceptions, governments and donors tend to focus more, with good intentions, on physical rehabilitation. We argue that perhaps this is due to insufficient knowledge or a lack of appreciation of the need to reconstruct the mind as a basis for a more lasting physical rehabilitation.

Granted, proven methodologies which are culturally appropriate are few and far between. To find hope is to have one's strength renewed so that one is more willing and better able to stay engaged with situations for which answers are not obvious. Unfortunately, with the aid of the powerful international media, scepticism about the possibilities for reconciliation are promoted relentlessly, while messages of hope are played down or simply ignored. As Peter Uvin has lamented when reflecting on Rwanda's history, "The development aid system still neglects most of the non-economic aspects of development in favour of a narrow economic-technical approach."[17]

The fourth lesson is that the Rwandans will not easily receive instruction about reconciliation from outsiders. However, those few Rwandans working effective projects can be encouraged and provided with models and resources as well as care to prevent burnout and/or vicarious traumatisation. Rwandans feel that the outside world does not fully understand them and therefore does not and cannot go far enough to reach where they hurt. They, themselves, need to drive this process of healing and reconciliation, and evolve local tools which suit their situation and can lead to a changed history, telling a new but equally valid story—the concept of conflict transformation. They need to look to their ancestors and celebrate the good in them, and local healing initiatives need to be promoted. It is important for Rwandans who are working effectively in reconciliation to "replicate" themselves, that is, to train up and mentor others in Rwanda who can promote healing and reconciliation. The role of the "outsider" may be to help with the development of workable models, work with Rwandans to test them, then leave them to adopt and run with the models.

The fifth lesson is the need to take what is good in the Rwandese culture and build on it. The workshops, for example, have shown how important and powerful rituals, symbols and ceremonies are in engendering healing and reconciliation. The use of the cross has become a very powerful symbol, accepted even outside of church circles (even civic leaders have fully participated in and been helped by the process). Clearly, spiritual ways of addressing healing are valid and effective. The use of small discussion groups is also very similar to community ways of problem solving. The only condition for success is that those who lead the process must have been exposed to it and been positively affected by it. The church can be restored to its effectiveness if it learns this lesson and spends no more emotional energy on the divisions which are currently plaguing it. The church has a much wider role—because Rwandan culture has been heavily influenced by its teaching—than has been exploited so far. No method should be left untried to open this channel of healing.

The sixth lesson is that not everybody is ready to begin the process of healing and reconciliation. There are people who will remain locked in a victim mentality. There will be also extremists, the die-hards who cannot be changed, those who are too hardened by their experiences. But their influence can be minimised by that of the critical mass of healed people who are willing to march forward, an anachronistic few overcome by the law of large numbers. Also, where enough care has not been taken, some people can be left worse off than before they began the process. It is extremely important that every programme of this nature be effectively supported by qualified persons in professions such as counselling, psychology, psychiatry and theology.

The seventh lesson is that the most effective healing workshops are those which are culturally adapted and facilitated by people from both sides of the main ethnic divide. Workshops need to be tailored carefully for the culture in which they are given and, where possible, use a common local language. The team of facilitators should be ethnically balanced to the extent possible, as this models the solution and helps people see that different ethnic groups can work together. The AEE workshops are facilitated by a Hutu, a Tutsi who has never left Rwanda, and a person who has returned from long exile. It is observable that the effort to help people from different sides of a conflict to process their feelings begins to convert negative feelings and energies into positive synergy. By jointly processing the negative, it is easier to tap the positive. People need to recognize their limitations but not be incapacitated by them.[18]

NOTES

[1] Washira George Assefa Hizkias, *Peacemaking and Democratisation in Africa: Theoretical Perspectives and Church Initiatives* (Nairobi: East African Educational Publishers Limited, 1996), 25.

[2] Danielle de Lame, "Understanding Collective Trauma and Healing in Post-Genocide Rwanda," unpublished paper (1996), 5.

[3] Jean Paul Lederach, *Building Peace: Sustainable Reconciliation in Divided Societies* (Washington, D.C.: United States Institute of Peace Press, 1997).

[4] Curt Reintsma, "Hope After Horror in Rwanda," *Front Lines* (September/October 1998).

[5] Warren Nyamugasira, Nigel Marsh and Lincoln Ndogoni, "Equipping Project Staff in Conflict Situations to Be Agents of Positive Developmental Energy," World Vision UK discussion paper no. 6 (Spring 1998), 6.

[6] In this context, "connectors" are activities or approaches that bring about increased connection and interdependency between different groups (see Mary Anderson, *Do No Harm—Supporting Local Capacities for Peace Through Aid* [Cambridge: Collaborative for Development Action, 1996]).

[7] This testimony, given in April 1998, was translated into English from Kinyarwanda. It has been condensed and also lightly edited for clarity and to preserve the anonymity of the author.

[8] "Drawings and Words by Abducted Displaced and Refugee Children in Northern Uganda," *Where Is My Home?: Children in War* (Kampala: AVSI, GUSCO, Red Barnet, UNICEF, World Vision, 1998).

[9] African Rights, "The Protestant Churches and the Genocide: An Appeal to the World Council of Churches' Meeting in Harare," unpublished paper (1998).

[10] Ibid.

[11] Ibid.

[12] African Evangelistic Enterprise, "African Evengelistic Enterprise Healing and Reconciliation Team Activity Description," unpublished paper (September 1998).

[13] Ibid., 6.

[14] Ibid.

[15] African Evangelistic Enterprise, "The Role of the Church in Healing, Forgiveness and Reconciliation: A Three-Year Report," unpublished paper (1997, rev. 1998), 12.

[16] Warren Nyamugasira, "Mending a Shattered People's Lives: Lessons from World Vision's Experience in Rwanda," paper presented at the World Vision International Council, Johannesburg (1–2 September 1998), 4.

[17] Nyamugasira, Marsh, and Ndogoni, "Equipping Project Staff," 6.

[18] The authors are grateful to all participants in the two workshops, who willingly undertook this often painful yet healing process, and to those who shared their testimonies with us. Also acknowledged are the contributions of Nigel Marsh, who compiled the reconciliation stories from Ruhengeri; John Steward, who dared to believe in, steered and documented the work of reconciliation and peacebuilding in World Vision Rwanda during 1997 and 1998; Frank Cookingham, who read through the draft and made valuable suggestions; Josephine Munyeri and Regine Uwibereyeho of World Vision's PDW team and Anastase Sabamungu and Joseph Nyamutera of African Evangelistic Enterprise, who shared their experience in the facilitation of the two workshops. We also thank the following donors for financial support: AusAID, WV Australia, United States, Canada and Taiwan and the Netherlands Government.

8.

Setting the Stage for Resettlement

Tuareg Women's Groups

BRIGETTE DELAY, M. A. HAMALOUTA AND REBECCA DALE

The 1990–96 civil conflict in Mali with its refugee flows to neighbouring countries and extensive internal displacement possesses many characteristics in common with situations that have come be known as complex humanitarian emergencies and lends itself to review when examining appropriate humanitarian response. This chapter documents one WV programme, the Malian Refugee programme (MRP), and its attempts to mitigate various social and economic factors in a refugee crisis by creating opportunities for women's growth and learning. MRP is an example of how a grassroots project targeting women had both a direct impact and a powerful indirect effect on refugees' efforts to rebuild their communities upon return.

Assessing MRP's impact more than two years post-repatriation provides an excellent opportunity to explore issues concerning the balance or mix of relief and development interventions in refugee and return situations, how external assistance can help or hinder, the feasibility of a participatory approach in complex emergencies, the potential for capacity building in refugee situations, and the role of women as agents of change for peace and reintegration.

The Malian situation exhibited a complex system of interlocking forces and players, of which assistance formed an integral part.

"In non-linear systems, small inputs can lead to dramatically large consequences."[1] From this comes the potential for assistance to have large positive and large negative effects. MRP appears to have been a project that found one of the critical points of leverage for useful interventions. This chapter considers how and why. A major difficulty we faced was isolating the effect of the project from the many factors that affect people's lives and coping strategies. In a complex conflict environment, this becomes even more difficult. Our assessment methodology using participatory techniques focused on the refugees and their communities and how they perceived the impact of the project and the ways their lives have changed due to the humanitarian emergency.

The chapter is divided into five sections. The first section gives an overview of the Malian crisis. The second section describes the project. The third section discusses methodology used in the study. The fourth section outlines findings on the direct and indirect impact of the project and the reintegration assistance environment. Finally, a fifth section makes recommendations and points out programming implications for field workers, organisations and donors.

OVERVIEW OF THE MALIAN CRISIS

The Malian conflict and displacement of 1990–96 was the culmination of many years of attrition in the North. Three principal causes have been cited: a one-party centralised government, which marginalised the North from development and the political process; a series of droughts creating economic hardship and mass migration; and unwarranted military force towards civilians. In order to understand the context WV was working in—and its beneficiaries are facing now—each of these is discussed below.

Historically marginalised from development and political process

The North of Mali was the seat of ancient empires, a focal point of the great trans-Sahara trade routes. Its prestige faded with time and most sharply with the modern world. Isolated from the South both physically and mentally, light-skinned Tuareg and Moor clans lived a traditional life as semi-nomads and nomads, resisting any form of centralised government. Northern populations did not demand or want to be part of what they saw as a colonial agenda.

Following Mali's independence in 1960 and the dictatorships of Keita and Traore, Northerners continued to be marginalised as the South continued the tradition of non-development in the North. Representation of Northerners in national and regional government was symbolic at best. There existed few schools and health facilities. The North remained isolated in terms of communication and difficult to access by road. A feeling among Northerners was that Southerners had now replaced the French as foreign occupiers.

Systemic economic collapse and prolonged food insecurity

Overall, Mali is one of the poorest countries in the world, ranking 174 out of 175 in the Human Development Index for 1998. The desert North, where life is highly vulnerable to climatic conditions, is one of the poorest regions of the country. In 1973 and again in 1984 serious droughts devastated Tuareg herds, destroying and crippling Tuareg economic capital. Traditional livelihoods collapsed, leaving families without animals and with few alternatives to generate income. Famine and high levels of malnutrition were reported.

With the increased poverty during the 1970s and 1980s, traditional survival mechanisms were overwhelmed. Thousands of young men migrated to neighbouring countries, including Algeria, Niger and Libya, in search of work. Disillusioned, many hired themselves out as mercenaries and were influenced by the spirit of rebellion. In the late 1980s, many young men returned to Mali eager to organise their own political movements declaring a free North.

Ethnic violence and flight

In June 1990, a newly formed Malian rebel group launched an attack on a government building to release four imprisoned comrades. Two days later, rebels killed two black farmers. Shocked by the direct attack on innocent civilians, the government reacted swiftly and brutally. A violent campaign by the Malian military began. Indiscriminate killing of light-skin nomads took place throughout the North. The military made no distinction between rebels and civilians, or between Tuaregs and Moors. Moors had not been involved in the rebel movement until after they were attacked during this period of reprisal. This violence fuelled more violence.

Tuareg and Moor communities began to flee the attacks. Most people scattered piecemeal, some in groups. The rich who still had herds were more able to vanish into the desert, surviving off their animals. Others sought refuge in the neighbouring countries of Mauritania, Algeria and Burkina Faso. An estimated 250,000 people were displaced, as refugees or within the country—about one-third of the Northern population and two-thirds of the Tuareg/Moor community. As a politically unglamorous conflict unfolded, these new refugees drew little international attention. A 1991 coup d'etat overthrew Moussa Traore's 23-year dictatorship, and a transition government made a commitment to building a new democratic government in Mali. Despite the new leadership, the North remained unstable for half a decade. Insecurity paralysed the region. Small-scale attacks by rebels against the government and counter-attacks against Tuareg and Moors continued. Loosely organised, rebels often acted more as bandits than as a political front. In 1994, frustrated by on-going insecurity, the Sonhrai farmers' movement known as GandaKoy, or "masters of the earth," began attacking Tuareg and Moor civilians in retaliation. Ethnic tension heightened the conflict to the brink of full-scale civil war.

Peace and return

A crucial turning point in the Malian conflict came in 1995, when the democratically elected government appointed a new minister of defence and put a more disciplined army in the North. This gave rebel leadership a new incentive to engage in discussion. As the divided rebel front continued to create havoc, one arm of the rebellion reconciled with GandaKoy. At the same time, the Malian government began efforts to integrate leaders and civil servants back into the government. In effect, the disorganised rebellion had lost touch with its civilian population, and civilian leadership began to push for peace. This was a remarkable period. As politicians ironed out details, communities began the process of reconciliation, and refugees began to consider going home. Grassroots movements conducted hundreds of community meetings to discuss the nuts and bolts of peace. Civil society played a major role in peacekeeping efforts. By 1996, all rebel groups had signed the National Pact, government efforts to integrate into civil service and military were under way, and the refugees began to return home.

The challenge of peace

The multiple tensions and their complex interactions, which caused the conflict, are still present to an extent, and limited banditry, such as hijacking cars, continues. "The question we are all asking is 'Will the peace hold firm?' The answer to this question is largely economic, depending partly on decentralisation and good governance, partly on annual rainfall and the river levels, and partly on the economy, and the relaunching of the North."[2]

The dramatic events of the 1970s through the 1990s confronted the Tuaregs' ancient way of life and inevitably resulted in remarkable change in the Tuareg and Moor communities. Exile fundamentally altered Tuareg culture and social norms. Leadership was challenged, refugees learned new skills, and children began to attend school. Many nomads experienced a more sedentary lifestyle and "community living" for the first time. This experience dramatically changed the Tuareg communities' priorities. MRP played a small but significant role in helping one group of women refugees in Mauritania play an active part in rebuilding their futures.

THE MALIAN REFUGEE PROGRAMME (MRP)

Laying the foundation

To flee persecution, more than 55,000 Tuareg and Moor civilians from the Timbuktu/Mopti region took refuge in south-eastern Mauritania in 1991. The first years in exile were harsh. With no international presence and minimal support from the Mauritanian government, the refugees survived by pulling together limited family resources, working as manual labourers and selling off their animals. In areas of concentrated settlement, there was little potable water, no public sanitation, no health services and no support for food assistance. In 1992, a measles epidemic killed hundreds, finally bringing the refugee situation to the attention of the international community. The United Nations High Commissioner for

Refugees (UNHCR) opened an office in the Bassikounou region providing and co-ordinating basic assistance, such as food aid, medical assistance and shelter. WV also opened a short-term emergency project to address high levels of malnutrition and rebuild animal stocks.

By 1994, under the co-ordination of UNHCR, four NGOs provided basic services in primary health care, education, community development and logistical support. For the most part, UNHCR and its implementing partners' interventions focused on large-scale assistance with little emphasis on development-oriented or gender-sensitive programming. To address this gap, UNHCR requested the International Catholic Migration Commission (ICMC) to initiate a small-scale project exclusively targeting women. A seed grant of US$50,000 was earmarked to assess, design and implement a programme. As a preliminary step, an exploratory study provided a basic overview of women's social and economic situation. Two major problems emerged among the women: the need to take on new responsibilities as money-makers and, in many cases, heads of households (some men were absent fighting in the conflict; others had stayed with remaining herds in the desert); and women's feelings of isolation, boredom and depression. Based on this information, ICMC focused its efforts on developing a technical skills and small-business training programme to assist women in their efforts to cope in exile.

Needs assessment

In August 1994, ICMC conducted an intensive needs assessment to prepare for the project. Three basic tools were used: a written survey conducted at the quartier (section) level; informal interviews with community groups, refugee leaders and individuals; and ongoing observation by the ICMC community staff while in the field. The survey was used to inventory women's education backgrounds, skills levels and aspirations for support. It was also used as a springboard for discussion on other important programming issues.

During this process, staff began to learn about women's frustrations and their complaints regarding the politicisation and lack of sustainability of past projects in the camps. Women interviewed provided concrete programming advice. Recommendations included maximising accessibility to services for women through decentralisation and organising the women on a quartier level, not a camp level, to avoid conflicts between different groups in the camps (both ethnic and nomadic clans.) Special care in avoiding community politics was key to future programme success. During the assessment period, women and men who represented all layers of the refugee community were consulted. These included formal leaders, informal leaders, housewives and youth. By cross-checking information at this early stage, the planning process was depoliticised.

Programme design

Based on the assessment results, skills training and small-business training programmes for women were designed. Three community training centres were established to teach two marketable skills, cloth dyeing and sewing. Sewing was selected based on popular request. Cloth dyeing was selected as an experiment based on informal feasibility studies. The brightly patterned cloth of Mauritanian style, which the refugees learned to produce, had high fashion value for the Malian women and there was a large market for it in the camps.

The original vision of the women's project was to use the centres as a training ground. ICMC started with the two skills but planned on incorporating others later. The staff recognised the importance of preparing women as business people, not just producers, and an integrated programme, including training in a marketable skill, functional literacy/numeracy and small business training was outlined. The last two components were not implemented until the second year.

Development approach in a relief setting

During this early planning period (June-July 1994), the refugee situation was still technically treated as an "emergency" by UNHCR. No long-term planning interventions were under way. ICMC staff chose to take a strong grassroots approach in all phases of the project cycle. This decision was grounded in the belief that refugees should be involved in their own programming. Developmental participatory grass-roots techniques—often seen as inappropriate or impossible in emergency settings—can actually be very effective.

As this grassroots approach was distinctly different from that of other agencies working in the camps, project staff dedicated time and effort to discuss ICMC's philosophy of self-reliance. Process-oriented development focused on building human capacity was paramount to the MRP approach. For the majority of refugees who had been isolated from development assistance in the past, this was a new and misunderstood way of working; refugees often expected handouts and quick and tangible project results. Consequently, staff maintained an on-going educational role with community members to explain the difference between programmes which stress self-reliance and participation[3] and traditional emergency assistance which often prescribed projects and only required passive or symbolic community participation. Over the project's two-year life, efforts continued to explain this "development" logic to refugee leaders and community members as grounding for each programming decision.

Staff's constant day-to-day contact with the refugee communities was crucial to programme success. This began to build trust and confidence between the NGO and the refugees. It provided refugees on-going opportunities to discuss their concerns with staff in both a formal and informal manner. The NGO was learning about the refugees and building relations with the leaders and women. The community also had a chance to learn about an NGO which focused on a two-way partnership with clearly defined roles and a high degree of motivation and commitment from refugees to participate in the project.

Training refugee women to train others

In consultation with the women leaders, 13 refugee women were recruited from the camps to be para-professional trainers in each of the three centres. The centre trainers were intensively trained over a three-month period at the ICMC office by a Mauritanian expert. They also received basic training in adult education techniques and lesson planning. At the end of the training, each candidate was required to pass a technical exam.

Organising women's groups and selection of beneficiaries

During the training of trainers, project staff began organising the women in the 121 quartiers[4] in the three camps. Women were

invited to organise in groups of 8–10. The only criterion for becoming a group was that the members had to be motivated to work
together. All women were encouraged to participate, and each
quartier was able to organise as many groups as desired. Groups
then self-selected one of their members to train at the centre. Each
group representative trained was prepared to return to her group
as a group trainer. The idea was to create a domino or ripple effect,
where a skill base was built within the refugee community and
passed down from the centre to the groups to each individual group
member.

As the centres could initially accept only 30 groups, all candidates' names were put into a hat and a drawing by a neutral party
was conducted in public in front of candidates and leaders. To avoid
conflict, the decision of who would have access to training was not
given to the refugee population. This was a conscious program-
matic decision related to the complex community dynamics in the
three camps. Groups who were not selected were given priority for
future space in the programme. Strategies such as this were used
consistently to avoid politicising assistance.

Once group trainers completed their programme, they returned
to their groups to train fellow members. Each group was given a
one-time material grant, valued at US$150, to begin its training.
This small grant consisted of basic start-up materials and enough
primary materials to conduct training at the group level. In turn, to
move the groups towards a functional business, each group was
required to manage available resources and raise approximately
US$50 for additional start-up costs. In most cases, the investment
money was raised by selling a portion of their food rations.[5] Centre
trainers also conducted outreach to groups to provide technical
advice and guidance.

Small-business skills

Despite original project plans to initiate a small-business training
programme, literacy and numeracy with the skills training, this
component of the project was not developed until after WV assumed responsibility for the project. This was mainly due to capacity issues and difficulty in recruiting a strong small-business project
officer/literacy expert. Despite these setbacks, by May 1995 an
initial staff of nine refugees were recruited and trained as small

enterprise development (SED) agents. SED agents provided out-reach support to more than 30 women's groups, providing infor-mal advice on group organisation, marketing and management.

A new emphasis on reintegration

WV assumed responsibility for the MRP from ICMC in June 1995 and committed to raising 50 percent of programme costs. ICMC was instrumental in facilitating a smooth transition of project staff and resources. Even before ICMC's closure, several joint initiatives with WV were conducted. This included training field staff in Par-ticipatory Rural Appraisal (PRA) and Rapid Rural Appraisal (RRA) techniques and a preliminary mid-term project evaluation. With-out this inter-agency co-operation, the project would have suffered unnecessary delays and a possible shift in focus. A majority of the original staff stayed on, facilitating project continuity.

Based on the preliminary mid-term project evaluations, WV fo-cused on refining ICMC's work. To do this, WV management staff organised a three-day workshop for all staff members to review mission, approach, project goals and objectives. The team defined its new field mission as promoting "economic security and per-sonal dignity of the community to ensure peaceful reintegration." The focus on reintegration was in direct response to the improving political situation between the Malian government and the rebels. With stability established in the North, refugees began to consider returning home. Unlike many mission statements, this common vi-sion symbolised more than a programme foundation: it was a firm commitment by WV managers to be as participatory on an organisational level as on the field level.

Although there was no dramatic change in specific programme activities as a result of WV's review, there was a distinct difference in project planning and a new vitality. A project which aimed to build self-reliance in the refugee setting and WV's new effort to build cross-border sustainability through human capacity building affected staff's attitude and outlook. Newfound enthusiasm to teach women essential skills that would help them during the reintegra-tion period spread among the staff, 75 percent of whom were refu-gees.

With an eye towards Mali, staff outlined four primary areas of intervention:

1. *Technical skills training:* Based on project evaluations, it was noted that substandard products had a direct impact on the marketability of women's products. As a result, centre trainers were offered a one-month refresher course. Trainers then organised a retraining for group members and their trainers. Twelve new groups were also trained.

2. *Small-business and enterprise development:* Traditionally, women had limited exposure to running businesses or managing money. This lack of business experience was compounded by women's extremely low level of literacy and numeracy.[6] Recognising the integral role of literacy to future small-business success, training was offered in small-enterprise development (SED) and functional literacy/numeracy.

SED training was a combination of classroom activities carried out at the training centres and interaction between group members and the SED agents at the quartier level. Activities were originally split into two levels, beginning and advanced. Literacy and numeracy classes were also organised into three distinct levels. Due to lack of resources, space in the literacy classes was limited to just over 200 women. Interest surpassed availability, and women often waited outside the classroom hoping to gain a space. A substantial amount of time and effort was committed to recruiting and training of staff and developing a training curriculum. This time spent on start-up activities (and the unanticipated premature closure of MRP) inevitably compromised the programme's impact. Training in these two critical areas was limited to teaching only the most elementary knowledge of business, literacy and numeracy.

3. *Building a professional refugee staff with participatory expertise:* Due to years of insufficient assistance in the northern regions of Mali prior to the conflict, only a small pool of qualified development workers existed among the Tuareg and Moor communities. MRP staff who were recruited from the refugee community had little to no development experience. Most commonly, refugee employees hired were former primary schoolteachers and the few literate women in the camps. Within WV's new framework of a reintegration programme, staff training was not only a means to ensure quality programming in the camps, but also a means to prepare professional development workers. WV recognised the staff's potential role in future efforts to reconstruct the North. Consequently, WV outlined an objective focused on professional development for

its staff. This included basic training in development principles, training in RRA/PRA, technical skills in sector work (SED, literacy), adult education techniques and teaching methodology, curriculum development, evaluation skills and project planning/management for refugee management staff. In total, over 40 refugee staff were trained.

RRA/PRA played a particularly important role in staff training and project definition. In effect, staff were given concrete tools, not just ideas, to conduct participatory work. In addition, RRA/PRA methodology reflected the project's philosophy through its implicit message, which stresses validation and respect for local knowledge. By using this methodology in all aspects of field work, the staff (the majority of whom were men or educated) witnessed illiterate women acting as full participants with valuable ideas and comments. This had tremendous impact on staff's underlying assumptions and attitudes concerning the uneducated and women. PRA transformed the staff's perceptions of women's ability as much as it transformed women's self-image.

4. *Attempting to ensure sustainability through cross-border linkages:* To assist MRP graduates start their business once they returned to their homes, MRP developed a cross-border assistance strategy for returnees. On a programming level, this included distributing basic start-up kits of hard-to-find material to each group, compiling a profile/tracking sheet of each group with group members' addresses in Mali, and providing NGOs in Mali with basic baseline data on existing groups. This was complemented with an effort to engage agencies working in Mali in MRP's efforts. In February 1996, the first cross-border trip was arranged. The purpose of this trip was to identify potential working partners among Mali-based NGOs. Each agency was informed of the project, its approach and the need to continue building women's capacities as business people.

To further the cross-border effort, MRP sponsored a meeting for Malian NGOs in the camp in April 1996. Twenty-two agencies participated, including UNHCR Mauritania (UNHCR Mali did not participate). Participating NGOs agreed to create an inter-agency co-ordination mechanism in Mali, agreeing in principle that refugee staff currently working for NGOs in the camps played a major role as an institutional memory and should be recruited to work with NGOs in the North of Mali. WV negotiated with participating organisations (including WV Mali) about continuing MRP's effort. Although several agencies were interested, by the end of the project there was no direct commitment. WV Mali, already active in another region in the North, decided not to expand its national programme to the Timbuktu region.

Premature closure and funding difficulties

By September 1995, most agencies' programmes shifted towards preparing for the repatriation effort. This translated into a devaluing of programmes such as MRP. In funders' minds, it was time to return to basic care and shift efforts and resources to the other side of the border. WV staff, however, recognised the tremendous opportunity to manage a repatriation programme situated in the camps. For instance, to complement standard repatriation kits given to refugees (food, tents, cooking supplies), WV provided groups with skills kits that would allow them to restart production when they returned home.

MRP now had two primary challenges. First, so departing groups could benefit, training was broken down into tight modules, each of which could be completed in a short period, not exceeding 10 days. Second, MRP tried to persuade UNHCR and other donors to provide support until basic training courses were completed. MRP argued that by providing women with basic skills, the programme would facilitate the women's reintegration. The women themselves saw their participation in such programmes as a direct factor in preparing for their return.

After unsuccessful attempts to secure funding for a 12-month programme, MRP changed tactics, asking donors to fund a programme which could "close well." Six-month "emergency" funding was finally secured after much direct advocacy with donors. This funding allowed staff to complete a first cycle of literacy for more than 200 women and a 10-day course on basic business skills for 1,000 women. Second-level courses were cut due to lack of funds. MRP closed in May 1996.

METHODOLOGY TO ASSESS THE IMPACT
OF MRP FOLLOWING RETURN

Did MRP accomplish its goal of promoting economic security and personal dignity of the community to ensure peaceful reintegration?

This question motivated the research team to conduct a case study two years post-return. This seven-day field study provided a unique opportunity for WV to gain insight into how a project such as MRP can affect a refugee community upon return.

A team of three people with different skills and levels of participation in the project formulated the study.[7] As in the camps, the research team used RRA as its research method. This was adapted to initiate what the team referred to as Rapid Reintegration Appraisal. Four sites were selected for research: Timbuktu City, as an example of women returning and working in an urban site, and three settlements in the Timbuktu region. The majority of women participating in MRP had resettled in this and the Mopti region. The three rural sites were small, averaging 300 settled habitants, and were fairly isolated from commercial centres. Each community was semi-nomadic.

The researchers agreed that the reintegration assistance available was an important mitigating factor in the women's efforts to rebuild their lives, so the primary criteria for site selection focused on access and the type of assistance for small-business development for women (material/money grants *vs.* credit). Using UNHCR's site profile sheets as an information base, the first site of Zin Zin was selected because it fell into an assistance gap and received little or no aid (Zin Zin was situated between two agency working zones). The second site, Gargando, was selected because it had received a large amount of assistance in the form of money grants. The last site, Tangata, was selected because it had been one of the few places which had received credit and outreach support.

The team was in each site for two days and used four standard RRA tools:

- ♦ a historical profile of the community's experience before, during and after flight (conducted with the site chief and settlement elders on arrival);
- ♦ a historical composite calendar of needs, production, resources and assistance since return (conducted in large groups of men and women, with much intracommunity debate);
- ♦ a matrix of women's activities before, during and after their refugee experience (conducted with women only);
- ♦ semi-structured interviews with former MRP participants, women who had not participated and community resource members.

Each tool was used to explore the reintegration phase and the impact of the project. This approach engaged the whole community and was key to establishing a context for our analysis.

In Timbuktu, the research team was able to conduct semi-structured interviews with two groups (20 women in total actively working as cloth dyers and tailors) and to construct a Venn diagram on socioeconomic relationships with representatives of 13 active MRP groups (about 40 women). Both Moor and Tuareg women were consulted.

The team recognised the field research as an extension of the work done in the camps and the philosophy of MRP. We decided to start directly with the population (following identification of the sites) and only as a second step to meet with representatives of agencies working in the Timbuktu region. This was to avoid a predominantly agency perspective of the situation. UNHCR, NGOs and government offices were consulted after the field research was conducted.[8] Findings in this case study reflect the refugees' perspective of their own reintegration.

FINDINGS

To assess how the MRP had fulfilled its mission of promoting economic security and personal dignity of the community to ensure their peaceful reintegration, the team focused on five areas:

- direct impact related to original MRP programme objectives, including whether women were able to start businesses using their technical skills;
- indirect impact of MRP, including whether MRP had helped women in their reintegration efforts and the impact on women's roles and self-perception;
- impact of the training of refugee staff;
- impact of cross-border work; and
- assistance environment upon return.

Viewing the women as part of a social system which they influence and which influences them, the researchers studied women's role in the reintegration process as members of a community, not in isolation.

Direct impact of MRP

MRP essentially prepared women to produce, organise and manage, and our findings on the direct impact of the programme have been synthesised into those categories:

Women as producers

Women's ability to continue practising cloth dyeing and tailoring as small businesses showed a strong correlation to their ability to access commercial centres, their organisational ability, availability of complete start-up kits (machines, gloves, dyes) and their ability to take risks.

In Timbuktu, team members visited several active cloth-dyeing groups.[9] Key to these women's success was their ability to access money grants, primary materials and a strong client base. An expatriate volunteer representing the embassy also played a key role in assisting the women.

Once groups were established, women secured local, tourist and international markets. In the Venn diagram exercise, women showed important socioeconomic ties to Niger, Algeria and Mauritania. Several groups often worked together to fill bulk orders from Niger (up to 200 veils). Although most women participated in these activities on a part time basis (due to their traditional family responsibilities), on average they earned $10–$14 a month. This gave them some financial independence and enabled them to purchase needed personal and family items. As a very scarce skill among Tuareg and Moor women prior to flight due to its "dirty nature," there was a fairly open market for those willing to break tradition.[10]

A surprising finding was that the large majority of the groups had changed profile considerably upon return. Although groups were self-selected in the camps, upon return most groups split and settled in several sites. In the three groups interviewed in Timbuktu, it was the group trainer who took the initiative to form a new group and trained new women after her return. Many new members included women who were in exile in Algeria and Burkina Faso and/or internally displaced. The team also learned of one woman who did not participate in MRP while she was in the camps, but upon return searched out a former trainer to learn cloth dyeing. Later, when she relocated to another site, she recruited eight new group members, built a workshop and is earning on average $20 a month.

The domino effect is continuing even after return, and new networks are being set up.

In contrast to the city women's experience, women living in the three settlement sites visited were not actively practising either skill. Several factors were cited by the women, including lack of start-up materials, difficulty in securing primary materials and a high degree of risk in an unknown market. Some women were practising the skills on an individual or sporadic basis. Most MRP participants outside the commercial area were involved in new activities, most commonly community stores and production of leather goods for sale, for which they used the business skills and experience learned in MRP.

Woman as organisers

"One twig cannot make an enclosure," as one women's group noted, using a Tuareg proverb. Women cited their experience of working in a group as one of MRP's most valuable contributions in their efforts to rebuild their lives. Prior to exile, women traditionally worked individually, producing items mainly for family use. In the camps, this changed. Survival strategies required individuals to pool resources to meet basic needs. This was particularly the case during the first 18 months in the camps, when no international assistance was available. Despite this new motivation to work in groups, women had little experience of it and many of the women's early initiatives floundered. Community leaders interviewed during the study noted that former MRP participants, however, showed a certain level of sophistication regarding organisational ability.

When asked why group work was so important in rebuilding efforts, women commonly cited three concrete advantages: (1) *A new sense of group solidarity.* As one women stated, "Before, I was alone and scared; now I feel I can do anything." (2) *Safety net.* In the groups visited (including alternative businesses supported by former MRP participants), cash boxes were used as a source of credit to members. (3) *External support.* Organising in groups helped women access external support.[11]

Women as businesswomen and managers
The research team found that most women who had participated

in the MRP had some notion of small-business management; the transfer of functional skills, however, has been piecemeal.

On a basic level, women benefited from their SED consultations and training. One significant change was that women are now actively searching out markets and approaching new ones. This has not only improved their income-earning potential, but also increased their exposure to new groups of people. In addition, most women are able to calculate the value of their work. This is particularly true in the commercial sites, where women tend to have a keener sense of selecting profitable items and marketing. They have also been able to transfer their knowledge of concepts into other areas, although illiteracy remains a strong obstacle. The project had not developed a system of bookkeeping for illiterate women. As a result, many women still relied on men for assistance in this area.

Indirect impact:
Changing voices, changing roles, changing communities

Individual empowerment
When asked why skills learnt in MRP had been useful during reintegration, women stressed their mental liberation and empowerment. MRP had taught them how to learn and had given them a "taste for work." This was a significant cultural shift; traditionally, leisure had been prized over work.

Impact on the household
Women explained that the economic power due to the new skills allows them to have a much greater influence in family decision-making; before, all decisions were made by men in the household. Women now have a sense of autonomy and credibility, and greater ability to assist the family in these times of hardship. And through their economic power, women have greater negotiating power.

Changing priorities
What women want for themselves, their families and their communities has changed as a result of the refugee experience, exposure to health and education services and participation in projects such as MRP. One of the most remarkable changes noted by the team is that women now see themselves as doers and learners. One said,

"Before, all we wanted for our daughters was that they get fat and ready for marriage and then have children. Now we have the spirit of development in our minds."

Women now place a tremendous importance on education for their daughters and themselves. In the past, formal education was not a priority for the Tuareg community, particularly for girls. Now the three communities we visited are participating in a community school programme and enrolment is high. Women are also seeking education for themselves to improve further their economic capacity and status.

Although MRP cannot claim credit for this dramatic new push for education and health services, it surely played a small role in redefining women's priorities.

Changing communities

Women now have higher credibility and therefore more of a voice in their communities. This change was noted and recognised as positive in all the meetings held during the evaluation (with single-sex and mixed groups). Economic hardship has been pivotal in changing the status of women. MRP helped some women while in Mauritania prepare to assume their new role. In Gargando and Tangata, women noted that now there is not a community assembly or meeting at which they are not represented. They believe they now have decision-making power. The experience of being businesswomen, and the feeling of empowerment and self-worth they gained both as individuals and as groups, are critical factors in strengthening and shaping their voice.

This is not to say that the effect of this has been uniform, or that there is no further progress to be made. The women themselves recognise there is a long way to go, and some are preparing to continue.

In giving a concrete example of how women have affected community decision-making, the president of the women's association in Gargando said, "On the return, the male family heads did not know where to start, they were overwhelmed. It was the women who took the first decisions and prioritised the school and mosque." When asked why the women had this role, two factors were cited. First, they had begun preparing for return in the camps, choosing to emphasize three areas: education, health care and social mobilisation. The second factor was that the women trained by MRP are much more open, aware and motivated to work together for development and have discovered ways of organising which they did not know before as communities. This was cited as a critical factor in moving communities forward, since former community structures had to be adapted to the new context. The ripple effect of the MRP programme and the way in which it engaged its beneficiaries (women, the refugee staff and the local leadership) and the tools this partnership gave them are being felt throughout the community.

MRP contributing development workers to the reintegration process

A significant number of women trainers have continued with their activities and have started groups, often involving women who were not in the original programme. One woman in Timbuktu even offers training courses for which women pay her. The training of refugee women as trainers for the other women was seen as essential to the sustainability and integrity of the project. Current activity levels of these women are a testament to the ability of trainers to continue affecting a large number of lives.

In addition to continuing as trainers, a number of women trainers who had minimal education are now themselves development workers in NGOs. This, for women whose traditional role was focused totally on the home, is a major change. Without their MRP training they would be unable to get these jobs.

Of the 40 refugee staff employed by MRP, many gained a position with a development agency upon their return. Returnee involvement in the planning and implementation of reintegration programmes (through staffing them) is an important part of ensuring Tuareg involvement in the development process.

Former MRP employees influenced the reintegration process as representatives of NGOs but also as community members. These professionals have acted as inside educators. They have become advocates for sustainable development.

The approach and methods taught by MRP and the training curriculum developed by technical staff continue to be used by field agents back home. One local NGO formed by former staff uses the

MRP literacy curriculum. During the study, a former camp leader, in collaboration with a number of former MRP staff members, showed the team a complete project document for a local NGO they are trying to set up, which is modelled after MRP.

Overall, MRP has succeeded in its third project goal of creating a new cadre of professional Tuareg and Moor development workers. This required an intensive focus on staff development, a central tenet of the MRP programme.

Impact of cross-border work

Although cross-border work informed a number of agencies of MRP's work in general, it did not lead to an optimum transfer of information and continuity back in Mali. This lack of information about, and relationships with, the returnees is a constraint on those who want to work with them. In this vacuum, agencies have looked where they can for the limited information available.

Informational continuity

The team found that MRP certificates have become a passport for assistance, playing an important role in signalling credibility to agencies seeking beneficiaries. All the women the team interviewed had carefully guarded and protected their certificates. This is, for many of them who are illiterate, the only certificate of training/ education they have. Still, some agencies have relied on the certificate too heavily. They have placed too high expectations on the business skills of the women, without having the necessary information about what the certificates denote or the resources for their own monitoring and follow-up.

Organisational continuity

Perhaps the ideal would have been for WV to cross the border with the community it had been working with; there were, however, capacity constraints on this. Staff who had been on the project for three years wanted to move on. WV Mali was not focused on the continuation of this work from another country office. The effectiveness of cross-border work was limited, as it was not an organisational priority or a priority for other organisations, including UNHCR. Systems were not in place to facilitate this cross-border approach, and putting them in place from scratch was difficult and time-consuming.

Impact of the reintegration assistance environment

The women and their communities are undergoing a further transition from the relative stability and norms built up during camp life to the task of reintegrating with the changed economic, social and environmental realities of their homeland. One of these changed realities is the way in which international assistance is given to the community; this was identified as a particularly important variable during the vulnerable period following return. Expectations of assistance have also changed.

The women and the agencies interviewed repeatedly emphasised that returnee women's success in continuing small-business activities depends on the overall assistance environment. Robin-Edward Poulton and Ibrahim ag Youssouf state that it is not large-scale, big-money projects that lead to reintegration, but rather "the small-scale, long-term grassroots development projects that will help the development of the North."[12] MRP built on, complemented and was crucially different from other types of assistance in the camp setting because other needs—such as food security—were already being met by other programmes. How different the current assistance environment is from that of MRP, and why, is an important consideration for assessing the impact of MRP. This has direct implications for project sustainability and usefulness in the overall context.

The research team came in at an important transition time; the initial reintegration programme co-ordinated by UNHCR was winding up operations. US Aid for International Development (USAID) is now a main funder for the North; its criteria for NGOs to receive assistance have been very different from those of UNHCR, which focused on large-scale, emergency reintegration projects. USAID has shifted the focus to development. The team looked at the impact of the initial reintegration assistance environment for the first two years following return, a period when agencies are trying to programme for the future.

The team found that the original MRP goals of self-reliance, partnership, ownership by the beneficiaries, development and women's empowerment have been difficult for women and their communities to sustain within the narrow reintegration-assistance environment. Paradoxically perhaps, we found that while MRP provided a passport for access to assistance for some of the women, this assistance has actually hindered them in some ways.

Focus on distributing funds rather than project follow-up and partnership

As frequently mentioned by the women and their communities, "It is not just about us being given money." Some women were actually ready for credit but received instead unwieldy levels of funding. Women's groups are now receiving thousands of dollars, as opposed to the small funding of MRP. Given their level of business training and experience, it is much harder for the women to cope with these sums.

The communities themselves recognise the shortcomings of this approach and are asking for greater support in terms of follow-up and evaluation. Women repeatedly identified their lack of education as a major constraint and were eager for follow-up training. Recognising that they need further training and that the projects should be carefully monitored, many interviewees suggested that some form of outside accountability be established until the skills are more internalised.

Political partnership as opposed to community and programming partnership

It might be supposed that in the post-emergency phase of reintegration there would be time for greater consultation with the community. However, the communities the team spoke with have not found this to be the case. They say they were consulted more often and had greater partnership, technical support and monitoring with camp-based agencies, in particular WV and MRP, during the refugee phase. Agencies such as UNHCR and GTZ attest that they have consulted the community. Where does this gap in perception come from, and how is the community-agency partnership different from that of MRP?

Many agencies working in the North appear to consider participation as consulting with traditional power structures and have given money directly to those structures, decentralising the use of funds without much technical participation. This creates a very different type of partnership than that under MRP. People complained that now money is given directly to the head of the satellite office for distribution within the community without consultations with the community and concerned groups within it. Political links are of course important, but in addition there should be some form of substantive partnership with the grassroots, not only with the formal leadership structures.

Mix, timing and sequencing of assistance

The women noted that continuing small-business activities requires a degree of stability and assurance that their families' basic needs are being met. Without this, women are not able to focus on money-making schemes requiring some degree of investment and risk. Instead, they must be part of an overall community strategy to survive in the short term. In the camps, a degree of food security allowed women to engage in new activity. This has had a major impact on the new businesswomen's decisions.

The timing and mix of assistance as part of coping strategies is key for communities to be able to engage in activities that can promote economic security. The initial emphasis on food security by UNHCR was an important contributing factor to stability on return. However, timing and mix have not been appropriate throughout this period for beneficiaries. For instance, the communities in all three sites explained that their most vulnerable time is the season of Ishasha, during which they have lowest resources and highest needs. During this critical period, they received little or no assistance, since this is when agencies and NGOs are closed for the holidays.[13] Sometimes communities received assistance at the wrong times; for example, seeds arrived in one of the settlements after the planting period. Occasionally the assistance itself was inappropriate. Implements which are not useable take up valuable storage space. During the discussions, it became clear that communities distinguish between the *quantity* of assistance they have received and its *quality;* they appreciate valuable and well-timed assistance.

Simple assessment exercises, such as those used by MRP, highlight periods of vulnerability for the community and what kind of assistance would be appropriate when. These nomadic and semi-nomadic communities, used to living in a highly vulnerable situation, very dependent on climate and seasons, are fully aware of these periods and have their own coping strategies—gathering wild fruits, stocking up food and products for sale, migrating to provide seasonal labour, borrowing from other families—which assistance could support and complement.

Impact of the current approach to reintegration

There is some evidence that the developmental building blocks transmitted by projects such as MRP are being undermined by the approach to aid during the two years following return. A representative of a development NGO trying to start community development work with women's groups said, "We are having to spend all our time with communities unlearning what people have been taught in the emergency phase since coming home."

Gains made in a project like MRP are fragile. The women have not had a long period in which to practice their skills and build on them. As one community leader noted, "What you did in the camps would have taken 10 years out here, but it can be undone very quickly, and that process has started."

Constraints on agencies

In focusing on the assistance environment, we also tried to discuss why, with agencies and others, the short-term approach appears to have been the norm. The following constraints on effective reintegration programming—common to many emergency reintegration phases—were found:

- *Pressure to disburse quickly.* Northern Mali embodies what is often typical in a post-return situation—a glut of short-term money available for reintegration and pressure to spend it quickly, before the funding is lost. This uncertain and volatile assistance environment acts as an immense constraint on carrying out developmental style programming.

- *Concentration on inputs and logistics.* The tendency of agencies to concentrate on logistics is compounded in Northern Mali, where transport and communications are so difficult. Seeing the situation from a traditional emergency approach inputs to meet certain needs quickly. A participatory approach is not a priority, partly because it is seen as highly time-consuming. But humanitarian emergencies do, in fact, last a long time; the traditional emergency approach was designed for short-term interventions.

◆ *Misunderstanding the dynamics of reintegration.* Much is made of avoiding dependency in literature, but exactly what dependency means in such contexts and how to programme against it in the field amidst a myriad of other pressures on field workers and organisations are unclear. Overall, the mechanics of reintegration and sustaining peace seem to be hazy.

RECOMMENDATIONS AND PROGRAMMING IMPLICATIONS

Recognise refugees and returnees as individuals with a past, a present and a future

The international community needs a new approach to refugee crises across borders and across time. In the refugee context, national borders act not only as a separation of states but also as a separation of response. Commitments need to be made to populations and regions, and not only to a population in exile. These include understanding and building on past development work; developing dual-level interventions in emergency situations which address basic needs and are able to support development-type goals in the traditional development sectors; and lastly, continuing to support refugees once they return. New funding mechanisms adapted to this approach are necessary.

Programming implications
◆ When possible, incorporate a reintegration objective into the projects in refugee settings, specifying activities which equip refugees for their return and resettlement.
◆ When an NGO office is present in both home country and host country, do joint planning from the outset of the project. When not possible, cross-border strategies should be developed early on, identifying collaborating partners in regions of return.

- If possible, move resources and staff with the population. Fund raisers will need to educate the donor community to the benefits of this "border-blind" approach.

See refugees/returnees as part of a larger community (in the country of exile with the host population; upon return, with local and displaced populations)

Equally important to working with refugees over time and space is work with host populations and home populations. Targeting refugees or returnees without responding to the needs of the whole community creates resentment.

Programming implications
- Peaceful refuge and peaceful reintegration require a regional approach, which looks at specials needs of refugee and returnee populations within the context of the larger community. This may involve support to host populations, those who did not leave and integrated projects.
- Equipping refugees with transferable skills can be an important part of facilitating integration at home.

Continually assess the reality of a refugee and returnee situation, be flexible in programming, and avoid being limited by traditional definitions which may preclude certain approaches

It is important for field workers, organisations and donors to remain alert and adapt programmes as the political and development climate changes. Agencies must also assess carefully the need for, and balance of, relief and development types of activities and must avoid general assistance packages ("cookie cutter" models) which rarely respond to the complex needs at the community level or build on community strengths and resources. A participatory, developmental approach and tools can be used in an emergency setting and during reintegration.

Programming implications
- Expect donors and agencies to be flexible during the project cycle. Change should not be the exception but the rule in people-centred development. Field people need national directors and

agency executives to assure them that it is acceptable and normal to make changes to a grant contract.

+ Plan exit strategies carefully and incorporate funds for this in original budgets, so projects can close well. Donors should consider the importance of such funding to avoid leaving projects hanging, caught between funding modalities.

+ Integrate participatory methods (such as RRA) into projects; ensure that the political and social context—and how it is affecting communities and livelihoods—is assessed.

Recognise that a refugee/returnee situation is a time of critical change for the community and can be a window for development and an opportunity to equip individuals and communities for their reintegration.

A refugee population is a concentrated audience. Crisis can create an impetus for change. People's traditional coping strategies have broken down, and they are looking for new strategies and skills. There is consequently a tremendous opportunity for traditional development goals to be pursued (such as literacy, primary school education, health education, women's empowerment).

Intensive capacity building can encourage people to return home, since they feel more equipped to cope. Concentrating on inputs to save lives can be complemented by activities that equip people to save their own lives in the future. On a practical level, development programmes can be more cost-effective in a refugee context than in a normal development context. This was particularly true for the Tuareg community, a traditionally nomadic people spread over a vast area where access is difficult but who as refugees were concentrated in one area.

Programming implications

+ Design training programmes in the camps with a "building blocks" approach. Small, manageable and flexible training modules allow more programme flexibility and more stability during the repatriation period. For instance, develop basic, yet adaptable training modules in several languages on key areas to help guide field workers in developing new programmes (school in a box, SED in a box, literacy in a box, public health, and so on).

- Provide permanent technical expertise/support within the organisation in special areas (small business, education, and so on). This will assist field workers to tap quickly into technical information and resources evaluation systems.
- Provide reintegration kits—portable skills kits—in addition to basic repatriation kits in order to support economic and social reintegration. For instance, offer start-up materials to continue practising skills developed. Also develop certificate programmes as part of training, backed up by information.
- Focus programme goals and indicators of success on capacity building and ripple effects, as well as the traditional sector's specific tangible results.

Recognise women as major agents of change, not just as receivers of inputs and as producers.

In Tuareg society, they say, "Train a man, and you train an individual. Train a woman, and you train a community." Despite wide recognition by development and emergency workers that women are central actors in changing communities, it is still necessary to stress the importance of targeting women in a useful way. It is important to encourage programmes that not only provide basic services but also create opportunities for learning. In particular, agencies should actively support projects that help women learn how to organise, be better decision-makers, and practice leadership skills. In addition, agencies should strongly support professional development and educational advancement for girls and women.

Programming implications
- Incorporate group and leadership skills and participatory methods into women's skills training programmes.
- Make taking on women trainers and staff a priority.
- Incorporate functional literacy and numeracy training into SED programmes for women.

Use a participatory approach on all levels

A participatory approach with beneficiaries and within organisations leads to better, more responsive programming and builds leadership. Participatory skills and processes can inform and be adapted to emergency/relief settings.

Programme planning and implementation based on such an approach not only leads to quality work in most cases but can also build important leadership skills within the community itself. Community ownership of activities is only ensured if the community chooses its own response. Programmes will be more efficient (in both short and long term), including in refugee situations, if communities are consulted about their needs and are fully involved.

In effect, NGO workers are empowered by being better informed to make concrete programming decisions, and beneficiaries are empowered by the opportunity to analyse their situation in a systematic and structured way. Participation can also be a vehicle to partnership between an agency and a community. As a parallel process, participatory work in the field will be stronger if participatory management is modelled at the organisational level as well. This integrity of approach can have powerful results.

Programming implications

- Ensure on-going community participation in all parts of the project cycle (needs assessment, design, monitoring and evaluation).
- Ensure that all staff (national and international) are trained in participatory techniques such as PRA/RRA.
- Encourage staff to maximise their day-to-day contact with the refugee/beneficiary community and to seek to develop partnership.
- Build in organisational accountability to the beneficiaries through periodic participatory evaluations.
- Foster participatory management and staff development within agencies' internal systems. Offer greater training and support of emergency management and human resources.
- Identify strategies to depoliticise assistance through broad-based consultation and interactions with all levels of the community. Also, recognise that being participatory does not mean that the community always makes all decisions. NGO workers can provide needed neutrality in divided communities, and technical criteria and standards can provide a neutral accountability outside the political.

Where possible, include a specific emphasis on creating a cadre of development professionals and community resource people as an integral goal of agency projects

Invest in refugee staff's professional development (especially women) as an integral goal of the project. Training of trainers in the beneficiary community can create a powerful ripple effect within the community and significantly increase the sustainable impact of projects. This training is also an important part of equipping communities for reintegration and involving them in the assistance environment.

Programming implications

- When appropriate, integrate a specific project objective and budget lines into the basic project design to support refugee staff recruitment and development.
- Adopt training of trainers as an approach in capacity-building programmes.
- Make participatory training of staff and trainers a priority.

Define and understand reintegration *more clearly and systematically for policy and programming purposes*

Despite WV's mission to assist women to reintegrate, the team was unable to determine whether, in fact, the women had reintegrated or whether they were still reintegrating. This was primarily due to difficulty defining the boundaries of the reintegration phase. Presumably this is a period following return up to a certain point when development begins, but where and what is that point?

At the field level, *reintegration* remains more of an ideal than an operational term—some kind of quasi-existence between *emergency/ relief* and *development*. Until the reintegration period is studied in more depth—the complex mechanisms of the system understood better in each context and indicators developed (particularly in relation to development)—assistance strategies attempting to balance emergency and development work will remain somewhat confused and disjointed. Donor funds remain restrictive and, many times, unresponsive. Although it is clear that the reintegration period is particularly important in emergencies, it remains poorly understood, particularly in regard to links among stability, return of refugees, peace and development.

Programming implications

- Develop methodology to assess the reintegration process (such as Rapid Reintegration Appraisal, piloted in this study) and to determine community needs or plans of action. This includes determining indicators and developing a series of tools that allow field workers to assess the situation quickly and accurately in order to determine appropriate assistance strategies.
- Assess populations periodically after return to evaluate the impact of projects.

NOTES

[1] Christopher Roche, "Operationality in Turbulence," *Development in States of War*, ed. Deborah Eade (Oxford: Oxfam, 1996), 24.

[2] Robin-Edward Poulton and Ibrahim ag Youssouf, *A Peace of Timbuktu* (New York and Geneva: United Nations Institute for Disarmament Research [UNIDIR], 1998).

[3] MRP defined *participation* as "interactive participation"—beneficiaries acting as joint decision-makers in all aspects of project planning.

[4] The number of quartiers changed over the life of the refugee camps. This was related to on-going reorganising of the camps.

[5] This raises interesting questions about how refugees choose to use their rations and how they may be converted to meet other needs and provide income support. Such issues need to be considered in organising rations.

[6] A 1994 UN study indicated that only 1 percent of the women in the camps were literate.

[7] The team consisted of the original MRP community service director; the MRP programme assistant (a refugee), who has continued to work as a development worker with WV in Mali; and an outside reintegration expert who had studied similar issues in Rwanda. Each team member brought a unique perspective to the research process. The familiarity of two team members with the communities and the project was key in establishing trust and co-operation in our research, but we were also aware of the potential for bias in this; having an outsider on the team was part of our strategy to minimise bias. We also triangulated our information in the communities and with other agencies.

[8] A meeting with NGO representatives was organised for the team by UNHCR. We also interviewed a number of agency representatives and staff.

[9] Twenty-three functional groups representing more than 230 women funded by the Canadian Embassy were identified (time constraints did not allow the team to identify other groups).

[10] Prior to exile, physical work for women was associated with the lower or slave classes.

[11] External support was key for a number of women in restarting a business. Some women told of how they presented diplomas, group lists and project plans to organizations for funding.

[12] Poulton and ag Youssouf, *A Peace of Timbuktu.*

[13] This is a season in which the women cannot produce goods, since they are concentrating on survival for their families and stocks are very low. The local market for their goods is also very reduced.

9.

Conflict, Repression and Politics

Dare NGOs Hope to Do Any Good?

ALAN WHAITES

In recent years the slide from politics to civil strife has been pronounced, particularly in a narrow group of relatively inflexible
states. This trend has seen the repeated pursuit of power (and much
less frequently, of principle) through the violent manipulation of
ethnic, religious and rural identities. In short, the study of recent
CHEs shows, not the importance of political failure per se, but the
tendency for modern political war to arise predominantly within
certain kinds of states.

That this path to conflict is more likely to be taken in an unaccountable state than in even the most heterogeneous low Human
Development Index (HDI) democracy has discernible roots in political logic.[1] Where the means of popular political articulation or
the ordered transfer of power are limited, the lack of safety valves
can force any pressure for change towards conflict until discontent
reaches a crisis point and explodes. Clapham and Wiseman have
observed that:

> None of those African states that have collapsed into anarchy
> could remotely be described as democratic and in most cases
> such as Doe's Liberia or Siyad Barre's Somali Republic political
> collapse can be directly related to the gross abuse of power. Con-
> versely even in a number of fairly surprising cases democratisation

has provided the means through which some forms of national political community have been re-established.[2]

Bringing this link between unaccountable government and civil
strife into focus is a reasonable cause for uncomfortable shuffling
by those groups committed to reconciliation, conflict prevention
and peacebuilding. There is little doubt, after all, that these issues
are usually well beyond an NGO's purview.

Despite this discomfort, those same development institutions and
large NGOs, especially those which work to publicise the prolif-
eration of conflict, must see the political causes of that trend as a
future challenge. Positively framed, this challenge is the need to
find ways at the micro-level to promote the peaceful process of
participatory political change. Even if we take a minimalist approach, there is an imperative that NGOs should at least not serve
to prolong the inflexibility and macro-political problems involved.
If NGOs are shy of working towards long-term solutions, they must
at least try not to confer benefits on the destructive political and
repressive forces that so often drag states to the point of collapse.

In essence, therefore, conflict and accountability pose a number
of difficult strategic questions for international NGOs. They cannot divorce themselves from the political contexts in which they
work. But, equally, can international NGOs really engage with the
dynamics which enable lack of political accountability to become
open bloodletting? This chapter argues that the alternative is to
continue to act purely as the ringside doctor, watching the violence
and waiting for a chance to rush in and wipe away the blood. From
our ringside seat, NGOs have grown used to three cycles of state
collapse, each of which involves a steady slide from political failure
to open conflict, and each of which presents opportunities for conflict prevention.

At the first level of these dynamics, NGOs have become wearily
familiar with the sight of governments in open hostility against
those portions of their own people considered most acutely to be a
threat. Genocide in Rwanda, ethnic cleansing in Kosovo—never
has it been clearer that states are willing to go to war against their
own citizens. Equally, for the victims of repression there is also a
second dynamic which presses the population towards use of force
against their oppressors—the process that leads from a Rugova's

peaceful resistance to the insurgency of a Kosovo Liberation Army (KLA).

The third path that leads from unaccountable government to civil strife is sometimes the most easily taken. It is in the nature of dictatorial and repressive regimes to suppress effective opposition and erode the popular understanding of political choice. Wherein lie the seeds of numerous problems when such regimes fall and a new approach to politics is required. From the debacle at the end of Portuguese colonialism in Angola to the fall of Barre in Somalia, transition has occasionally left the heirs fighting over their inheritance.

NGOS, UNACCOUNTABLE STATES AND CONFLICT

It may seem to be stating the obvious to suggest that the unaccountable state, particularly when repressive, leaves few options open for the expression of opposition other than rebellion, conflict or coup. Few relief workers will doubt that political repression and civil strife can go hand in hand, twin forces creating the environment for CHEs and the human misery which follows. Mengistu's Ethiopia, Mobuto's Zaire and the stasis of Sudan have underscored the ease with which lack of political discourse can be translated into conflict, refugees, infrastructural collapse and famine. But are the generic political trends within conflicts really relevant to NGOs? Issues of accountability can seem far removed when knee deep in mud and the trauma of war.

Nevertheless, NGOs have increasingly set themselves on a course of addressing both the seeds of conflict and the challenges of reconciliation. Some of this work has been astute in exploring the possibility that development activities themselves can play a positive role in easing the primordial divisions, those based on fundamental social identities, which all too often are manipulated as causes of conflict.[3]

This chapter recognises that such ethnic and religious divisions are critical to any progress in avoiding future CHEs. It seeks, however, to relate our existing understanding of conflict to the inability of unaccountable systems to manage such divisions. In addressing the increased likelihood that lack of political participation and accountability will push heterogeneous societies towards civil strife, this chapter suggests that NGOs need to broaden the vision of their role. To a degree, this means a natural progression of thought, for NGO approaches to such issues can centre on the nurturing of civil society—frequently seen as a panacea for all political development ills.

While not a panacea, in reality civil society does matter. The flowering of civil society after democratisation takes place is well observed; indeed, some 100,000 new charities arose in former Eastern Bloc states in the first seven years of democracy.[4] But is civil society really as essential to the initial process of political change as often suggested? And if it is, what should be the response of international NGOs? In pointing to situations where NGOs have struggled with these issues, this chapter draws on case examples from four African and Asian countries.[5]

Just as the strength of the authoritarian state is a potential CHE to be feared, the greed and competition fuelled by the weak unaccountable state also can lead to the use of force. Erosion of the state has created dynamics of its own,[6] and recently more work has been done developing the thinking of Migdal[7] and others on the weak state as a catalyst for crisis. The legacy of two decades of external conditionality and the nature of globalisation have combined to erode states until some provide only a show of government while vested interest groups vie for resources and control. The histories of Sierra Leone, the Congo and even Nigeria would seem to provide ammunition for this frequently made point. The lack of accountability this helps to create only strengthens the potential for these would-be leaders to seize all spoils; the state reduced to the point of being no more than a criminal enterprise[8] is still a profitable prize. Sam Jones, in a World Vision report, has explored state erosion with particular reference to Africa, detailing the processes by which economic and political forces have left some states progressively bereft of the means to fulfil their functions.[9]

In the case of Africa, Clapham and Wiseman have suggested a basic set of criteria which might characterise a more accountable state.[10] A temptation this chapter intentionally avoids. Prescriptions for democracy, like discussions of beauty, often reveal more about the biases of the beholder than the reality of the form. This chapter rejects Western democracy as the sole model for the recommended aims (indeed some Western democracies offer no model at all).

Emphasis within this discussion is instead on participation—the right to a voice and a semblance of choice. By focusing on these areas the aspiration for democracy, whatever its final form, can be seen as it is played out every day in an NGO's own projects and work.

LACK OF ACCOUNTABILITY, THE LIMIT FOR NGOS?

NGOs might recognise the link between repressive contexts and the eventual conflicts and rebellions that frequently bring such regimes to an end. But, are we equally able to do anything which might lessen the pressures pushing a country towards the eventual humanitarian emergency to follow? To what extent do we stretch the humanitarian principle that NGOs must do all in their power to save lives?[11] Hugo Slim has urged the NGO community to remember its prophetic vision in pushing forward the boundaries of humanitarian action[12]—but can we really see peaceful transition from repression to popular accountability as yet another addition to our duties? This chapter does not claim that a different operational approach by NGOs would have prevented genocide in Rwanda or violence in East Timor. Nor does this chapter argue for a specific responsibility on the part of NGOs to right all wrongs, create a perfect world and rid our planet of injustice (although some NGO advertising literature might have us believe it possible).

This chapter does, however, argue that NGOs cannot ignore the implications of repression either for increasing the propensity towards conflict or hindering poverty alleviation. As a result, NGOs do need to take seriously the potential impact of their work on the wider political context, encouraging real, if small, steps towards popular accountability (and peaceful transition)—a process which this chapter suggests requires neither a new type of programme nor a radical change in philosophy. In essence, NGOs have little choice but to opt for intentional action—the only alternative is a hollow pretence.

REPRESSION, NGOS AND DONORS

Taking a fresh look at the possible links between NGO interventions and the aspirations of the poor for popular accountability is a natural progression in any comprehensive attempt to address long-term causes of conflict. The potential for NGOs to play a positive, peacebuilding role through the nurturing of constructive civil society is real. NGOs must also go beyond concern for conflict alone to look at our overall developmental and ethical imperatives—a process that will inevitably mean being frank not only about the role of NGOs, but also in regard to pressures originating with that other critical audience, the donor community.

The developmental implications of unaccountable regimes are fundamental to the operating environments of NGOs in constrained contexts. The ability of development NGOs to make an impact on poverty is dependent upon the constraints faced by the communities concerned. NGO interventions are therefore complicated when these constraints include not only lack of credit, or access to the market or agricultural inputs, but also policies of a brutal and control-orientated regime. At the local level, the author remembers the frustration as an Asian village watched new irrigation channels being dug past their dry fields, bypassed for being associated with the political opposition. Indeed, in some contexts, such as Mobutu's Zaire, the greatest cause of prolonged poverty seems to be not lack of resources but prolonged bad government policies. Sadly, Organisation for Economic Co-operation and Development (OECD) governments and transnational corporations are sometimes complicit in this.

Ethically this has always created an immediate dilemma for NGOs: no matter how distasteful they might find it, NGOs can only rarely avoid interaction with the regime concerned. Indeed through their operational programmes, NGOs might even be accused of sustaining the very regime that is a significant cause of the problem they are seeking to solve. This forms the starting point for a range of dilemmas faced by many relief and development organisations, dilemmas which begin with the most basic issue of all: Should an NGO be operationally active in a system governed through repression and brutality? Increasingly, these dilemmas are being recognised and discussed, certainly to an extent not previously seen. The naivete of Biafra and Vietnam seems to have waned, with NGOs at least debating the ethics of the best approach to famine in Sudan or to food shortages in DPRK (North Korea), the world's last surviving Stalinist state.

For donors, the issue of repressive regimes has caused dilemmas of an entirely different kind, as they have sought to bring this factor within the scope of increased aid conditionality. Renewed certainty over the merits of Western political norms (regardless of the realities of Western politics) has led to the inclusion of liberal democracy as a policy objective by donor states who have brought the issue firmly within the remit of what Mark Robinson terms the "New Policy Agenda."[13]

Promotion of democracy has included much being made of the part played by local civil society and, by proxy, the role of international NGOs in strengthening civil associations. Harry Blair, an American political scientist, has both written on the role of civil society in underpinning any sustainable move to democracy and also directly advised the US administration through the U.S. Agency for International Development (USAID) on how democratisation could be included within donor programmes. Blair suggests that there are two basic strategies for supporting civil society. Basic Strategy 1 (BS1) centres on the donor working to "improve conditions in which it [civil society] can function effectively" (that is, working with the government to create a civil society–friendly state). Basic Strategy 2 (BS2) involves direct support of civil society organisations (CSOs) in order to strengthen the generally accepted composite parts of civil society.[14]

Blair believes that BS1 logically precedes BS2, in that the latter is made easier by a supportive environment. However, in many contexts the harsh reality of political constraints has forced USAID to pursue BS2 as its initial strategy. Elsewhere, BS2 has been favoured in the belief that a "trickle-up" approach might, by increasing civil society activity, create a more enabling environment. An argument can be made that in today's Western democracies, the development of CSOs took place in relatively inhospitable environments before triggering further democratic reform. Despite this caveat, Blair's framework does provide a useful model for NGO planning and strategy.

NGOs are all too familiar with those contexts in which Blair's BS1 approach of assisting governments is made impossible by the human rights abuses and repression of the regime. This is underscored by the tendency of Western donors to react to such contexts through the faithful adoption of Blair's BS2 approach—in effect, they identify these contexts as prime candidates for the delivery of assistance through international NGOs. The recent development of specialist "democratisation" budget lines by these donors has at least added a small element of clarity to the motives of USAID, the Department for International Development (DFID) and others, even if the very transparency of such mechanisms can render them impractical for NGOs.

POPULAR ACCOUNTABILITY AS AN OBJECTIVE

This idea of using NGO programmes as a step towards popular accountability is therefore not new. The danger, however, is that the discussion has been focused on the agenda of other actors and not the policy objectives of NGOs themselves. The drive to consider NGO programmes as part of the process of political change has been driven by the New Policy Agenda, which has opened up new resources for NGOs from politically motivated donors.[15] There is a need for NGOs to clarify and reclaim the macro issue of popular accountability on their own (and hopefully their local partners') behalf. For some NGOs, therefore, the donor's concern for democracy has been useful for funding purposes without directly leading to a reappraisal of what role an agency should play in long-term processes of change within the framework of the context.

To some extent, NGOs can claim that pressures have existed in recent years for them to become mired in the immediate and tragic consequences of crisis. The length of the list of conflicts—Angola, Sierra Leone, East Timor, Kosovo, Chechnya . . . —has mitigated against humanitarian agencies addressing the contextual political issues. Even so, if NGOs have an operational presence within constrained contexts, then facing up to political realities should be unavoidable. Failure to have a clear approach to the context can, after all, mean drifting into support for the status quo.[16]

More positively, NGOs, by having an analysis of their context and a commitment to ownership of development by communities, can try to make their own development activities a contribution to positive change. These contributions include small steps discussed below which NGOs can take towards the promotion of popular accountability, which do not necessarily mean coming into conflict with the state. The alternative—avoiding the issue altogether—represents NGO short-sightedness at its worst and a denial of the reality that national accountability is a very real issue for project sustainability. Those who doubt the link between politics and project sustainability should look closely at the exacerbating effect of political prevarication on top of economic crisis in Indonesia in 1997–98.

Accountability offers at least some hope to communities that they will be able to improve the wider conditions which shape and mould their own efforts at local development. The ability of citizens to choose governments and to remove the incompetent from office is important; this "democracy enhances efficiency" argument was adopted in the early 1990s by the World Bank as well as Western donors.[17] By 1995 this view had become an orthodoxy, with James H. Michel of the OECD stating:

> Both long term evidence and the growing commitment of citizens in all parts of the world support the existence of a positive correlation between the quality of political and civil rights in a society and economic and social well-being. The capacity of any country to formulate, implement and sustain sound policies over time is enhanced by that country's capacity for good governance and the ability of its citizens to participate in the processes and decisions that affect them.[18]

NGOs may view the platitudes with scepticism, but it is still important to recognise that there is no inconsistency in identifying civil society growth and popular accountability as objectives of developmental activity.

NGOS AND ACCOUNTABILITY

The actual role of NGOs in promoting popular accountability is difficult to define. Direct political action by foreign organisations is invariably undesirable and full of potential pitfalls. However, NGOs can help to create an environment in which democracy might prosper and where people feel more able to articulate political aspirations. Jeffries has outlined a socioeconomic environment for democracy based on the interaction of civil society with a strong, well-defined state.[19] This process is the product of developmental processes of which NGOs are increasingly aware (such as civil society and embourgeoisement, that is, becoming middle class).[20] The role of the NGO, as with most good development, becomes that of facilitator responding to community goals. There are several ways in which NGOs can work towards this facilitating role, three of which are outlined below:

NGOs and civil society

The author has written elsewhere both on the pitfalls of a simplistic approach to civil society and on the need not to confuse the strengthening of people's groups with the improving of the state.[21] Even so, the evolution of conflicting political theory has not helped NGOs to grapple with a subject apparently of considerable relevance to their work. Instead, NGOs have too often fallen victim to the temptation of analysing civil society issues in light of their own existing strengths and weaknesses.[22]

One view is that civil society emerges as part of the development process, a school of "civil society" studies derived from the work of de Tocqueville.[23] Sometimes caricatured as Euro-centric, and often associated with a Weberian modernisation approach, this view is challenged by contextualists such as Bayart. Yet when applied fully, de Tocqueville's thought does help to point to the changing nature of civil society as development takes place, a historical progression the author has sought to illustrate through a more detailed study of civil society and social change in Pakistan.[24]

While avoiding the idea that civil society is inherent in every society, this chapter suggests that development workers can draw on de Tocqueville's legacy for definitions of social defences against despotism of the state. These defences rest both on distribution of political power through democratic institutions and on organisation of civil society through civil associations. For NGOs in constrained contexts, it is the importance of civil society organizations (CSOs) to the growth of civil society which provides the key linkage to development projects. The role NGOs play in promoting participatory issue-focused community groups such as credit unions, health education clubs and co-operatives is one that has tremendous potential to enhance the development of civil society.

In Pakistan under Zia, examples of such groups included the Bonded Labour Liberation Front (BLLF), which, in order to achieve its long-term goals, had little choice but consistently to promote the concept of Rule of Law. The BLLF was built on an often loose structure of local projects, groups and workers associations, which survived considerable duress. Equally the coalition of Pakistani women's groups which emerged to fight negative, gender-based constitutional change was rooted in a tradition of non-political women's NGOs stretching back to the nineteenth century.[25]

Real impact from nurturing local civil associations can also be seen at the grassroots level. It is not surprising that the political repercussions of NGOs can be most powerful, initially, in the village, slum, commune and district. This is true particularly where time has been taken to help communities to unite internally. In one country with a brutally repressive regime, a simple tube well project brought a community together to discuss its own long-term interests. A new community committee quickly identified itself closely with the "collectivity" of the slum. This led to project decisions that NGO staff considered remarkably bold for the context. The committee, in choosing a contractor for one part of the project, rejected outright a bid by repressive local government authorities because of doubts about the quality of work that would be provided. In another decision, the committee decided to provide a basic service to local dwellers at a fraction of the rate charged by local monopoly business in order to force an across-the-board price reduction.

NGOs and leadership building

An assumption made regarding some of the world's worst regimes is that all aspects of the administrative system are automatically tainted by the nature of the government. This can be ironic since, for example, in a planned economic system, the majority of the population can work in some form or other for the state. In one notable example, civil servants made up a significant proportion of street demonstrators during unrest at the end of the 1980s but have been labelled by external groups as pariahs for accepting state pay. There is therefore a need for discernment in dealing with government structures. NGOs, by working with middle- and lower-level bureaucrats in social welfare ministries, are often dealing with people who are passive or even active supporters of the opposition.[26] By introducing such counterparts to participatory principles and methods, such views hopefully can be nurtured.

The capacity building of local indigenous NGOs and even a foreign agency's own staff also opens up the potential for the promotion of participatory principles amongst potential leaders and administrators. This capacity building may ultimately prove to be a crucial service following political transition.[27] A problem that can become very real in contexts with particularly brutal regimes is the absence of an effective opposition. In such contexts, vocal opposition is largely limited to a small number of known dissidents and students. Following collapse of the old regime, therefore, there can be a vacuum of trained leadership. Just as serious, during gradual transition, oppressive regimes can be left stranded without any truly representative opposition with which to negotiate.

Enabling others to articulate ideas of rights and standards can have drastic effects on the elite circles of closed contexts. The author enjoyed the humour of the local staff of one NGO who developed their own euphemisms for the "official" concept of participation (which included everything from labour levees to military conscription) and for the "real" participation they practised in projects. But, without euphemisms, the same NGO staff later staged a local conference for members of the political elite to explain the benefits of planning developing interventions only after listening to the poor. Eventually the group won the right to teach the same methodologies to a cross-section of local NGOs.

NGOs as witnesses

NGOs working in politically constrained contexts have a witness function which they should not take lightly. The presence of NGOs can in some instances act as a brake on local repression by opening up the possibility of external condemnation. Equally, NGOs can make available to other groups information the NGO itself might not wish to use. In this way NGOs can facilitate the work of campaigning organisations in maintaining pressure on repressive regimes.[28] This is a role that NGOs are now confronting more systematically.

Baseline survey reports on the health conditions of a local community have enabled at least one NGO to provide insights to specialist groups on everything from domestic violence to forced labour. NGO access also provided some local leaders a route through which to speak. For one country, a network of both humanitarian and human rights NGOs enabled the mobilisation of external political concern over persistent human rights abuses against a particular ethnic group in a remote, specially administered military zone. It may be that the ability of NGOs to act is restricted during a period of repression, but this does not preclude their role as witness at some point. In something of a unique statement, the UN International Tribunal for the Former Yugoslavia has made clear its own reliance on the help offered by relief and development groups on the ground.[29]

This trend of mutual concern and co-operation should continue to be nurtured by both humanitarian and human rights NGOs. The conference Co-operation Between Humanitarian Organisations and Human Rights Organisations (Amsterdam, 9 February 1996) concluded with a draft statement aimed at practical steps towards co-operation.[30] Such practical steps continue to be needed and, at one level, human rights NGOs must look closely at their usual reluctance to engage constructively in the training of their humanitarian counterparts.

Hopefully, those NGOs that do undertake operational activities in environments shaped by oppressive regimes will consider local aspirations for autonomy and popular accountability in relation to their own thinking and planning. But this constructive role depends on adherence by development agencies to firm standards for engagement with the state and clear goals for participatory capacity building. Full consideration to the need for ethical parameters should therefore be the first task of potentially operational agencies.

SHOULD NGOS COPY DONORS IN WITHHOLDING ASSISTANCE?

The very complexity for NGOs of co-existing ethically with the unaccountable state can make the idea of distance very attractive. Some NGOs have therefore chosen to remain absent from politically

difficult contexts, hoping that their denial of help might itself has-
ten change. The idea of denying aid and humanitarian assistance as
a tool in achieving accountability is not new. Indeed, the economic
punishment of repressive states has long been viewed by the international community as a means to provoke internal change—albeit
often via civil strife and conflict.

Denial of aid does not therefore necessarily promote peaceful
transition. The costly humanitarian consequences of the sanctions
imposed on Iraq come with an implicit hope on the part of the
imposing states that deteriorating socioeconomic conditions will
prompt unrest. The humanitarian scandal of seeking to starve people
into rebellion represents a clear signal to NGOs to be wary of all
attempts to use humanitarian assistance as weapons in undeclared
wars. Punitive economic action against regimes invariably involves
a reduction or cessation of aid even where trade sanctions are not
used (the UK drastically cut aid to Burma whilst continuing to run
"British Trade Weeks" in Rangoon). Cessation of aid is a background principle within guidelines accepted by the Development
Assistance Committee (DAC) group of large donors, based on the
fact that

> members wish to rely to the maximum extent on measures of
> positive support, but they also wish to be clear about the po-
> tential for negative measures affecting the volume and form
> of their aid, in areas of serious and systematic violations of
> human rights and brutal reversals from democratisation.[31]

Where bilateral government-to-government aid is concerned, this
cessation has in the past had occasional impact on the resources
available to repressive regimes. Examples where this alone significantly contributed to change, such as Malawi, are rare. Even so,
some impact has been felt, mainly through the reduction of economic options available to the regime. Economically, large aid grants
do provide a significant source of foreign exchange for developing
state governments. If those grants are spent directly through state
structures, they are usually received in hard currency and converted
by the state into local payments for staff and contractors. Often
the entire hard currency amount is then available to the regime for
other purposes, including the purchase of military hardware.

Large bilateral grants can also directly subsidise operational expenses of state structures. The use of foreign grants to fund health and education services frees up resources of the regime for other purposes. But even if it might be effective to include cessation of bilateral, government-to-government aid as part of a package of punitive economic measures, does this mean that NGOs should consider similar action? Those governments most rigorous in the implementation of punitive measures against the apartheid regime in South Africa were also amongst the most generous donors to NGOs working with communities in the townships. The contradiction was a recognition that bilateral (state-to-state) and NGO aid are not like and like. Indeed there are sufficient differences between bilateral government-to-government aid and the work of NGOs to reduce significantly any benefits to the repressive regime involved.

Qualitative differences between state and NGO aid become crucial at this point in any discussion of the role of development assistance within unaccountable environments. Therefore, at the risk of covering ground already familiar to development professionals, it is nevertheless worth restating the points of divergence. The differences can be felt particularly in the crucial areas of foreign exchange and subsidies discussed above. These problems are less pronounced for NGOs for two reasons: first, the issue of scale; and, second the issue of delivery.

Scale

Scale seems an obvious question when dealing with the ethics of sending aid to countries in conflict or governed by oppressive regimes. The scale of resources made available through foreign currency gain and the freeing up of state resources may be a very real issue with bilateral and multilateral or IFI (International Financial Institutions) aid initiatives, but for NGOs, it is unlikely that the levels of assistance involved will reach a threatening level. During the 1980s Cambodia was denied bilateral aid by many large Western aid donors, and several NGOs spent disproportionately large sums in the country to try to meet the high levels of needs. Even in this instance, the two largest NGO programmes (those of World Vision and Oxfam) averaged a combined value of less than US$20 million. The small scale of NGO assistance is, however, not guaranteed, and, as we shall see below, it is still important for NGOs to minimise the economic benefits regimes might directly derive from NGO involvement.

Delivery

There is no neat distinction between government and NGOs in terms of delivery options open to them, but there is a tendency to differ in terms of the "favoured" means of delivery. Both can deliver through state organs or through local NGOs/CSOs/CBOs (community-based organisations). However, where repressive regimes are concerned, NGO delivery of aid should be evaluated in light of four generally applicable characteristics:

1. *Delivery targeted at the grassroots:* NGOs are usually community—rather than institutionally—orientated. This means that projects are planned from the community level and that institutional structures such as health-referral systems are dealt with from the perspective of community requirements.

2. *Close monitoring:* Even where state structures are involved in project implementation, such as a local health department, NGOs usually have the freedom to negotiate the method of payments (that is, direct to contractors or staff, rather than direct payments to government structures). Similarly, the proximity of NGO involvement facilitates close scrutiny as to whether expenditure is utilised as agreed. Failure in this regard can lead the NGO to withdraw funds.

3. *Local presence:* The proximity of the implementing NGO enhances not only the monitoring of expenditure, but also facilitates awareness amongst the community of where expenditure originates. It is important to note that the presence of NGO staff reduces the ability of the regime to take credit for the programme.

4. *Community structures:* The participatory, grassroots approach favoured by NGOs is possible only where some form of community organisation exists, and often NGOs give priority to strengthening such bodies as a key project goal. As James Midgley rightly states: "Non-governmental organisations are

not only more likely [than the state] to serve the interests of the poor but they are capable of initiating schemes that increase the organisational power and consequently the political pressures that can be exerted by poor people."[32]

CO-EXISTING WITH THE REGIME

NGOs, more often than not, decide to try to work alongside the poor within the borders of an unaccountable or, worse, a repressive state. The decision to work in a context where political accountability is absent places a series of moral choices before any humanitarian group, especially if that NGO is pursuing goals for constructive participatory change. Otherwise, an NGO can simply become counter-productive. Lack of such goals or of engagement with moral choices leads NGOs to accommodate their own developmental principles to the wishes of the regime. Their programmes can simply become means through which a poverty-exacerbating government gains political and economic benefit for itself.

For NGOs to have any claim, therefore, to being able to operate in politically unaccountable contexts and to promote participation, they must first adhere to guidelines addressing key dangers for the NGO in its relations with the state. This is particularly true where that unaccountable state is also routinely repressive in its relationship with the civilian population. Indeed, NGOs should always have guidelines and rules in their relations with the state in any country, precepts that simply become more extensive the more problematic the state.

Once operational, NGOs face several pressures to keep programmes and projects running, even if the guidelines are not being kept as strictly as was hoped. This is a dangerous time for any agency. To allow implementation of ethical guidelines for constrained contexts to slip is to negate the constructive role NGOs might have been able to play in social and political development. It is therefore beholden on NGOs in these circumstances to be clear on the ethical objectives of their role within the country. If these are undermined by the failure of their guidelines, then their ability to assist communities may be no more than providing a palliative. Guidelines have to be seen as the "bottom line" below which NGO assistance becomes part of the problem rather than a solution, and a decision to withdraw must always be a realistic and accepted option.

This chapter suggests that where an unaccountable state is also repressive, guidelines must define the type of development work to be undertaken and the modus operandi of the NGO in relation to the state. Where practical, an NGO can best guide its staff by deciding its own limits in relation to the regime. An example of some basic issues are given below, but this is an area where every development group must examine its own rationale and ethos. Ideally, the NGO should be willing to negotiate with the regime, testing the limits and waters in hope of securing agreement on the participatory nature of development work. In some contexts this has been clearly articulated to line-ministry counterparts. It is to be hoped that guidelines would deal with the following issues:

1. *Minimising economic gain:* Within constrained, politically unaccountable contexts, there are direct and indirect economic benefits regimes seek to derive from foreign NGOs. The main direct benefit is provision of any NGO funds that go directly to government ministries such as health departments. Where possible, NGOs should therefore avoid such funding relationships. A more vexing avenue for state gain are instances where unrealistic official exchange rates are imposed. If NGOs are forced to exchange hard currency at a rate that significantly overvalues local currency, then the state derives dollars, yen and so on to increase its own purchasing power, including purchasing power for military hardware. In these instances, some NGOs have gone to great lengths, including carrying suitcases of cash into the constrained context, in order to exchange currency on the black market. This is a high-risk approach that potentially allows the state a source of leverage should it decide to make an issue out of the illegal nature of the transactions. A safer alternative is to reduce the hard-currency element of the programme to the lowest level possible. In one NGO programme, where the official exchange rate was some 20 times the market price, aid was limited to duty-free gifts-in-kind until exchange rates were normalised. If duty-free shipment is not possible in a highly repressive state, and

exchange rates are unrealistic, then the context may be inappropriate for any NGO involvement.

2. *Legitimisation:* Regimes can seek to use NGOs for propaganda purposes through any number of mechanisms and almost certainly will take advantage of their opportunities. NGOs in dealing with this issue may be fortunate enough to be able to lay down clear ground rules with their counterpart. But, even where the subject cannot be broached officially, NGO staff can consider to what extent they can minimise legitimisation. Steps might include ensuring that there are no photographs with officials, full accreditation of the NGO as project donor, and free contact between the NGO and community. It is rarely possible to counter the government's propaganda machine entirely, but a strong point can be made. It should also be remembered that communities in constrained contexts are rarely as gullible as outsiders assume. In one country visited by the author recently, the fact that foreign NGOs were providing the only real health assistance was seen as an indictment of the regime. The question becomes, Why should we need to get help from foreigners when we have a government that does nothing? In another context, where a relief distribution was made, a photograph of an NGO worker handing goods over to a community leader was juxtaposed in the official newspaper with a picture of two soldiers exchanging the same goods at the same spot but several hours later. The picture was seen by the community as evidence that the NGO had shunned the military.

3. *Participatory development:* In countries where the rule of law is loosely understood, Memorandums of Understanding (MOUs) sometimes have the same contractual force as an annual letter to Santa Claus. Even so, these agreements can provide key benchmarks in establishing the direction in which NGOs will seek to develop. Even if an NGO feels unable to complain about lack of adherence by a government to the MOU, it can often point to the document as a statement of principles signed by counterparts. It is therefore worth pressing for an MOU that conforms most closely to the developmental style and principles genuinely held by the NGO. Before entering a constrained context, NGOs should negotiate

detailed MOUs which lay ground rules for the types of NGO project to be undertaken. MOUs should stipulate that the NGO will be final arbiter of beneficiaries and that these decisions will be made regardless of ethnicity, religion, gender or other factors. MOUs must also state that NGOs will have free access to projects, automatic visa rights and duty-free importation of goods. Communications issues such as international direct dialling should also be addressed, as well as the right to employ and select local staff.

It is crucial that MOUs make clear the NGO's intention to undertake development work in a participatory, community-led way that will be responsive to local priorities and input. Ambiguities associated with the term *participatory* can be partially offset by reference to United Nations Economic and Social Council Resolution 1929 as a minimum definition.[33] Having negotiated an MOU on this basis, the agency should be focused on working towards the level of participation and community control that is possible in normal developing contexts. This may be gradual while the agency educates counterparts and its own staff on the processes involved, but progress made should be closely monitored.

4. *Choosing partners:* A fellow political scientist and friend commented on his country's close alliance with the crumbling Soviet Union by stating that one should not climb into a taxi for a long journey without being sure the driver will be with you until the end. When embarking upon work in complex and politically charged contexts, NGOs should choose their local partners (other NGOs or ministries) with care. At face value, local NGOs often seem the most ethical groups with which to link, although these can themselves be government-run. From local relief and disaster prevention groups staffed with retired generals to women's clubs led by the president's wife, local NGOs need considerable examination and care.

The most obvious ministries (such as social welfare) may also be too weak to protect the NGO's right to abide by an agreed MOU. In many instances, it is specific line ministries (education and health) that bring a combination of some degree of leverage and genuine concern for the poor. Genuinely non-governmental NGOs are also an important group, and where such bodies do not exist, the nearest equivalents (including medical and professional associations, churches and mosques) should be reviewed. On the question of partners, however, no hard and fast rules exist; rather, there remains a duty of care on the part of every NGO to research its MOU and other partners with great diligence.

Ultimately guidelines must be found for each unique context in question. Experience from one repressive state may help but is unlikely to be exactly replicable elsewhere. The key for any NGO seeking to pursue ethical as well as developmental objectives is itself the willingness to develop guidelines at all. A commitment to doing whatever is possible at the micro-level to promote positive change is the essential starting point, following which extensive research, review and dialogue will be needed. Such commitments represent brave decisions by NGOs willing to face difficult challenges in order to provide clean delivery of well-targeted aid to communities in countries with oppressive regimes. If this aid is to be delivered without the regime deriving unacceptable benefit from its expenditure, then the degree of moral responsibility rests with the NGO. Where ethical guidelines are concerned, taking internal ethics, mission and accountability seriously is all-important.

CONCLUSIONS

Unaccountable regimes usually have a limit to the level of repression to which they will subject their populations. The role of the military in seeing itself as defender of the state will also often lead to disillusion in the ranks if suppression of democracy continues for too long (a factor observed by Stepan in Brazil[34] and Jalal in Pakistan[35]). Unfortunately for NGOs, these are unpredictable processes and without a timetable for change, humanitarian agencies are left to consider how best to deal with the realities of the present. Few NGOs would willingly wish to be used as part of a "hearts and minds" legitimisation campaign either by an unaccountable government or by an occupying power.

Neither do NGOs wish to offer economic support to the less enlightened governments with whom they must interact. But, given the scenario outlined above, there is room for agencies to consider creative involvement on a case-by-case basis. In making this consideration, NGOs also must be willing to act with a full appreciation of the potential consequences of their involvement and a commitment to a responsible mode of operation. Ultimately for NGOs, inaction holds little attraction. The consequence of repression is often a violent collapse, and for NGOs, the experience of these provides considerable incentive to do what little we can to promote a more peaceful transition.

In undertaking operations in such politically constrained contexts, NGOs should seek to reclaim conceptual ownership for the civil society–nurturing parts of our work. The agenda we pursue for positive change should not be that of donors, but rather an extension of our principles of development. NGOs can and should attempt to maximise the participatory characteristics and effective monitoring of their projects.

The potential of agencies to take advantage of characteristics that ensure effective and well-targeted delivery of assistance is a strength for encouraging participation, complemented by the relatively small scale of resources involved. The level of NGO assistance to developing countries is unlikely to reach a scale that would prevent any overall punitive economic action from being effective. The crucial caveat is that the capability of NGOs to provide a channel of assistance to the oppressed is dependent upon those NGOs facing up to implications of their operational context and consequently adhering to a set of guidelines designed to minimise any benefit operations could confer on the regime.

This chapter has suggested some parameters within which NGO development assistance can be made possible to communities in constrained contexts, whilst also arguing that NGOs can play a positive role in the political development of the context in question. Significant factors are the potential civil society–enhancing role of NGO operations, coupled with their leadership-building work. When planning involvement within such contexts, NGOs should be encouraged to recognise these factors and to respond to them in their style of operations. The potential for direct assistance to communities in a form that enhances conditions for local popular accountability is also noteworthy for those outside the NGO community.

This is not to say anything can be guaranteed, but inaction will not cure the illness. In addition to promoting special projects for capability building and civil society–enhancement, NGOs should also emphasise those aspects of good development work likely to promote these as a side-effect. It is unfortunate that constructive action is rare where these regimes are involved. Amongst Western policy makers the tools of first choice have become negative and punitive (for example, sanctions). Without addressing whether this wider macro approach is effective and appropriate, it does suggest that even when this approach is taken, NGOs can provide positive steps towards a solution.

Ultimately, individual agencies must wrestle with the issues and determine their own ethical position on such questions. NGOs should not allow the priorities of their own or any other government's policy to affect their decisions on allocation of aid. Although agencies might sympathise with reasons for economic and other actions taken against certain regimes, that sympathy should not develop into automatic inclusion of government policy as a factor in NGO thinking.

NOTES

[1] As always, there are notable exceptions, such as Sierra Leone, although a comparison of heterogeneous less developed countries (LDC) democracies and recent LDC conflicts bears out the point.

[2] Christopher Clapham and John A. Wiseman, "Assessing the Prospects for the Consolidation of Democracy in Africa," in *Democracy and Political Change in Africa*, ed. John A. Wiseman et al. (London: Routledge, 1995), 224.

[3] Siobhan O'Reilly, *The Contribution of Community Development to Peacebuilding: World Vision's Area Development Programmes* (Milton Keynes, UK: World Vision UK, 1998).

[4] *Monday Developments* [InterAction, Washington, D.C.] (22 November 1999), 8.

[5] The countries in question are not named in order to protect the NGOs involved.

[6] The author has developed this theme in "NGOs, Civil Society and the State: Avoiding Theoretical Extremes in Real World Issues," *Development in Practice* 8/3 (August 1998).

[7] See Joel S Migdal, *Strong Societies and Weak States: State-Society Relations and State Capabilities in the Third World* (Princeton, N.J.: Princeton University Press, 1988). Also Joel S Migdal et al., *State Power and Social Forces: Domination and Transformation in the Third World* (Cambridge: Cambridge University Press, 1994).

[8] Jean Francois Bayart, et al.,"The Criminalisation of the State in Africa," *Africa Issues* (1998).

[9] Sam Jones, *Stolen Sovereignty: Globalisation and the Disempowerment of Africa* (Milton Keynes, UK: World Vision UK, 1997).

[10] Clapham and Wiseman, "Assessing the Prospects for the Consolidation of Democracy in Africa," 220–24.

[11] The International Committee of the Red Cross (ICRC) definition of this principle states a desire to "prevent and alleviate human suffering wherever it may be found . . . to protect life and health and to ensure respect for human beings" (see Hugo Slim, "Sharing a Universal Ethic: Spreading the Principle of Humanity Beyond Humanitarianism," paper presented at the ECHO/ODI Conference entitled Principled Aid in an Unprincipled World: Relief, War and Humanitarian Principles, 7 April 1998).

[12] Hugo Slim, "Sharing a Universal Ethic."

[13] Mark Robinson, *Governance, Democracy and Conditionality: What Role for NGOs?* (Oxford: International NGO Training and Research Centre [INTRAC], 1993).

[14] Harry Blair, "Donors, Democratisation and Civil Society: Relating Theory to Practice," in *NGOs, States and Donors: Too Close for Comfort,* ed. David Hulme and Michael Edwards (London: MacMillan, 1997), chap. 2.

[15] Michael Edwards and David Hulme, "NGO Performance and Accountability: Introduction and Overview," in *Non-governmental Organisation: Performance and Accountability, Beyond the Magic Bullet,* ed. Michael Edwards and David Hulme (London: Earthscan/SCF, 1975), 4–5.

[16] For the extent of donor analysis, see OECD (Organization for Economic Co-operation and Development), Development Assistance Committee (DAC), *Participatory Development and Good Governance,* Development Co-operation Guidelines Series (Paris, 1995).

[17] World Bank, *World Development Report 1991* (Oxford: Oxford University Press, 1991), 132.

[18] James H. Michel, foreword to OECD/DAC, *Participatory Development and Good Governance.*

[19] Richard Jeffries, "The State, Structural Adjustment and Good Government in Africa," *The Journal of Commonwealth and Comparative Politics* 31/1 (March 1993).

[20] These issues have featured in several key NGO meetings from the Manchester University Scaling up Conference of 1991 through to the BOND conference, Building Capacity in the South: Partnerships, Policies and the Role of Donors, 18 September 1995.

[21] Alan Whaites, "Let's Get Civil Society Straight: NGOs and Political Theory," *Development in Practice* 6/3 (August 1996); idem, "NGOs, Civil Society and the State: Avoiding Theoretical Extremes in Real World Issues," *Development in Practice* 8/3 (August 1998).

[22] Whaites, "Let's Get Civil Society Straight."

[23] Of the alternative definitions available, the understanding of civil society expounded by Hegel has enjoyed some support for developing contexts. Hegel identified civil society as a product of economic development, which consisted of competing self-interests requiring state regulation. The Hegelian definition therefore asserts that it is civil society which threatens and the state which safeguards. The Hegelian view accepts that civil society represents many aspects of society that are desirable and welcome, but the root of civil society is in self-interest, and this undermines the benefit of its own pluralism. This concept of civil society does have its parallel in the study of less economically developed states. The belief that third-world societies possess an array of competing interests (primordial and induced by "clientelistic" networks) and that this requires order provided by the state has been a recurrent theme. Huntington's vision of the chaos produced by the process of development, not least increasing participation without strong institutional channels of articulation, is resonant of Hegelian assumptions (see Samuel P. Huntington, *Political Order in Changing Societies* [New Haven, Conn.: Yale University Press, 1968], 28–41). The belief that ultimately some form of stable institution of state (such as a single governing party) must take the lead in political development reflects the belief in the need for the regulatory state.

[24] Alan Whaites, "The State and Civil Society in Pakistan," *Contemporary South Asia* 4/3 (1995).

[25] Ibid.

[26] The complexity of state-society relations in this respect reflects the discussion of Joel Migdal, "The State in Society: An Approach to Struggles for Domination," in Migdal et al., *State Power and Social Forces*, 8–9.

[27] The dilemmas which can face elites in these circumstances are discussed in Merilee S Grindle and John W Thomas, *Public Choices and Policy Change: The Political Economy of Reform in Developing Countries* (Baltimore, Md.: Johns Hopkins University Press, 1991), chap. 5 and conclusion.

[28] See Oxfam, "Human Rights in Development and Relief Work," *The Oxfam Handbook of Development and Relief,* chap. 2, esp. sections 2.3.1 and 2.3.2

[29] UN, "Co-operation Between Non-Governmental Organisations and the International Criminal Tribunal for Former Yugoslavia" (The Hague, Netherlands).

[30] Draft Final Statement of the Conference on Co-operation Between Humanitarian Organisations and Human Rights Organisations, Amsterdam, 9 February 1996.

[31] OECD (DAC). *Participatory Development and Good Governance.*

[32] James Midgley, "Community Participation, the State and Social Policy," in James Midgley et al., *Community Participation, Social Development and the State* (London: Methuen, 1986), 154.

[33] For a useful discussion of the definition issue, see ibid., 23–38.

[34] Alfred Stepan, *Rethinking Military Politics: Brazil and the Southern Cone* (Princeton, N.J.: Princeton University Press, 1988).

[35] Ayesha Jalal, *The State of Martial Rule* (New Delhi: Cambridge University Press, 1993).

World Vision

Other New Titles from World Vision Publications

World Vision Security Manual, *Charles Rogers and Brian Sytsma,
editors*
Global trends and recent events signal the growing vulnerability of international humanitarian workers. This pocket-sized manual is designed to
help organizations create a complete personnel safety policy that increases situational awareness, simulates attack and hostage scenarios and
develops security assessments. 148 pp. **$14.95**

**Walking With the Poor: Principles and Practices
of Transformational Development** by Bryant L. Myers.
The author says those who want to alleviate poverty need to walk with
the poor, see their reality, and then look for solutions. He explores
Christian views of poverty and looks at how it is experienced in different
cultures. Draws on theological and biblical resources as well as secular
development theory and practice to develop a theoretical framework for
working alongside the poor. 288 pp. **$21.95**

**Working With the Poor: New Insights and Learnings from
Development Practitioners,** Bryant L. Myers, editor.
Christian development practitioners explore how to express holistic
transformational development. As they struggle to overcome the problem
of dualism, they articulate a genuinely holistic approach to helping the
poor. 192 pp. **$16.95**

Toll Free in the U.S.: 1-800-777-7752

Direct: (626) 301-7720

Web: www.marcpublications.com

World Vision Publications • 800 W. Chestnut Ave. • Monrovia, CA • 91016
